THE TYNE COAL KEEL

THE TYNE COAL KEEL

A UNIQUE BRITISH WATERCRAFT, 1400–1890

by

ADRIAN OSLER

Design, typesetting and publishing by UK Book Publishing

www.ukbookpublishing.com

ISBN: 978-1-915338-39-6

For my wife, daughter, and sisters

CONTENTS

LIST OF ILLUSTRATIONS

FIGURES

MAPS

PLATES

SOURCES OF ILLUSTRATIONS

Author as Originator or Collector

Figures: 1.1; 1.4; 2.1; 2.2; 2.3; 2.4; 2.5; 2.6; 2.7; 2.8; 2.9; 2.10; 2.11; 2.12; 2.13; 2.14; 2.15; 2.16; 2.17; 3.1; 3.2; 3.3; 3.4; 3.5; 3.6; 3.7; 3.8; 3.9; 3.10; 3.11; 3.12; 3.13; 3.14; 3.15; 4.1; 4.2; 4.3; 4.4; 4.5; 4.6; 4.7; 4.8; 4.9; 4.10; 4.11; 4.12; 4.13; 4.14; 4.15; 4.16; 5.1; 5.2; 5.5; 5.6; 5.7; 5.8 (top); 5.10; 6.1; 6.2; 6.3; 6.4; 6.6; 6.7 (left); 6.8; and 6.10.

Maps: 1; 2; 3; 4; and 5.

Tailpieces: Chapters 1, 2, 3 and 4.

Bridgeman Images (TWAM, Laing Art Gallery collections)

Plates: 2; 3; 4; 5; and 6 (cover).

Davison Art Center, Wesleyan University, open access collection

Tailpiece: Chapter 5 (Thomas Bewick, 1753-1828).

Michael Greatbatch

Figure 5.9.

Professor Jon Adams

Figures: 6.5; and 6.7 (right).

Northumberland Archives (SANT collections)
Figure 6.9.

Royal Museums Greenwich (© National Maritime Museum)
Plate 1.

The Common Room (NEIMME)
Figures: 1.2; 1.3; 5.3; 5.4; and 5.8 (bottom).

Tailpiece: Chapter 6.

ACRONYMS

AC   Alnwick Castle Archives/Collections
NA   Northumberland Archives
NCL   Newcastle Central Library (Local collections)
NEIMME   North of England Institute of Mining and Mechanical Engineers
NMG   National Museums Greenwich
PP   Parliamentary Papers
SANT   Society of Antiquaries of Newcastle upon Tyne
SDJ   *Smith's Dock Journal*
TIC   Tyne Improvement Commission
TWAM   Tyne & Wear Archives and Museums
TWCMS   Tyne and Wear County Museums Service

ACKNOWLEDGEMENTS

THE MATERIAL PRESENTED IN THIS BOOK was gathered as opportunity offered over a period of more than 30 years, and one fears that lapse of time and memory may have allowed the assistance of a few individuals to be forgotten; if so, I heartily apologise. Many people, however, remain within the author's sphere of gratitude and, pleasingly, these include several like-minded friends and former colleagues. Of those who have freely offered support and helpful comment during the work's lengthy passage especial mention must be made of archaeologist Alan Williams and former maritime history curator Ian Whitehead, their expertise and patience has been greatly valued throughout. Correspondingly, Mike Greatbatch gave rare insight into one of the keel's heartlands, the Ouseburn, whilst fellow sailor Dr Peter Wright's doctoral thesis and published research gave invaluable context for eighteenth-century, water-trade matters.

Within the field of vernacular boat studies the author is also beholden to the work of leading individuals who have sadly 'crossed the bar'. Their knowledgeable discourse is greatly missed, especially that of Dr Basil Greenhill, Cdr. Eric McKee, and my old friend and colleague, Michael Stammers (Curator Emeritus, Merseyside Maritime Museum).

Amongst others who have contributed either directly, or even barely knowingly, over the past three decades it is with particular gratitude I mention: Lindsay Allanson-Jones; Dr Tony Barrow; Dr John Broadwater (USA); Dr Marc Chivers;

the late Joe Clarke; John Clayson; Bob Elsey; the late Ron French; Ian Friel; John Gall; the late Dr Bill Griffiths; Trevor Hipperson (Norfolk Wherry Trust); the late Dick Keys; Dr Stafford Linsley; Robert Malster; Grace McCombie; Dave Pennington; Katrina Porteous; Sarah Richardson (Laing Art Gallery); Derek Tree; the late Duncan Towns; and last but by no means least, Les Turnbull.

And, as always, sincere thanks are given for the assistance and source material provided over the years by dedicated staff at the following institutions: Newcastle Library; Newcastle University Library (Special Collections); The Common Room (NEIMME); Northumberland Archives (especially the SANT collections); and Tyne & Wear Archives and Museums. Regrettably, the Covid pandemic curtailed access to Durham Record Office and the British Library – some things must be left to others.

Writing this book has proved a *lang tide*, one that could not have been undertaken without my wife, Dorothy's, understanding of the peculiar nature of 'boats and boatmen', and the unselfish application of her professional editorial skills when preparing it for publication. 'Thanks', is not a big enough word to express my gratitude; there must have been many an occasion when, to mix maritime metaphors, she would willingly have 'keel-hauled' me . . .

ADRIAN OSLER

PREFACE

THE OPENING UP OF DRIFT MINES for coal in the steep-sided tributary valleys of the River Tyne to the west of Newcastle in the early fourteenth century marked the commencement of a trade – the Coal Trade – that increasingly came to dictate the economy and infrastructure of North East England for the next five centuries. It was the crucial role played by water transport that made the movement of this low cost, bulk mineral to consumers not only possible but profitable. The significant profits that accrued from coal were shared not only by the landowners who held the mining rights but also by the Crown, which quickly recognized the revenues that might be raised from taxation, at source, of this much sought-after fuel.

From the beginning, a crucial element in the transport chain from coal pit to distant marketplace, especially London, was the fleet of River Tyne lighters known as 'keels'. These craft were employed to tranship the coal some dozen miles downriver from the collieries' riverside storage depots – staiths – to be loaded aboard the seagoing vessels that lay in deep water nearer the river mouth. Although the exact origins and nature of these early keels is unclear, what is known is that by the early fifteenth century they were sufficiently numerous and of such regular form that their customary lading was designated, by national statute, as the (taxable) unit of measure for the region's coal shipping trade. Indeed, local shippers universally used this transaction unit – the 'keel' of 21.2 tons of coal – until 1869.

For more than 500 years keel owners were obliged to submit to a statutory, annual 'admeasurement' procedure in which the displacement of each individual vessel was determined and unequivocally marked. This process, it is argued here, stultified the keel's technical development for it gave owners no scope to practice economies of scale by increasing a vessel's capacity, and encouraged a conservative outlook among both owners and operatives. Variations in demand and the trade's subsequent expansion were simply met by an overall increase or decrease in the number of keels which coal shippers deployed. Consequently, the keel long retained a suite of old-established features, for instance, retaining the use of a steering oar – not a rudder – for control, and employing an unchanged mix of propulsion with crews utilizing: the river's tidal flow; shallow-water poling; a basic squaresail rig; rowing (the famous 'Keel Row'); and man-hauling.

Surviving into the era of steam afloat, the keel's nineteenth-century owners were eventually obliged to adopt practical improvements in pursuit of efficiency but, for implacable economic reasons, the keel fleet continued to decline and the last genuine Tyne coal keel was reputedly built about 1860. The few coal-carrying keels that still remained at work under sail and oar became obsolete during the next decade. By 1890, contemporary local observers agreed that the traditional working keel was actually extinct, the last survivors having either been discarded, reduced to general purpose dumb lighters, or ignominiously converted to ferry-landing stages.

As a subject for study in its own right the keel has significance for many reasons, not least for the fact that the North East Coal Trade helped to underwrite national security in wartime and prosperity in peace, and the keel fleet was critical to coal's expansion. An understanding of the keel as a transport mechanism also helps to explain why the developments which modernised bulk water transport elsewhere, in particular canalisation, river improvement and steam propulsion, were late to make a mark on the economically strategic waterway of the Tyne. And from a somewhat different perspective the forensic appraisal of the keel presented here allows insight, by proxy, into the technologies and operational routines of other pre-seventeenth century rivercraft. In like manner, this study provides regional archaeologists with a set of physical criteria against which to assess any future discoveries of historic watercraft along the river. Similarly, at a national and even international level, it provides students of Medieval and Early Modern boat technology and boat handling with a well-founded, quantitative set of comparative data for a typologically and commercially important class of British rivercraft.

Finally, in this day and age it does no harm to reflect upon the paradox of an energy regime founded upon a fossil fuel which, for centuries, was reliant upon the renewables of tide, wind, and muscle-power for its transport to millions of consumers.

ADRIAN OSLER
Northumberland, 2022

Lower River Tyne

Newcastle

Shields Hbr.

Stella

Coals from Newcastle

N
W   E
S

NEWCASTLE

R. Tyne
R. Wear

Shields Hbr.

R. Tees

Humber

R. Trent

DISTANCES:

Stella to Newcastle   6 statute miles
Newcastle to Shields   9.5 statute miles
Shields to Gravesend   293 nautical miles

R. Great Ouse

R. Bure & R. Yare

LONDON

R. Thames

Gravesend

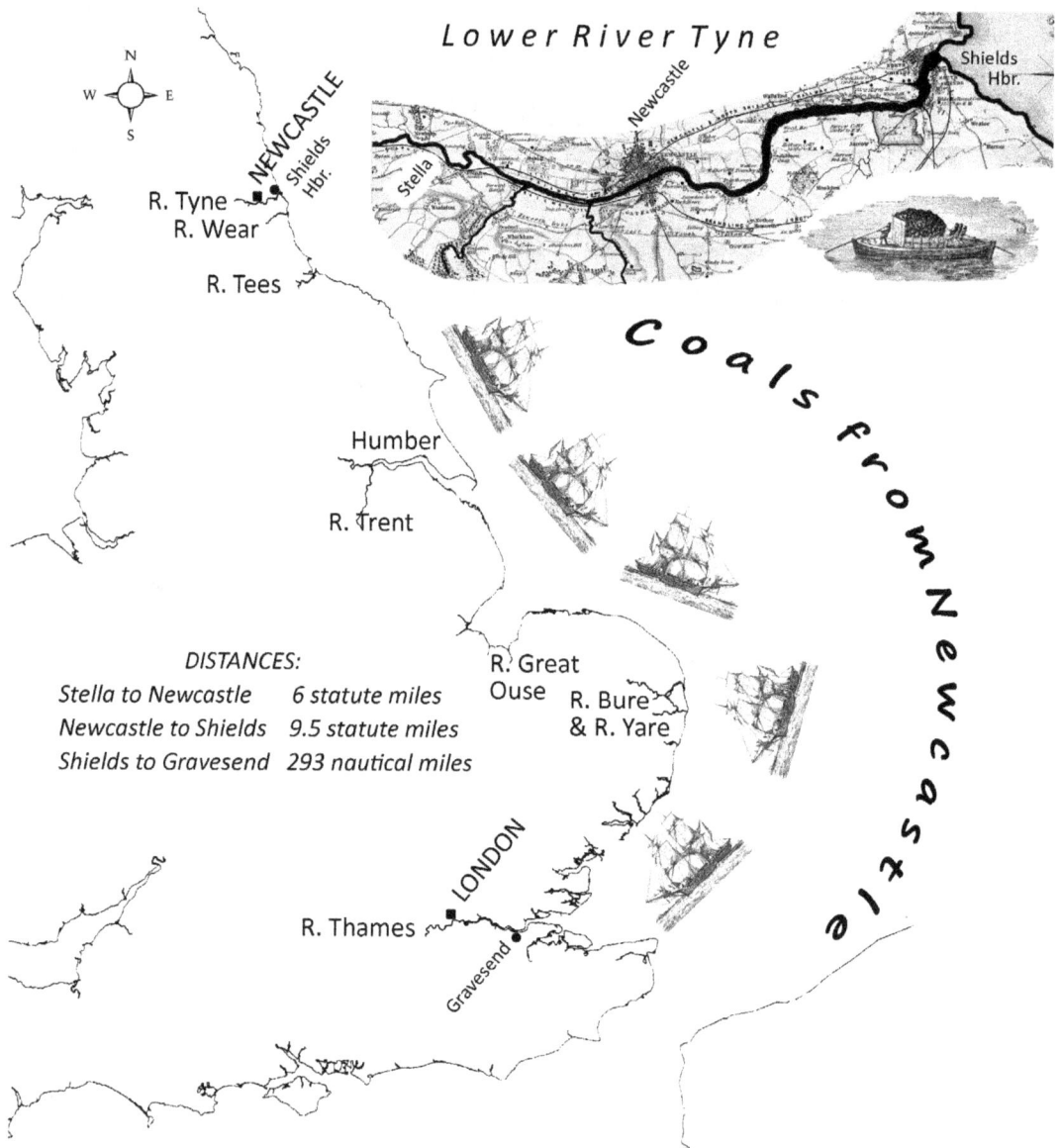

MAP 1 From the early-fifteenth century to the early-nineteenth century, the principal destinations for 'coals from Newcastle' were London, East Anglia and South East England. The Tyne coal keel was the essential first link in the waterborne transport chain of all coal shipments, both home and abroad.

ONE

THE ELUSIVE KEEL

AS THE PENULTIMATE DECADE of the nineteenth century ended, a contributor to the *Newcastle Chronicle* reported sympathetically on the rapid decline of this once ubiquitous watercraft – the Tyne Coal Keel – concluding that, 'The number is gradually becoming smaller, and before long the advisability may have to be considered of arranging space, in our largest museum of antiquities, for the reception of an undoubted specimen of the old Tyne Keel'. [1] Predictably perhaps the concerns of the writer, J I Nicholson, elicited no published response or action, not even by local antiquarians – of whom there were many. [2] Indeed, had his bold and percipient suggestion been acted upon, there would have been no need for a book like this over 130 years later. But, since no 'specimen of the old Tyne Keel' was preserved by Nicolson and his fellow citizens, posterity has largely been denied the opportunity to study and appreciate this now distant Tyneside icon, one that was unique in form and dedicated function, and which was of exceptional economic importance. This book seeks to redress that deficiency, presenting for the first time a comprehensive appraisal of the keel as a watercraft, its design, construction and performance, the nature of its builders, the variety of ways in which it was propelled and managed over time, and its potential paths of evolution from the *Ceol* of early medieval times. And the reader will soon find that Nicolson's 'Tyne Keel' was, in

1

reality, something far removed from the crude, ungainly and archaic flat-bottomed barge generally portrayed by contemporary observers – an impression that lingers erroneously yet.

THE STORY SO FAR . . .

The continued lack of detailed investigation of the nature of the keel and its everyday management by twentieth- and twenty-first century historians is a little surprising. This deficit is all the more notable since the last decade delivered two comprehensive published works – based on assiduous documentary research – by Joseph Fewster (2011) and Peter Wright (2014) respectively, that deal with the keels' manual operatives (the Tyneside keelmen), and the large variety of water trades that were exercised on the river during the seventeenth and eighteenth centuries. Fewster focused on 'labour organisation and conflict', and consequently gave scant consideration to the actual nature of the watercraft itself, although including a brief intriguing description of keel handling from a previously uncited source.[3] Correspondingly, Wright's published work based on his doctoral thesis, provides no fresh insight into the keel's material form, although his exemplary original findings about the Tyne's distinctive 'water trades' offer a fine frame of reference through which to view the keel's pre-nineteenth century milieu and development.[4]

Both these authors relied largely on the analysis and interpretation of conventional documentary research, but quite different methods were applied by Patrick Taylor and Alan Williams (2010) to their restricted study of the late nineteenth- and early twentieth-century Tyne wherry, a late contemporary of the Tyne keel. Their investigation was field survey led with surviving artefacts, in the form of foreshore hulks, rather than documentary sources being afforded priority.[5]

Viewed in a wider geographic context, all the above-mentioned writers had opportunity to benefit from the national perspective provided (2008) by Michael

Stammers' succinct and authoritative compendium work that described cargo-carrying sailing barges throughout Britain.[6] Nevertheless, when it came to the Tyne coal keel even Stammers was indebted to the well-rehearsed texts of Tyneside historians of the eighteenth and nineteenth centuries, from John Brand (1789) through Eneas McKenzie (1827) to R J Charleton (1885) and others. But the limitations of such local commentators are clear, their descriptions are generalist and qualitative in nature, lacking the consistency, practical detail and measurement that would allow the keel's form, construction, and handling to be defined to the same level as comparable watercraft recorded elsewhere, for instance, the similarly named – if apparently unrelated – Humber keels or Norfolk keels and wherries.[7][8] With respect to the keel this descriptive deficiency also reflects a lack of appreciation by waterways' historians of the Tyne's role as a major inland navigation.

Reviewed objectively even the most adroit combination of recent published research, earlier printed sources, and surviving archival material still falls short when challenged to bring the keel alive as a physical working entity – the 'white van' of its day and locale. To do so a more inclusive, evidence-based approach accompanied by rigorous quantitative analysis of formerly unnoticed, largely non-documentary, material is required.

In searching for more information about the elusive keel, four sources recommended themselves: texts, both printed and archival; iconographic representations, either as original works of art or as published images; authentic three-dimensional representations, i.e. models; and lastly, full-size artefacts including analogous watercraft. Of these four, textual sources had received by far the most attention hitherto, but even there recent advances in digitization opened-up areas effectively denied to previous researchers. By comparison, the iconography of the keel was little explored, with previous writers relying upon the interpretation of a few clichéd images, or nothing at all. And, with two exceptions – Mitcalfe and Viall in 1935 and 1942 respectively – there had been only superficial examination of the few authenticated contemporary keel models that have survived.[9][10] Lastly, the comparative evidence gained from recent ethnographic and historical studies into the survival and use of vernacular British boats, had not been applied to the puzzle that was the keel.

It is time now to consider the potential, and limitations, of those four sources where some answers to that puzzle might be found.

WHAT PEOPLE WROTE . . .

The considerable volume of archival and primary printed material – largely held in North East England – that relates directly to the practices of the Tyne's keelmen and their employers, has been the subject of detailed scrutiny, analysis, and listing by: Fewster, 1957–58, 1962–63, 2011; Rowe, 1969; and Wright, 2011, 2014, so is not rehearsed here. Suffice it to say that within the scope of this book's remit the yield from such material proved limited, although always contextually helpful. However, the author was fortunate to discover two manuscripts by the antiquarian and dialect scholar, R Oliver Heslop (1842–1916): his pre-publication draft 'Keels and Keelmen', c.1902, now in the collections of The Common Room (North of England Institute of Mechanical and Mining Engineers); and his earlier rough draft 'Notes on Keels' now held by Newcastle's Discovery Museum (Figs. 1.1, 1.2).[11][12]

A degree of previously unremarked practical detail about the keel has also emerged through re-examination of select printed primary sources, including the published report of the Admiralty Inquiry preceding the River Tyne Conservancy Act of 1850, together with legal disputes about naval impressment or local riparian issues, including the cases of Robert Softley (1801) and *Rex v. Russell & Others* (1828) respectively.[13][14][15] Access to eighteenth and nineteenth century newspaper reports and advertisements in digital searchable form also opened up a wealth of previously hard to find incidental detail.[16] Indeed, such contemporary newspaper accounts of keel sales, losses and accidents provided fresh insight into the supply and demand factors within the keel 'fleet', and occasionally gave insight into everyday practices regarding the keel's management, rig and equipment.

FIGURE 1.1
Extract from R. O. Heslop's draft manuscript (TWAM F7675), 'Notes on Keels', showing his uncertainty over the Tyne keel's dimensions.

FIGURE 1.2 A keel and its crew by R J S Bertram, c.1902. Intended to accompany Heslop's proposed paper, this pen-and-ink sketch was clearly based on the model then held by the Society of Antiquaries of Newcastle upon Tyne and later transferred to Tyne & Wear Archives and Museums: TWAM H5441 (courtesy of The Common Room, NEIMME).

. . . AND WHAT THEY DREW

Although keels occur as compositional elements in the work of several Tyneside artists, historians have generally considered such images as illustrative devices only, rather discounting them as utilitarian evidence. However, new evaluation of topographic river scenes by local nineteenth-century artists demonstrates that, collectively, their work offers much in the way of technical detail or validation of descriptive texts. Notable in this respect are works by: T M Richardson Snr (1784–1848); J W Carmichael (1799–1868); B B Hemy (1845–1913); R Jobling (1841–1923); and book illustrator W J Palmer (active 1870–80). Similarly, at a more mundane level the engraved, often naïve, vignettes used in contemporary advertisements and the *pro forma* 'coal tickets' (receipts) issued by individual collieries to shippers, also helps to establish a visual confirmation of the keel's characteristics and handling over time (Fig. 1.3).

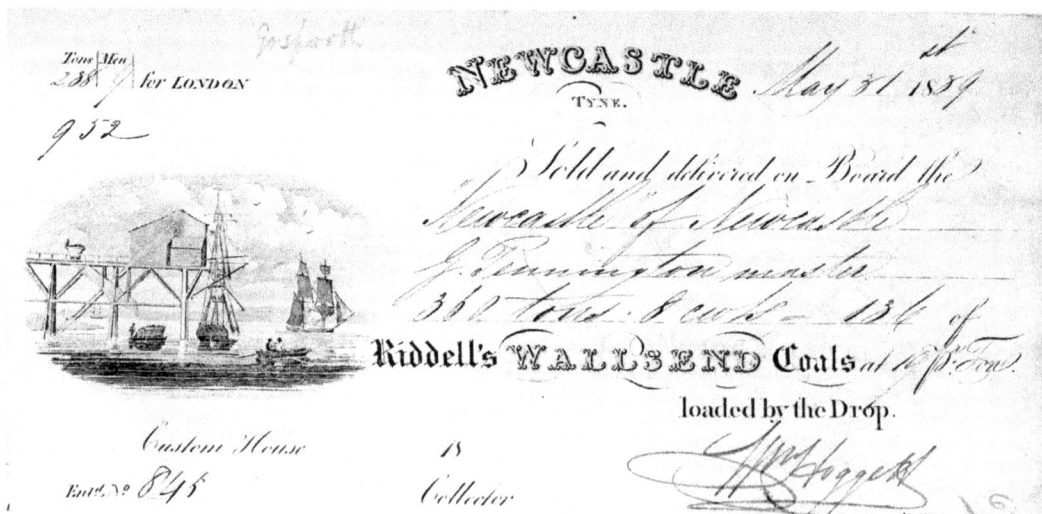

FIGURE 1.3 A typical coal ticket, its cartouche depicting a keel being loaded from a chaldron wagon via a spout, whilst a seagoing collier-brig waits to load at the mechanical 'Drop' (courtesy of The Common Room, NEIMME).

One must recognize however, the chronological and stylistic limitations of such graphic works. Those produced prior to the early nineteenth century, for example, require particular caution since their representation of watercraft – as distinct from the built environment – may owe more to convention or a remote engraver's interpretation than literal, on-site depiction. Whilst at the nearer end of the timescale, it is disappointing to find that no verifiable photographs have come to light of keels at work under sail and oar, although from the turn-of-the-century onward various images of the river record 'strings' of unrigged watercraft – largely Tyne wherries – towed by steam tugs.[17]

KEELS IN MINIATURE

Only four contemporary models of keels survive, and all are now housed (2021) in the Discovery Museum of Tyne and Wear Archives and Museums.[18] The origins of three of the models is not known, whilst the fourth – which exhibits the most detail – was transferred from the collections of the Society of Antiquaries of Newcastle upon Tyne to the present location in 1977 (Fig. 1.4).[19] None are specifically dated, although one at least was reputedly made by an inmate of the Keelman's Hospital, c.1850 (TWAM B9779). And on the grounds of materials and technique the author's curatorial judgement is that all four can be attributed to 'amateur' makers of the nineteenth century. To a greater or lesser degree each model offers useful technical insights and, given their rarity, it is not surprising to find that two already hold the status of figured specimens (TWAM B9779; TWAM H5441).[20][21][22] Nevertheless, it has to be recognized that the motives and skill-levels of the makers are unknown, with visual representation rather than technical accuracy probably their priority.

FIGURE 1.4 The only surviving rigged model of a Tyne Coal Keel, date unknown, but presumed late nineteenth century. Originally acquired and preserved by The Society of Antiquaries of Newcastle upon Tyne, it is now (2021) displayed in the Discovery Museum, Newcastle: TWAM H5541.

A 'SPECIMEN OF THE OLD TYNE KEEL'?

As previously indicated, no full-size keel has survived ashore, afloat, or even as an identifiable hulk. And considering that several hundred remained in use until the mid-nineteenth century, this seems an extraordinary total extinction. The explanation rests on the premise that during the third quarter of the nineteenth century there were substantial improvements in direct (shore-to-ship) coal loading systems, and their subsequent spread allied to the unexpected collapse of the sailing collier fleet, c.1875, helped trigger the keel's final fall and obsolescence.[23] [24] The concomitant occupational 'decline' of the keelmen has been well documented by historians but the fate of the dozens of iconic craft that they worked in seems to have barely merited mention.[25]

As Nicolson suggested, the remaining evidence implies that the keel's disappearance was swift and near total, occurring largely in the period 1870–1890.[26] Newspaper comment late in the century suggested that 'the working article is now [1893] so scarce that soon the only actual specimen of the genus keel will have to be looked for by antiquarian shipbuilders away among the few remaining mud banks on the river's brink'. More specifically, it was indicated that, 'There are only six working on the river at the present day [1889] and they are towed to and fro by a tug'.[27] An official survey by the Tyne's Harbour Master in November 1883 revealed something of the latter day keels' typical fate.[28] Of the dozen listed amongst the 'Wrecks and Unserviceable Vessels laid on the Shores or Banks' of the navigation between Shields and Newcastle, almost a half were rated as either 'condemned', 'falling to pieces' or being 'broken up'. Only a couple had some prospect of repair, the rest but little. Regrettably, the situation in the keel's final stronghold – upriver of Newcastle bridge – went unrecorded, although it might be supposed that by then (1883) many disused keels lay by Stella shore at Blaydon and along the banks of the locality's once busy coal shipping tributaries, the rivers Team and Derwent. Some fifty years later, in 1925, no keels were officially recorded as being active on the Tyne, not even as dumb (towed) lighters.[29]

Furthermore, amateur enthusiast H R Viall's assiduous regional 'quest for the keel' in the mid-1930s failed to reveal even a foreshore hulk.[30] And when advised of that, the curator of Newcastle's newly established 'Municipal Museum of Science and Engineering' did not attempt to look further. Some fifty years later, as a curatorial successor, it fell to this author to continue the search for the elusive, historic keel.

NOTES

[1] Nicholson J I, 'Keels and Keelmen', *Newcastle Weekly Chronicle Supplement*, 9 November 1889.

[2] At the time this was published the semi-retired, intellectually minded Joseph Innes Nicholson resided in a middle-class area of Heaton and often contributed articles to the *Newcastle Chronicle* and *Weekly Chronicle*. Although originally a schoolteacher, he later became a partner in the flint glass manufactory of Liddell, Henzell & Co. on the Ouseburn – an industrialized tributary of the lower Tyne that was serviced by watercraft.

[3] Fewster, *The Keelmen*, 2-3.

[4] Wright, Thesis, 98-103.

[5] Taylor P & Williams A, 'The Newburn wherries: remnants of the River Tyne's industrial past', *Archaeologia Aeliana* Fifth Series, Vol XXXIX, (2010) 401-425.

[6] Stammers, *Sailing Barges*.

[7] Schofield, *Humber Keels and Keelmen*.

[8] Malster, *Wherries and Waterways*.

[9] Mitcalfe W S, 'The History of the Keelmen and Their Strike in 1822', in *Archaeologia Aeliana*, v.14 (1935).

[10] Viall H R, 'Tyne Keels', *The Mariner's Mirror*, Vol. 28, No.2, 1942, 160-162.

[11] Heslop R O, manuscript 'Keels and Keelmen', NEIMME, D/71. This is a 'printer ready' manuscript, but the book for which it (and other papers) was prepared was never published by the Institute.

[12] Heslop R O, manuscript 'Notes on Keels', TWAM F7675. As a curator the author consulted this (then newly acquired) document in the early 1980s but was unaware of the Mining Institute's related manuscript until 2011. This, much corrected, draft undoubtedly represents Heslop's initial thoughts on the subject.

[13] Admiralty Inquiry Under the Preliminary Inquiries Act, 11 & 12 Vict., cap. 129. River Tyne Conservancy Bill (1849, 1849).

[14] English Reports Decisions, 1801, *Ex parte* Robert Softley.

[15] *Newcastle Courant* 23 August 1828: The King *v.* Russell and Others.

[16] https://www.britishnewspaperarchive.co.uk/ (accessed variously, January 2017 to December 2019).

[17] A twice published photograph (*Country Life*, 22 November 1962; 21 April 1966) purporting to be an 'ancient keel' under sail is in fact a clinker-built Tyne wherry with a makeshift tarpaulin rig, post-1920.

[18] In order of acquisition by Tyne & Wear Archives and Museums : TWAM B9780 (1932); TWAM B9779 (1935); TWAM B9757 (1958); TWAM H5441 (1977).

[19] Owing to its previous location this has sometimes been referred to as the 'Black Gate' model. R O Heslop was joint curator of the Society's museum in the Black Gate building at the turn of the century.

[20] TWAM B9779: Mitcalfe, 'The History of', 5.

[21] TWAM H5441: Viall, 'Tyne Keels', plate 9.

[22] TWAM H5441: Stammers, *Sailing Barges*, 31.

[23] Powell, *Staith to Conveyor*, 28-31, 66-75.

[24] Osler, Thesis, 228-238.

[25] By comparison the coal keel's complementary transport partner, the bulk goods carrying Tyne wherry, survived for much longer and in considerable numbers. Today there is just one well-preserved museum example (*Elswick No. 2*) of the type, together with archaeologically documented hulks (Taylor & Williams, 2010) and published outlines of its use (Mannering J, 1997; Stammers, 2008).

[26] Regrettably there are no official statistics to confirm this; a pasted note in the Tyne's earliest surviving Customs register for craft under 50 tons simply indicates that: 'The Old Keel Register is Lost'.

[27] *Newcastle Weekly Chronicle*, 9 November 1889; *Newcastle Weekly Chronicle*, c.1893 (Newcastle Library: Newscuttings Vol. 2, 105, letter to editor signed 'Tyne, Morpeth').

[28] *Tyne Improvement Commission, Annual Report, 1883*, Table 'A return of Old Vessels Laid up etc.'; most of these craft lay at Whitehill Point and Jarrow Slake.

[29] Newcastle Library: Ms, 'List of Lighters and other small craft on the River Tyne as at May 1925', Tyne Improvement Commission (River Police); over 170 'wherries' and 'lighters' were then in commission, but no keels. I am grateful to Alan Williams for drawing this item to my attention.

[30] Viall, 'Tyne Keels', 160-161

TWO

FORM AND CONSTRUCTION

FROM AT LEAST 1421 ONWARD, various State directives ensured that the keel's maximum load capacity remained at a fixed (taxable) figure, eventually comprising eight 'Newcastle' chaldrons, equivalent to 21.2 tons. Consequently, it is frustrating to find that no contemporary writers recorded or even referred to specific details of the keel's dimensions and precise form. Most, however, did infer that Tyne keels were of a single, conformable type. Indeed, it is reasonable to hypothesize that in the extraordinarily competitive environment of the Tyne's sailing era 'Coal Trade' which spanned six centuries, c.1350–c.1850, and which regularly saw keel fleets numbering several hundred, the builders and users of such vessels would have progressively improved the type's configuration. Since every keel's loaded displacement and its homogenous cargo (coal) was defined by statute, and its area of operation was confined to the lower River Tyne, it seems likely that a watercraft of optimum dimensions and design would have evolved over time. That is, a dedicated design would have gained acceptance which promised its users cost effectiveness through carrying efficiency, economy of manning and, perhaps, low-cost series construction.

SIZE

Historical Uncertainty

Some of the quantitative measures by which a watercraft's size are usually expressed prove inappropriate for the keel, so consideration here is confined to just two parameters: the hull's principal linear dimensions; and its volumetric displacement.[1] But given even these two limitations, the establishment of definitive figures is problematic. Eighteenth- and early nineteenth-century commentators were often vague about these quantitative matters, whilst upon close examination the statistics put forward by writers in the post-keel era frequently prove derivative or inconsistent, leading to much uncertainty (Table 2.1).[2] For example, the keel's beam (breadth) is variously cited over time as between 19 feet and 15 feet 6 inches, a difference of over one-fifth. Despite extensive documentary research even Wright (2011) was forced to resort to Viall's estimate of 70 years earlier, not appreciating – as indicated later below – that Viall's figure of 19 feet was self-contradictory.

TABLE 2.1 Tabular summary indicating the uncertainty about the keel's dimensions and the dependence of twentieth-century authors upon earlier sources. None gave the keel's light draught.

Source		Dimensions (feet and inches); (Beam/Length, %)					
Author	Date	Length	Beam	Depth	Load draught	Light draught	B/L (%)
Dodd R	1795	max. 45' 0"	c.19' 0"		c.5' 0"		
Hails W A	1806	48' 0"	18' 0"				38
Brockett (2nd edn)	1829	c.50' 0"	c.20' 0"				
Heslop R O (draft)	c.1902	41' (dg) 42'	22' 0"		4' 6"; 5'		
Heslop R O (final)	c.1902	42' 0"	19' 0"		4' 6"		45
'A H'	1911	30' to 40'					c.50
Warrington Smyth	1929	42' 0"	19' 0"		4' 6"		
Smith's Dock Journ.	1932	c. 40' 0"					c.50
Mitcalfe W S	1935	c. 40' 0"	15' 6"	6' 6"			39
Viall H R	1942	42' 0"	19' 0"	6' 0"			45

However, such ambiguity is excusable for various reasons. Firstly, none of the early published commentators (except for Dodd, 1795) were directly connected with the river trades: secondly, a variety of Tyneside craft were colloquially termed 'keels' during the nineteenth century. Added to this, lay observers frequently confused the river's dedicated coal keels with its multipurpose lighterage wherries. Lastly, and as a generality, a working boat user or owner was (and still is) often hazy about their boat's precise dimensions.[3]

Length is perhaps the most obvious criterion for establishing a vessel's size, and all the published authorities agree that the length of a keel was between 40 and 50 feet, a range which exhibits a similar variance (one fifth) to that collectively given for beam. The upper end of this range can immediately be discounted because the upper length of a coal keel may be estimated through examination of contemporary legal agreements that record the length of riverbank afforded to a keel for a loading 'room' or 'birth' (berth). From the early seventeenth century at least, the characteristic length of a loading berth was 15 yards (45 feet).[4] Throughout the eighteenth century this seems to have remained the norm, for example, an agreement in 1740 for wharfage on the river Derwent specifies: six keelrooms totaling 88 yards in length (14½ yards each); four others totaling 60 yards (15 yards each); and four of 61 yards (15¼ yards each). Correspondingly a plan, c.1780, of 'keel births' along the same tributary lists in succession: two 'births' of 15 yards; one of 15 yards; three of 13½ yards; and two (by scale measure) of 14½ yards (Fig. 2.1).[5]

Overall these records imply that, although 15 yards (45 feet), was the preferred space for loading a keel this might be reduced to as little as 13½ yards (40½ feet) if circumstances required, as in the case quoted above where the total length available was curtailed by a bend in the river. A 45-foot working norm also accords with Ralph Dodd's statement in 1795 that the locks on his proposed 'East to the West Sea Canal' (Newcastle-to-Carlisle), which was to commence at Stella (Blaydon), should be 'not less than 90 or 95 feet. On this scale two keels might pass at a time'.[6] A nominal 45-foot berth space also accords with the estimates of Heslop and later authors that keels were around 40 to 42 feet in length, a measure in

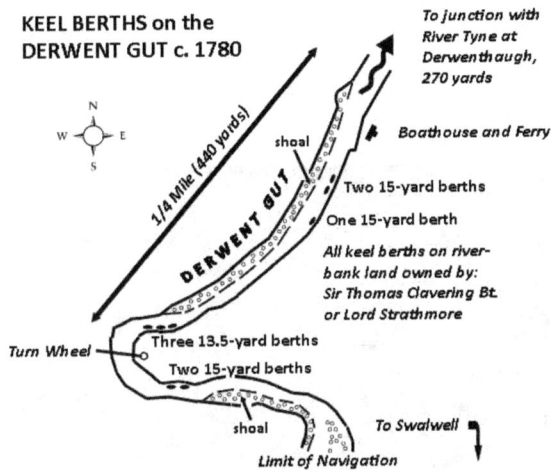

KEEL BERTHS on the DERWENT GUT c. 1780

To junction with River Tyne at Derwenthaugh, 270 yards

Boathouse and Ferry

Two 15-yard berths

One 15-yard berth

All keel berths on river-bank land owned by: Sir Thomas Clavering Bt. or Lord Strathmore

shoal

1/4 Mile (440 yards)

DERWENT GUT

Turn Wheel

Three 13.5-yard berths

Two 15-yard berths

shoal

To Swalwell

Limit of Navigation

FIGURE 2.1 Location and size of keel berths on the River Derwent close to its conjunction with the River Tyne, c.1780 (from TWAM, DT.BEL/2/31).

which they probably included the rudder.[7] At that overall length, a standard 15-yard berthing arrangement would have provided a gap of approximately a yard between the extremities of adjacent keels, allowing them sufficient margin to be worked in and out as required. Since riverside space suitable for coal staiths and keel berths was costly to acquire, the length of a keel berth will have been kept to a practicable minimum, a supposition reinforced by the congestion shown in some early illustrations (Fig. 2.2).

The matter of the keel's beam is rather more difficult to resolve since all estimates, excepting Mitcalfe's in 1935, appear to derive either from vague reports by earlier writers to the effect that the keel's beam was 'half the length', or by Dodd's late eighteenth-century statement that 'coal keels . . . are on an average nineteen feet in the beam' (see [6]). Dodd's figure should be treated with caution, however, for he was energetically promoting a broad-gauge canal with locks 19½ feet wide that would accommodate 100-ton barges and seagoing craft as well as 'coal keels', thus outclassing his competitor, William Chapman, whose projected narrow-gauge canal had locks only 12 feet-wide. A hundred years later Heslop (c.1902) surprisingly adopted Dodd's 19-foot figure without question, even amending his manuscript's original estimate of 22 feet (i.e. roughly half the keel's supposed

15

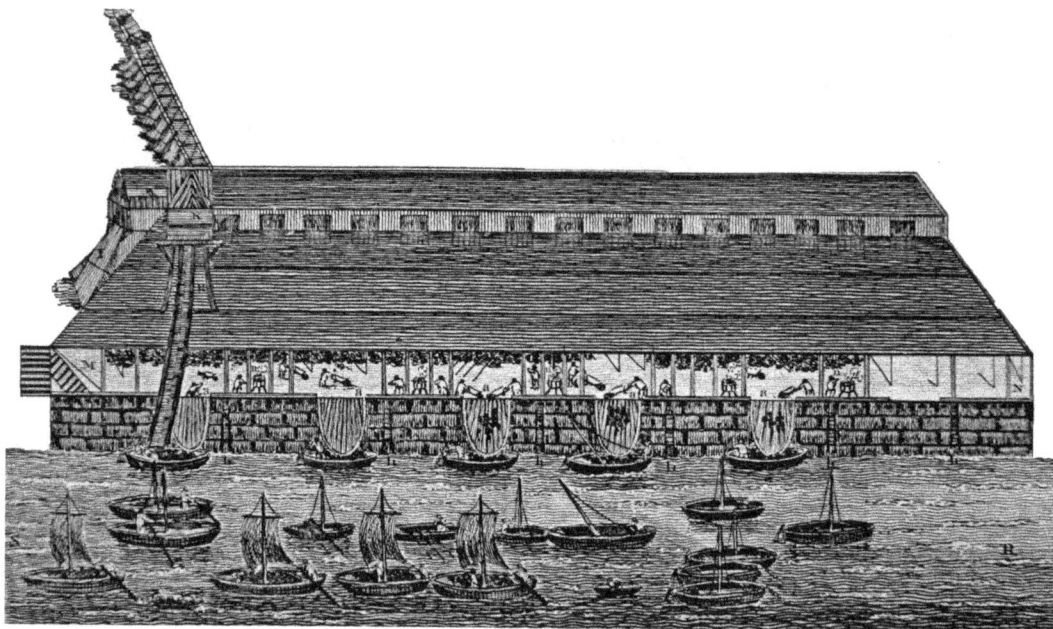

FIGURE 2.2 Five keels load from the 'shoots' of a large Wearside staith whilst a crowd of others wait in mid-river (from Barras's 'Description of a Coal Staith' in *The London Magazine*, 1766).

length) to do so.[8] Forty years on, in 1942, the otherwise reliable Hugh Viall even more surprisingly reiterated the figure of '19 feet' even though his own measured drawing of the Society of Antiquaries of Newcastle upon Tyne model (SANT; Table 2.2) and Mitcalfe's recently published paper (1935) indicated it was significantly under that.[9] Mitcalfe and his technically competent illustrator, 'H.L.H.', had used an authentic keel model now held by Tyne & Wear Archives and Museum (TWAM B9779; Table 2.2) to calculate a lower beam measurement for the keel: some 15 feet 6 inches on a nominal hull length of 40 feet.[10] This figure produces a beam-to-length ratio of approximately two-fifths (40%), markedly less than the one-half (50%) or more suggested by early commentators.

That two-fifths ratio has since been corroborated by the author's re-examination of the model used and illustrated by Mitcalfe, and this conclusion is also supported by comparative measurements taken – between 2012 and 2017 – from three more contemporary models (Table 2.2). Analysis reveals that not only is the beam-to-

TABLE 2.2 Measurements of the four contemporary keel models now (2021) held in the collections of Tyne & Wear Archives and Museums.

TWAM No.	H5441	B9780	B9779	B9757
Designated as:	SANT	Caverhill I	Mitcalfe	Marr
Acquired	<1902	1932	1935	1958
Length	19.25″	12.5″	15″	25.5″
Breadth	7.75″	4.75″	5.75″	10.00″
Depth	3.06″	c.2.75″	2.38″	3.69″
Keel	14″	n-m	12″	21″
Beam/Length (%)	40	38	38	39
Depth/Beam (%)	39	59	41	37
Keel/Length (%)	73	n-m	80	82

Note: 'n-m', not measurable

length ratio of two-fifths remarkably consistent throughout, but it is matched by a corresponding level of agreement for the depth-to-beam ratio which – with one reasonable exception – again approximates two-fifths.[11] Similarly, and with due allowance for the difficulties of establishing uniform datum points, the length of keel (from stem- to stern-rabbet) is proportioned at around three-quarters to four-fifths of the vessel's overall length. Lest such proportional consistency be thought of no consequence, it is emphasized that the concept of constructional ratios is a well attested and ancient one in wooden ship- and boat-building practice, having especial practical and economic benefit when the series production of a specific type of vessel is anticipated.[12] [13]

Methodical Measurement

Although conceptually useful, the discovery of these proportions does not actually help to establish a standard keel's full-size dimensions. For that it is necessary to determine the scale of each of the four models concerned. And this process must take into consideration the fact that although each model represents a full-size craft of the same (or similar) dimensions, the four models vary greatly in size, ranging from 25½ inches to 12½ inches in length. Furthermore, long professional experience of models and modelmaking suggests that the makers of vernacular models of this kind commonly kept a couple of dimensional factors in mind. Firstly, the use of a commonplace linear scale that allowed a sufficiently realistic representation of the vessel concerned, and secondly, the maker's need to work within the size constraints imposed by the modelmaking materials cheaply to hand. Exotic or irregular scales (Table 2.3, row 6) seem unlikely, for the occasional modelmaker intuitively applies Occam's Razor – simplest is best – as well as a 'jack-a-legs' (keelman's clasp knife) to the job in hand! (Table 2.3).

TABLE 2.3 Proposed imperial scales for surviving keel models.

TWAM No.	H5441	B9780	B9779	B9757
Designated name	SANT	Caverhill 1	Mitcalfe	Marr
Length	19¼"	12½"	15"	25½"
Scale	1:24	1:36	1:30	1:18
1 inch scale	2ft	3ft	2ft 6in	1ft 6in
Scaled @ 42 ft length	1" ≡ 2' 2" 1:26	1in ≡ 3' 4" 1:39	1in ≡ 2' 10" 1:34	1in ≡ 1' 8" 1:20

After rigorous analysis, the author has concluded that all four models were indeed purposely worked to common imperial scales. Further, it is suggested that the choice of each model's scale was influenced by their respective makers' appraisals of the materials available and, perhaps, the model's anticipated display point. It may be no accident that the two smallest models, the plain but very naturalistic block-carved models designated Caverhill I and Mitcalfe here (TWAM B9780 and TWAM B9779 respectively), were reputedly made within the spatial limitations and domestic confines of the Keelman's Hospital by an occupant named Robson Caverhill around the year 1850.[14] By comparison, the Marr model (TWAM B9757), designated after the donor, is a much larger, two-foot long, technical showpiece comprising an eye-catching, varnished, plank-on-block constructed hull which, although showing some deck details, seemingly represented an un-rigged type of keel (Fig. 2.4, bottom). To the modern eye the most complete surviving model is the fully rigged and detailed SANT model (TWAM H5441) which may, with some justification, be described as an iconic representation of the nineteenth-century Tyne coal keel, but unfortunately is both unprovenanced and undated.

Following extensive analysis and consideration, the author concludes that the scales of the four models are as follows: Caverhill I, 1:36 (one inch ≡ three feet); Mitcalfe, 1:30 (one inch ≡ two feet six inches); Marr, 1:18 (one inch ≡ one foot six inches); SANT, 1:24 (one inch ≡ two feet). Scaled up, these ratios give consistent full-size lengths for the hulls of the craft represented of between 37 and 39 feet (Table 2.4, column 6). Conversely, at an assumed length of around 42 feet, as cited by Heslop and others, all attempts at scaling result in awkward ratios that seem unlikely to have been adopted by untutored modelmakers versed in imperial measures (Table 2.3, row 6; Table 2.4, column 7).

TABLE 2.4 Length of full-size keels at the scales variously calculated by the author, 2012-2019.

TWAM	Designated name	Length (inches)	Scale ratio	Common scale	Full-size keel	Scale @ 42 ft in length
H5441	SANT	19¼	1:24	1in ≡ 2 ft	38ft 6in	1in ≡ 2ft 2in
B9780	Caverhill 1	12½	1:36	1in ≡ 3 ft	37ft 6in	1in ≡ 3ft 4in
B9779	Mitcalfe	15	1:30	1in ≡ 2ft 6in	37ft 6in	1in ≡ 2ft 10 in
B9757	Marr	25½	1:18	1in ≡ 1ft 6in	38ft 3in	1in ≡ 1ft 8in

Further credence is given to the 37- to 39-foot figure by an artist's marginal annotation on one of the two (unpublished) illustrations commissioned for Heslop's proposed paper, c.1902, which reads: 'Keel 36ft [long], Sail 12ft high'.[15] The artist concerned, Robert J S Bertram (1871–1953), may be regarded as an informed source for he was the graphically talented son of a Newcastle ship chandler and, as a boy, had at first been put to work in the 'coal trade' at a time when some keels still remained in use. Several details within his lively pen-and-ink sketches also indicate that his work for Heslop was informed by close study of the SANT model – apparently then held in the society's Black Gate Museum.[16]

A further line of model-based evidence useful for determining the keel's length would be through scaling up deck or rig fittings of recognized size and pattern, e.g. cleats and blocks. But the ancillary fittings installed on Tyne keels were not only few in number but are generally atypical of those used on river lighters elsewhere, making comparisons unrewarding. Just one reliable comparison seems possible, namely, calculation of the width of the keel's two square hatch covers, or scuttles, for the size of such an aperture is related directly to the human frame. Hatch covers are depicted on three of the four models, and when scaled up give full-size dimensions as follows: SANT (forehatch only, aft hatch may not be original), 1 foot 10 inches; Mitcalfe, 1 foot 10½ inches; and Marr, 1 foot 6 inches. These measurements accord closely with the known dimensions of nineteenth-century hatches intended for crew access and, for that matter, with those found on modern yachts too.[17] That confidence can be placed in the accuracy of these model hatches seems assured. For example, on the Mitcalfe model the maker has even represented the recess for the 'cat band', the hinged and lockable iron strap which secured the hatch cover in place, and which remained a distinctive fitting on Tyne wherries until the mid-twentieth century.[18][19]

In the absence of any full-size survivals or archaeological findings, the conclusions on the all-important matter of the keel's size can now be summarized

TABLE 2.5 Calculated dimensions of full-size vessels represented by the four surviving contemporary models of Tyne Coal Keels.

TWAM	Designated name	Length: including rudder	Length: over stems	Length: on deck	Breadth: maximum outside	Depth: keel rabbet to sheer
H5441	SANT	40ft 4in	38ft 6in	37ft 3in	15ft 6in	6ft 1½in
B9780	Caverhill 1	no rudder	not measured	37ft 6in	14ft 7½ in	8ft 3in**
B9779	Mitcalfe	40ft 0in		37ft 6in	14ft 4½ in	6ft 0in
B9757	Marr	40ft 1in		38ft 3in	15ft 0in	5ft 10½in *

Notes: column 7: *corrected for hogging of model's keel; ** anomalous depth of model

through comprehensive analysis of the scant evidence found in documentary sources, combined with a rigorous examination of the four surviving contemporary models. This leads the author to deduce that the hull of a nineteenth-century Tyne coal keel was typically around: 38 feet length (on deck); 15 feet beam (to outside of planking); and 6 feet depth (internal). The overall working length, including rudder, was probably slightly over 40 feet (Table 2.5).

HULL FORM

The keel's historically unchanging and specialized function as a coal-carrying lighter suggests that its mature, late-eighteenth to mid-nineteenth century hull form might usefully be considered from two perspectives. Firstly, a comparison with select British river and estuarine craft which performed a similar function in the pre-steam era. Secondly, determination of the keel's three-dimensional form through quantitative, evidence-based analysis, leading (by extrapolation) to an appraisal of its likely performance as a carrier.

Comparison and Contrast

Although lighters known as 'keels' were employed for the trans-shipment of coal to seagoing ships on all four of the North East's major coal loading rivers – the Blyth, Tyne, Wear and Tees – it was widely acknowledged by contemporaries that the keels used on the Tyne were of a distinct kind. This was particularly obvious when compared to the keels of its chief competitor, the adjacent River Wear. Heslop, for example, explained that 'the shallows of the Wear required the least possible draught . . . the Wearside keel became a flat bottomed construction, characterized by great breadth of beam forward, narrowing aft, and terminating in a square stern'.[20][21] Indeed, throughout Britain during the long era of 'oar and sail' the twin issues of maximizing carrying capacity and exploiting shallow waterways shaped a response in the form of river lighters and barges that were preponderantly flat-floored, shallow of hull, and had relatively narrow beam in respect to their length. But within this generally accepted pattern there was a remarkable variety of regional types.[22][23] The Tyne coal keel was, however, amongst a handful of localized lighters whose hull forms lay outside the common run outlined above.

Unfortunately, many early comments about the Tyne's keels originated from travellers who lived outside the region, visitors who generally observed the vessels briefly and superficially from the riverbank, and thus gained little or no appreciation of their underwater shape and efficiency. Keels were thus branded with published epithets such as 'clumsy and ungainly', 'like half a walnut' or, slightly more descriptively, as 'oval and shallow draughted'. Most famously of all perhaps, they were labelled negatively in print by the popular, ardent industrializer Samuel Smiles as 'a very ancient model . . . a tubby, grimy-looking craft, rounded fore-and aft'.[24] Luckily, the legacy of the Tyne's own topographical and marine artists provides a more informed and appreciative perspective, for they sometimes depicted the keel's aesthetically satisfying underwater hull form with precision. Three examples depicting beached keels suffice (Fig. 2.3; Plate 1): a detail from an engraving after J W Carmichael (1799–1868) c.1830; an unfinished watercolour by Thomas Richardson Snr (1784–1848) c.1840; and a topographical view of 'Forth Banks', dated 1835, by the same artist.[25][26][27] These select bow-on views emphasise the keel's well rounded, bowl-shaped underwater sections and flat sheerline to perfection, characteristics that are fully endorsed by the contemporary models already described above (Fig. 2.4).

Correspondingly, the measured lines plan (hull contour plan) generated from the SANT model emphasizes that the keel was no angular, block-ended barge but a craft that possessed a subtly rounded, streamlined form. Technically however, a more objective, quantitative mode of description is required. This can be achieved in accord with Eric McKee's widely recognized 'Conventions Used to Describe Boat Shape' and the accompanying taxonomy, 'A Classification of Shapes', as developed in his seminal publication: *Working Boats of Britain* (1983).[28]

FIGURE 2.3 A few contemporary artists depicted keels aground, helpfully recording their shallow, bowl-shaped hulls (after: J W Carmichael, top; and T M Richardson Snr, middle & bottom).

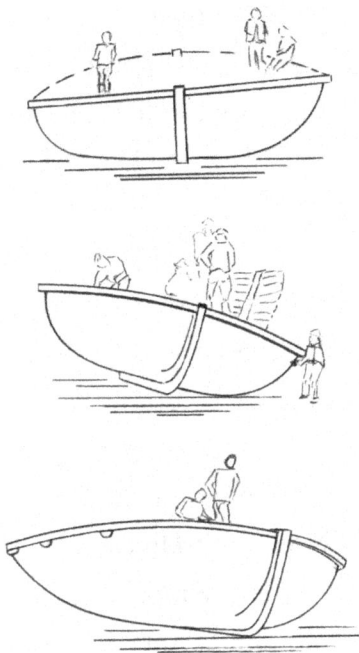

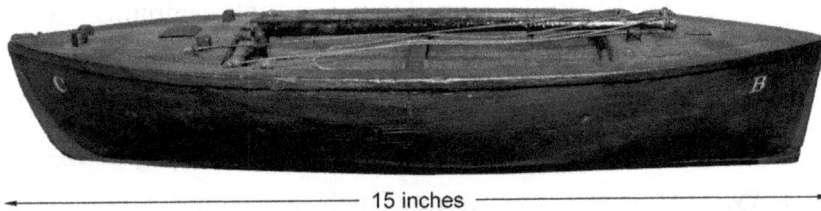

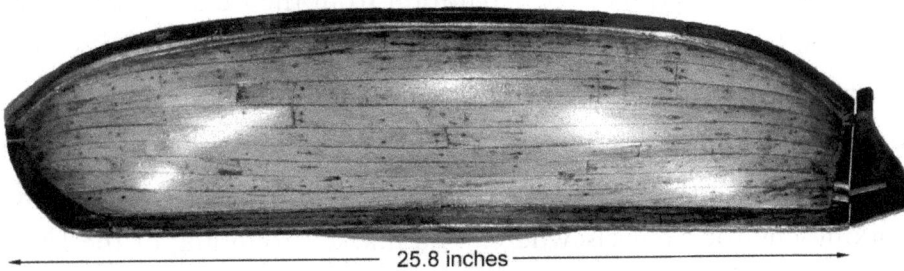

15 inches

25.8 inches

FIGURE 2.4 Top, with mast lowered, the Mitcalfe model exhibits the keel's characteristic flat sheerline and simple deck layout; below, the strake pattern of the Marr model emphasizes the keel's rounded hull form.

As per McKee's definitions, and based upon the SANT model, the Tyne keel's descriptive 'Profile' is as follows: length overall, 38 feet 3 inches; the (external) keel line, 'Straight'; the length of keel, 34 feet 6 inches; draught forward and aft (loaded), approx. 5 feet 3 inches; keel disposition, 'Level'; sheerline, 'Flat'; freeboard (at ends and amidships), 1ft 3in; stem shape forward, 'Raked and Curved'; and the stem shape aft, 'Raked (c. 10°) and Straight'. Likewise, the keel's 'Boat Shape' can be described as follows: Bow, 'Pointed End, Bluff'; Stern, 'Pointed End, Bluff'; midship section exhibits 'Flam'; bilge, 'Round' and barely 'Slack'; floor, 'Flat' and 'Curved'. Dimensionally, the block ratios calculate as: length to beam ratio 2.5, barely 'Beamy'; and beam to depth ratio 2.5, 'Normal' (Fig. 2.6).[29] When entered into McKee's taxonomy (classification) system the Tyne keel's relevant characteristics key out as: Class (median type) – 'Keelboat'; Division (midship section) – 'Round'; Sub-division (topsides, ends) – 'Stem-ended', i.e. double-ender; Category (keel profile) – 'Level'; Sub-category (block ratios) – 'Beamy' and 'Normal'; but the Taxon (label) itself exhibits no precise match. Nevertheless, McKee placed the keel within his disparate 'Hoggy' sub-category owing to its block ratio description of 'Beamy, flatter floor'. But that original categorization is arguable, for McKee's evaluation was based in part on incomplete and questionable information.[30]

A strong case can now be made for the Tyne keel as a specific taxon within a new sub-category.[31]Although rather arcane, such taxonomic discussions do serve to highlight the keel's typological separation from the bulk of British estuarine craft of similar function. That separation is defined by two, probably evolutionary, characteristics; firstly, the adoption of a round-bottomed mid-section; and secondly, the carriage of a specific amount of cargo loaded *upon* – rather than *within* – the hull. The first point is reinforced through comparison with craft of similar function and working environment elsewhere. The marked rounding of the keel's bilge in the mid-section is unusual, for river lighters characteristically displayed hard bilges or single chines in order to reduce draught and maximize internal capacity (Fig. 2.5). Likewise, the keel occupies a discrete position in the block ratio spectrum, appearing unusual among lighters by combining a high value for beam with a 'normal' (median) depth of hull (Fig. 2.6).

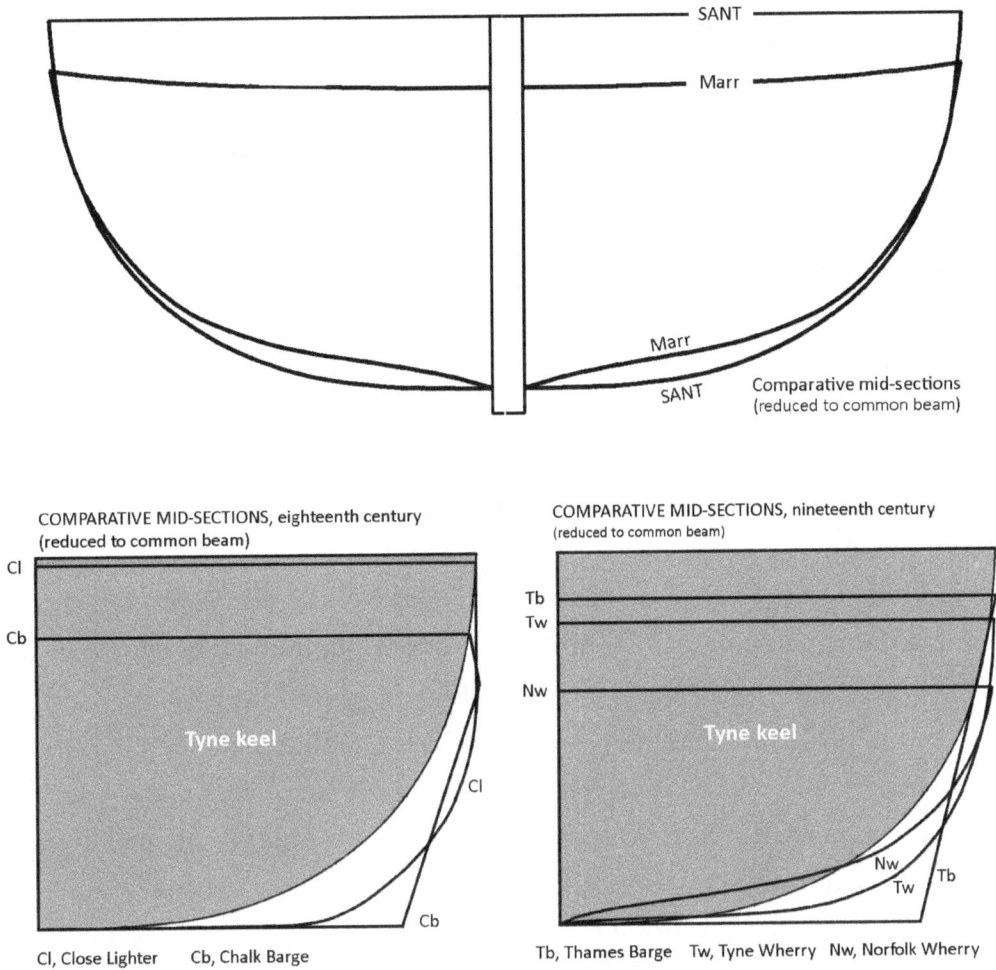

FIGURE 2.5 Top, the mid-sections of the SANT and Marr models drawn to a common beam. The Marr model's reduced depth possibly reflects lighter construction and weight reduction consequent upon the loss of sailing gear; bottom, the mid-sections of 18th century and 19th century East Coast lighters compared with the mid-section of a Tyne Keel (the latter based on SANT model).

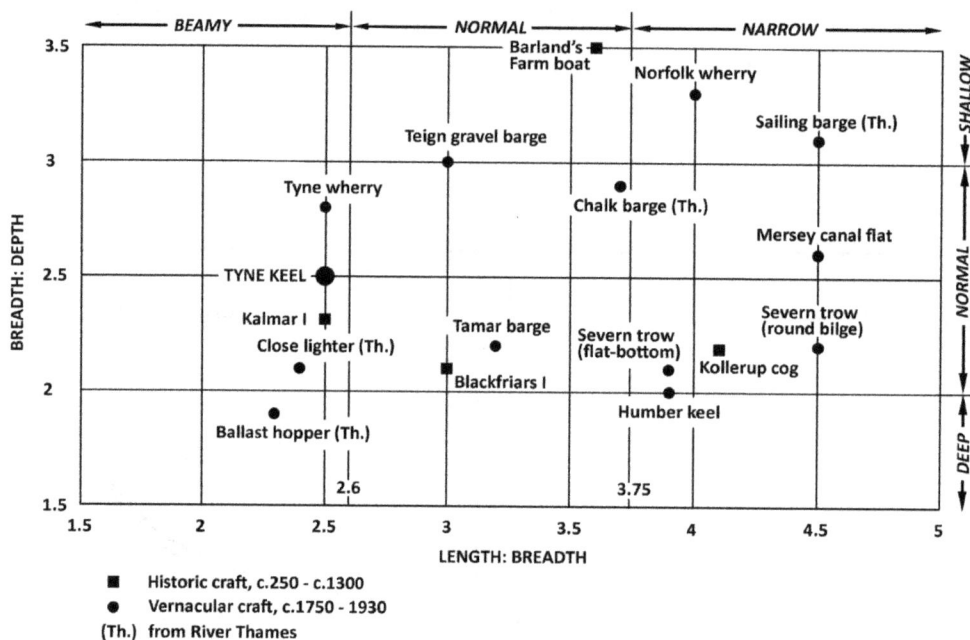

FIGURE 2.6 Comparative block ratios: the Tyne keel positioned against commonplace British lighters and select historic craft with reference to the categorizations suggested by McKee (1983).

In respect of the second point mentioned above, the keel's burden, there is significant divergence again. Within the limitations imposed upon lighters by, for instance, the volume of trade, environmental considerations (such as waterway width and depth), and manning costs, the historic trend was for operators to gain economies of scale by increasing a local type's carrying capacity and size to an upper manageable limit. But a keel owner on the Tyne was denied any such evolutionary gains since his vessel's cargo was regulated by national statute at a fixed, unchanging volume of coal from the late fourteenth century onward.

Although such centralized regulation was far from perfect at first, after 1695 a series of more consistent and effective Acts of Parliament concerning the 'admeasurement' of keels effectively restricted the keel's burden to 21.2 tons.[32][33] Over the long term it was these statutory constraints that apparently fashioned, or even stultified, the keel's evolution in respect of its size, capacity, and design.

Description and Analysis

On the evidence of the three most dependable surviving models, i.e. SANT, Marr, and Mitcalfe, together with information derived from contemporary visual sources, the principal external features of the keel's hull by the nineteenth century were as follows: in profile, there was a noticeably flat sheerline; the fore stem was strongly curved and of near radial form, its rabbet intersecting the sheer at an angle of approximately 60° at the top and merging smoothly into the keel line below; characteristically, the stem featured a broad cutwater, sometimes of unusual width; but the sternpost was slender, upright, and tapered slightly from bottom to top, with a straight rabbet line that raked aft by only around 10° (Figs. 2.7 and 2.10). The after edge of the sternpost accepted a wedge-form, median rudder of moderate breadth, hung by means of a long rod (pintle) passing through paired gudgeons on both the post and the blade. This arrangement allowed the rudder to be readily shipped (lifted aboard), as was frequently required. The rudder head itself was generally socketed to accept a short, but substantial, upwardly curved tiller.

In plan-view the keel was broadly oval in form with quite evenly disposed ends and carried its point of maximum beam close to two-fifths of the vessel's length from the bow. In the nineteenth century at least, the space occupied by the shallow hold amounted to nearly half or, alternatively, just over two-fifths of the keel's length on deck. This difference arose from a structural choice, the longer hold incorporated a transverse centre-beam whilst the shorter type had none, though in both cases the hold was bounded fore and aft by substantial transverse beams.[34] The port and starboard sides of the hold commonly matched the deck's curved edge and consequently lay symmetrically about the vessel's fore-and-aft centre line, but there was an asymmetric variant in which the port side of the hold was brought well inboard and aligned parallel to it – as seen in the SANT and Marr models (Figs. 2.7 and 2.10). Earlier, however, the keel appears to have exhibited cargo-carrying arrangements that were based upon an open hold in which the coals were carried within the full depth of the hull (Fig. 2.8; see also Chapter 6).

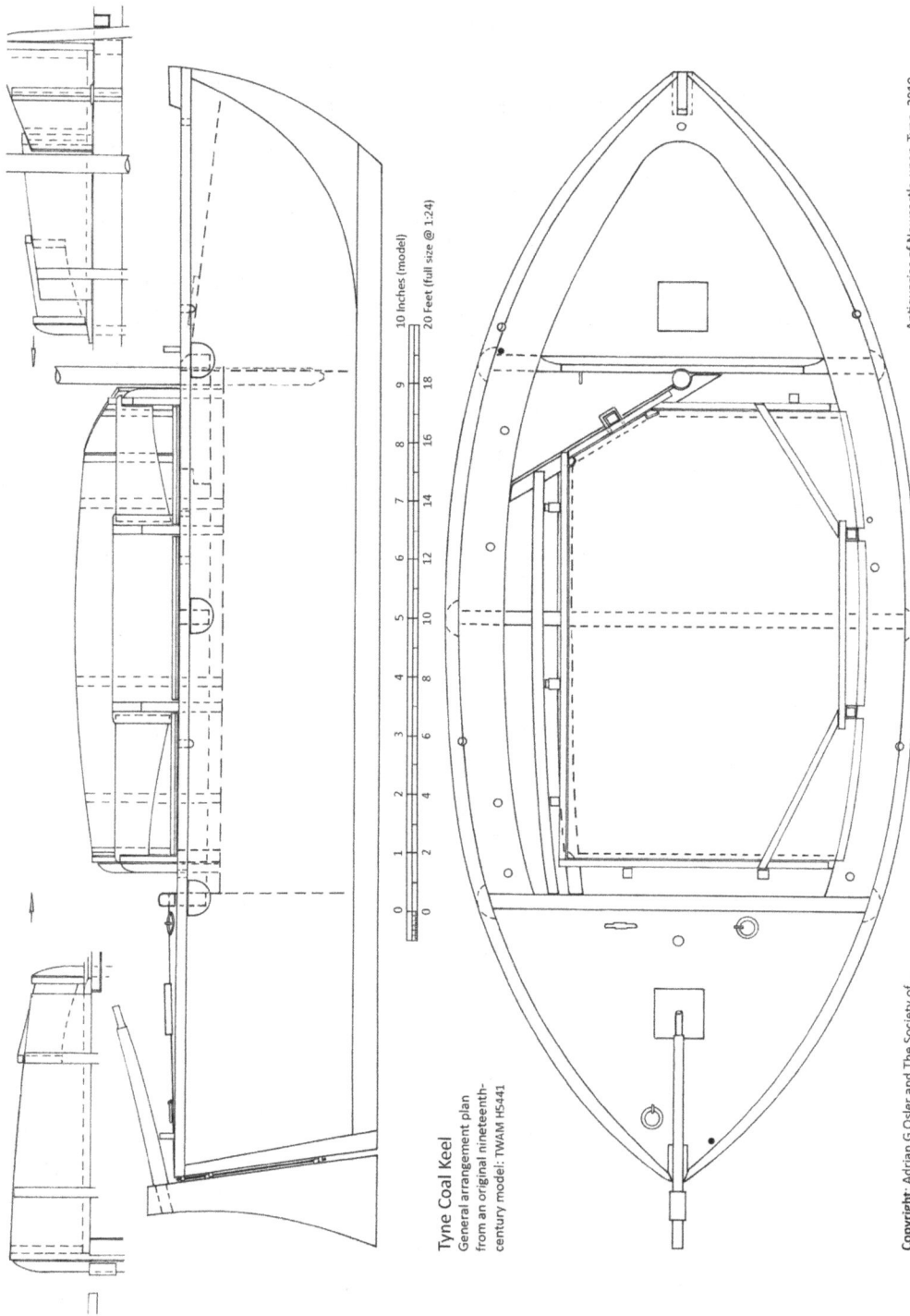

Tyne Coal Keel
General arrangement plan
from an original nineteenth-
century model: TWAM H5441

10 Inches (model)

20 Feet (full size @ 1:24)

FIGURE 2.7 General arrangement plan – excluding rig – of a Tyne Coal Keel (SANT model, TWAM H5441).

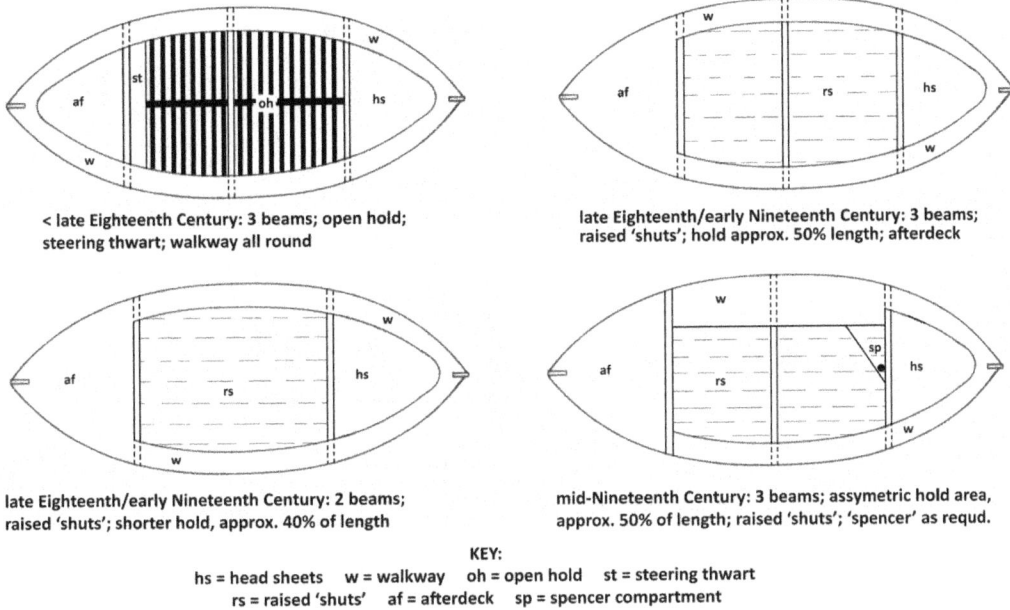

< late Eighteenth Century: 3 beams; open hold;
steering thwart; walkway all round

late Eighteenth/early Nineteenth Century: 3 beams;
raised 'shuts'; hold approx. 50% length; afterdeck

late Eighteenth/early Nineteenth Century: 2 beams;
raised 'shuts'; shorter hold, approx. 40% of length

mid-Nineteenth Century: 3 beams; assymetric hold area,
approx. 50% of length; raised 'shuts'; 'spencer' as requd.

KEY:
hs = head sheets   w = walkway   oh = open hold   st = steering thwart
rs = raised 'shuts'   af = afterdeck   sp = spencer compartment

FIGURE 2.8 Deck and hold layouts (bow to right) as evidenced by contemporary descriptions, illustrations, and models; other variations probably existed.

Considered aesthetically, the keel's hull form was pleasingly well balanced (Figs. 2.9 and 2.10). And, although within McKee's criteria the keel's bow might be considered 'bluff', it in no way resembled the rotund 'apple-cheeked' bows of the typical seagoing collier brig of the period, for the underwater bow was wedge-shaped throughout and displayed a modest angle of entry (35°- 40°). In the Marr model there is even a hint of concavity in the entry below the light waterline. The maximum breadth of the load waterline lay slightly aft of the vessel's midpoint, from where it ran in an easy (near-symmetrical) convex sweep fore and aft, above which the topsides were well disposed at bow and stern. Towards and below the light waterline the stern narrowed perceptibly (25–30°), producing a smooth concave 'run' into the sternpost and rudder blade.

Only two of the surviving keel models are sufficiently well fashioned to give confidence in their representation of hull form, so any attempt to determine a full-size keel's hydrodynamic character from them requires qualification and caution

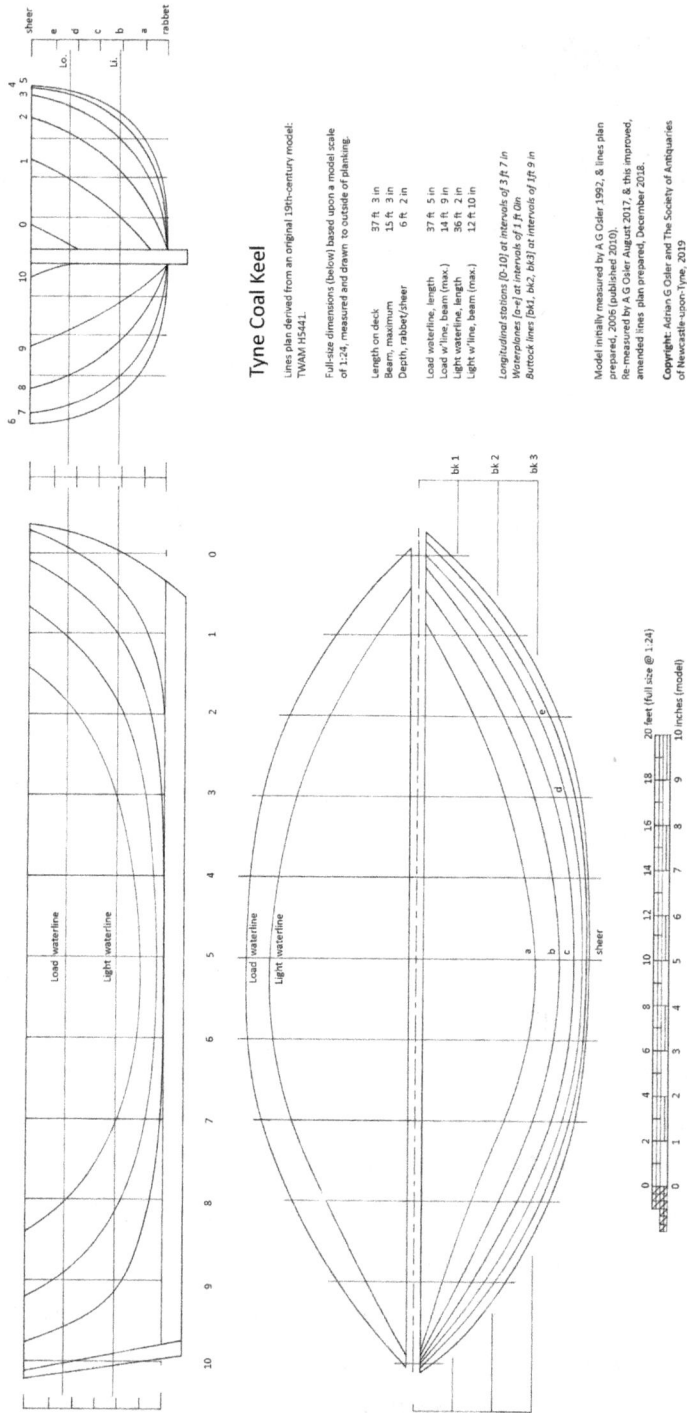

Tyne Coal Keel

Lines plan derived from an original 19th-century model: TWAM H5441.

Full-size dimensions (below) based upon a model scale of 1:24, measured and drawn to outside of planking.

Length on deck	37 ft	3 in
Beam, maximum	15 ft	3 in
Depth, rabbet/sheer	6 ft	2 in

Load waterline, length	37 ft	5 in
Load w'line, beam (max.)	14 ft	9 in
Light waterline, length	36 ft	2 in
Light w'line, beam (max.)	12 ft	10 in

Longitudinal stations (0-10) at intervals of 3 ft 7 in
Waterplanes (a-e) at intervals of 1 ft 0in
Buttock lines (bk1, bk2, bk3) at intervals of 1 ft 9 in

Model initially measured by A G Osler 1992, & lines plan prepared, 2006 (published 2010).
Re-measured by A G Osler August 2017, & this improved, amended lines plan prepared, December 2018.

FIGURE 2.9 Lines plan and dimensions of a Tyne Coal Keel equipped for sailing (SANT model, TWAM H5441).

Tyne Coal Keel, non-sailing type

Lines & half-breadth plan derived from model TWAM B9757 (uncorrected for hogging of original, approx.1/4 inch over 25 inches)

Measured with preliminary draught in 1992, revised and re-drawn 2021.

Full-size dimensions based on a model scale of 1:18 (1 in = 1 ft 6 in)

Length overall   38 ft 8 in
Beam, maximum   15 ft 0 in
Depth, rabbet/sheer   5 ft 6 in

Waterplanes @ 9 in & 1 ft 6 in intervals
Longitudinal stations @ approx 7 ft 2 in
Buttocks @ 1 ft 6 in intervals

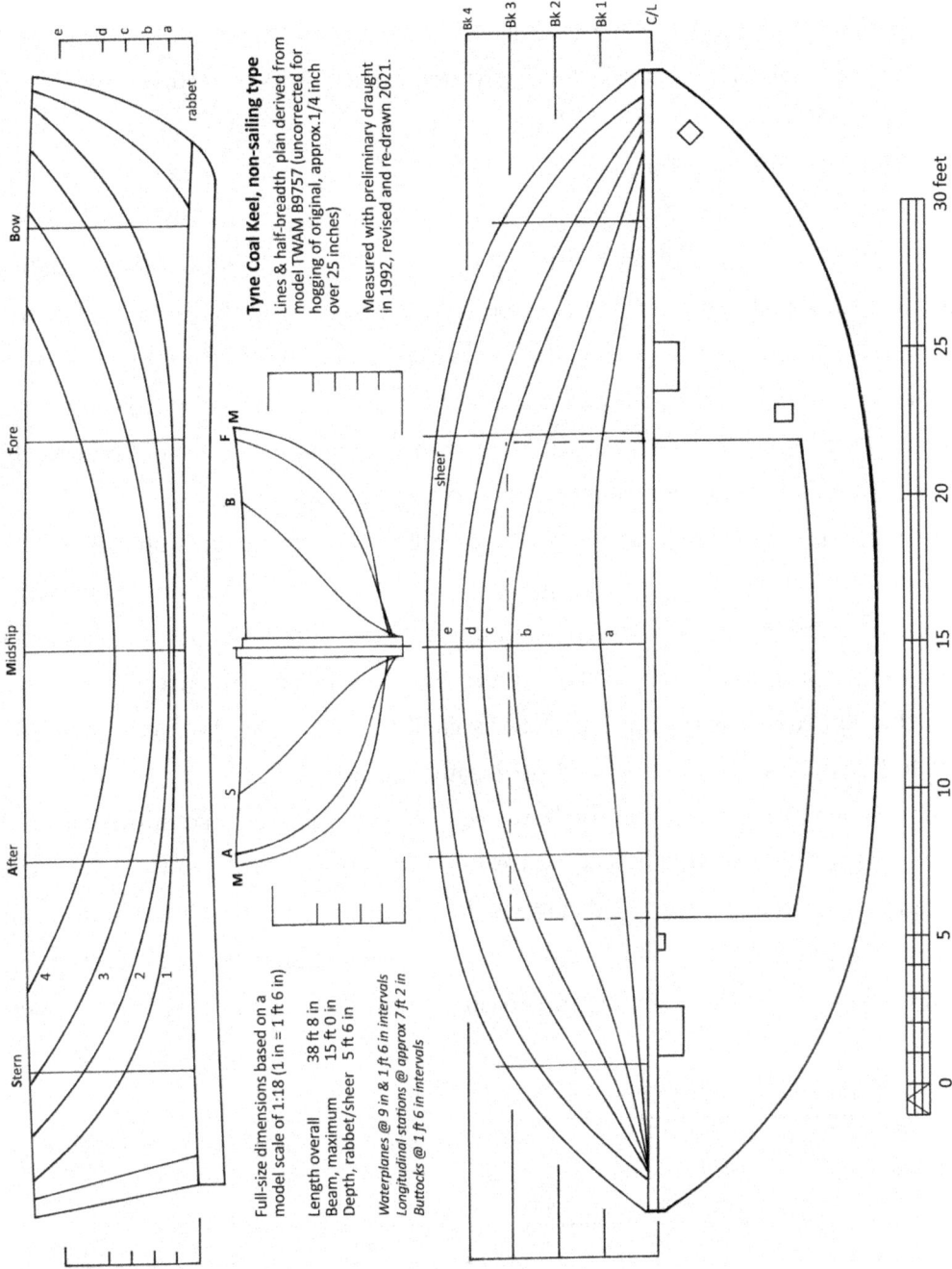

FIGURE 2.10 Lines and half-breadth plan of a Tyne Coal Keel of shallow-hulled, non-sailing type (Marr model, TWAM B9757).

(Figs. 2.9 and 2.10). Nevertheless, calculations based upon detailed measurements of the SANT model combined with quantitative information derived from a few reliable contemporary reports allows for a degree of confidence in select results.[35] For example, in 1828 an experienced witness, keelman Wm. Hume, indicated that the draught of a 'light' (i.e. unladen) keel was around 3 feet or slightly less, a figure that provides an initial datum point for displacement calculations.[36] At 3 feet draught the full-size keel represented by the SANT model would have displaced 12.8 tons in freshwater, sinking to a loadline draught of 5 feet 3 inches when carrying a statutory 21.2 tons of coal.[37] Although slightly deeper than the 5 feet loaded draught for a keel also cited by Hume, this is well within the margin of error for such model-based calculations, providing a working freeboard of around 1 foot 9 inches. This dimension accords well with the visual evidence of laden keels' topsides provided by nineteenth-century paintings and illustrations.

Uncertainties as to the nature of the scantlings and internal construction of the keel render any estimation of the weight of the hull and its equipment (as actually built) problematic. But calculations based upon its identifiable structural elements and the weight profiles of comparable watercraft renders a total of around 14 tons, a figure that approximates to the unladen displacement calculated above and would appear to be well within the range of probability (Table 2.6).

A significant characteristic of the bowl- or dish-like hull section exhibited by the keel was that it had a relatively low 'wetted surface area' in relation to the vessel's displacement, presenting up to 20 percent less surface area than a flat-bottomed lighter of comparable size. This marks an important efficiency gain, since at its normal working speed the 'skin friction' arising from a lighter's wetted (underwater)

TABLE 2.6 Hypothetical weight of keel hull, based on SANT model.

Item	Hull planks	Frames	Deck & hold planks	Keel & keelson	Stem & sternpost	Hold beams	Rubbing strakes	Fastenings & fittings	Total (Tons)
Tons	3.4	5.1	1.5	1.5	1	0.4	0.5	0.7	14.1

Note: calculated for three-inch hull planking with all oak construction at 51 lbs. per cubic foot

surface area comprises around three-quarters of the total resistance encountered. Corresponding analysis shows that the keel's 'prismatic coefficient' (P_C) – 'the numerical measure of the fullness of the ends of a hull in relation to the middle' – was advantageously low for a mundane working lighter. Indeed, the Tyne keel's P_C of 0.62 is theoretically optimal at velocities of around 3¾ knots and thus appears well suited to the speeds attained in everyday use on the tideway.[38] However, these gains regarding propulsive efficiency were, to an extent, offset by the relatively modest levels of transverse stability provided by a hull with bowl-like (semicircular) hull sections. That is, the keel's ability to resist capsizing forces was limited, added to which only a modest angle of accidental heel, less than 15°, would put the deck edge dangerously under the water.[39] Regrettably, further quantification of the keel's degree of stability is not possible, for a lack of detailed knowledge of the keel's internal components and their weights precludes calculation of its vertical centre of gravity (VCG) – a critical figure.[40]

From at least the early nineteenth century the keel can be considered as having carried a 'deck cargo', with all the safety issues that such cargoes carried for ships' crews throughout history. But that is not to imply that keels, especially laden ones, were inherently unstable. Newspaper reports of keels capsizing when at work are infrequent, but on the other hand sinkings caused by sudden leakage, accident, collision or (one assumes) poor maintenance were relatively commonplace events, events that might be anticipated in a fleet of several hundred, hard worked, parsimoniously operated craft. That the keel's stability record appears no worse seems attributable to two things: firstly, to the accumulated empirical knowledge of keel builders; and secondly, to the generally high level of experience amongst the senior crew members, especially the annually contracted skippers. Although the keelman was popularly portrayed in 'verse and worse' as a figure of fun, there are more reliable views of his competence. For instance, although he was hardly a disinterested observer, the testimony of a naval officer in 1801 was that 'he should prefer as a seaman a person bred to the keels, to one who had been two voyages to the East Indies' – a professional view that should be allowed credence.[41]

CONSTRUCTION

The last dedicated coal keel was reputedly built around 1860, so it is not surprising to find that little written evidence survives regarding the techniques used in the building of keels, their wooden fabric and even the nature of their builders.[42] What little incidental information did find its way into secondary sources in the latter part of the nineteenth and early twentieth centuries was already well removed from firsthand experience and, consequently, was often reliant on hearsay, a situation which has left much open to interpretation.

Builders

Formal references to keel building and repair initially occur in the late seventeenth century, where they were among the activities anxiously protected by a minor guild: the Company of Shipwrights of Newcastle-upon-Tyne.[43] This guild not only set strict daily rates for all kinds of shipbuilding work but constrained its members to practice either within 'the liberties of Newcastle [town]' or, by special dispensation, along the river elsewhere. But in the early eighteenth century changes in local social conditions saw the Company's authority weaken, and encroachment on the shipwright's craft by non-members became a serious problem. Furthermore, the Company's own brethren increasingly sought to evade the guild's strictly prescribed rules. For example, so as to avoid regulations that prohibited fixed price contracts guild members might spuriously buy-back keels that they had built, or they would covertly undercut the Company's agreed minimum rate of £14 per annum for hiring out any 'new keel, or keel fitted with furniture [equipment]'.[44] And the Newcastle-based guild's monopolistic position continued to worsen. By 1720 the right to build ships and keels at South Shields had been established, added to which a lengthy shipbuilding recession caused a decline in guild numbers that was exacerbated in mid-century by the Navy's wartime demands for skilled tradesmen. One consequence of the guild's decline seems to have been that, in the late eighteenth century, the building of keels became a more dispersed activity – both professionally and geographically. By the turn of the nineteenth century keel building appears to have lain in the hands of three kinds of business concern: large, well established shipbuilding companies; small local shipyards; and individual, specialist keel builders.

This diversity of supply is reflected in the fact that a quarter of the 37 Tyneside 'master [ship] builders' listed for the hundred years from 1720 to 1820 occasionally advertised keels for sale including, for example, Thomas Reed of South Shore (Gateshead) as early as 1705.[45] Similarly, in mid-century, apprentice hostman Ralph Jackson's journal for 1756 is replete with mention of keels being repaired and maintained by 'carpenters' at the 'landing' of a local shipbuilding partnership: Messrs. Robert and John Gothards, at North Shore (Newcastle).[46] Jackson also refers to another prominent North Shore shipyard, that of Edward Trewhitt, who advertised two working keels for sale in 1755 and where a total of five 'Keels, Coal Boats or Lighters' were offered upon his decease in 1767.[47] That a corresponding level of involvement by shipbuilders continued on into the early nineteenth century is indicated by the fact that at least a quarter of the two dozen 'Merchant Yards' enumerated in an Admiralty survey of 1804 are known, through newspaper evidence, to have built keels.[48] [49] Such establishments ranged in size from Francis Hurry's complex at Howdon employing over 150 shipwrights and apprentices, to Miles Hall's modest 'North Shore' (St. Lawrence, Newcastle) venture with just 12 employees. But their annual output of keels (as distinct from ships) is hard to estimate, although incidental reports indicate that the levels were modest. For example, Francis Hurry's extensive assets at closure – due to bankruptcy – in 1805 included two 'new coal keels', whilst Hall advertised a single keel for sale that same year and another 'new-built keel lately launched' two years later in 1807. The same year also saw recently widowed Ann Young forced to sell two 'strong and remarkably well-built keels' at her North Shore yard, together with the sparse inventory of equipment and materials that had made up 'all the stock' of her late husband, whose workforce had comprised just four shipwrights and nine apprentices in 1804.[50]

Specialist keel builders appear to have been relatively few and are only occasionally designated as such in print, though a handful of Newcastle- and Gateshead-based family concerns do stand out during the late eighteenth and early nineteenth century. In Newcastle, the Petrie family's business was located at the heart of the keelman's milieu 'on the Shore-side behind Sandgate', adjacent to the eponymous Petrie's Close. At least two generations of the Petrie family built keels there, Alexander Snr (d.1815) and Alexander Jnr, although the latter's activities were cut short in February 1826 by a dreadful fire which cruelly destroyed not only his workshop 'owing to the combustible materials it contained' but 'a considerable quantity of wood'– that is, his stockpile of building materials too.[51] On the opposite shore at Gateshead, keel- and boat- building was notable not only in the town itself along Hillgate Quay but also just upriver at Dunston-on-Tyne, where Enoch White and George Bowlt have been cited as likely keel builders during the mid-eighteenth century.[52][53] The Bowlt (or Boult) family were certainly amongst the Tyne's most prominent boatbuilders from about 1790 to 1830 and John Boult's (d.1827) workforce numbered 14 in 1804, although his involvement if any with keel building at that time is unclear.[54] That, however, was not the case with Thomas Sadler of Dunston who, if relatively late to this specialist work, explicitly styled himself as a 'keel builder' and advertised coal keels for sale both 'new' and 'at work' in 1819.[55] Upon Thomas's death in November 1836 (Fig. 2.11), he was succeeded after a brief interval by Robert and William Sadler, presumably his sons, who continued to occupy the family's 'commodious' rented quay at Dunston

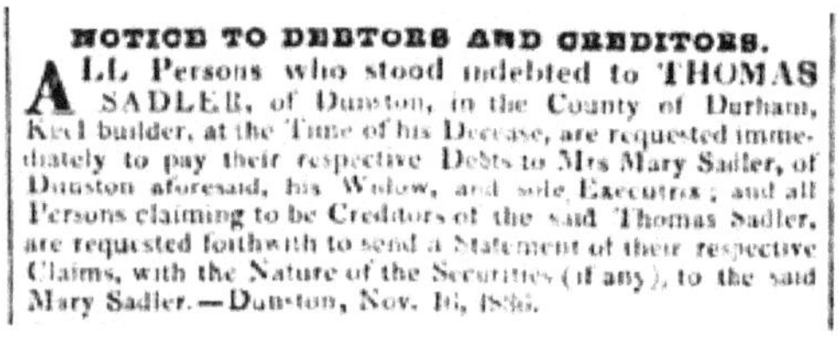

FIGURE 2.11 Formal notice to the 'Debtors and Creditors' of the late Thomas Sadler 'Keel builder' of Dunston, Gateshead, November 1836 (*Newcastle Courant*).

NOTICE TO DEBTORS AND CREDITORS.
ALL Persons who stood indebted to THOMAS SADLER, of Dunston, in the County of Durham, Keel builder, at the Time of his Decease, are requested immediately to pay their respective Debts to Mrs Mary Sadler, of Dunston aforesaid, his Widow, and sole Executrix; and all Persons claiming to be Creditors of the said Thomas Sadler, are requested forthwith to send a Statement of their respective Claims, with the Nature of the Securities (if any), to the said Mary Sadler.—Dunston, Nov. 16, 1836.

as 'keel builders' and keel owners, petitioning the Tyne Improvement Commission for permission to 'lay down a new slipway' as late as 1856.[56]

Though now lost to the record, similar enterprises clearly existed elsewhere.[57] For instance, in 1817 the lease of a 'Keel Builder's Yard' with a large drying foreshore and 54 yards of deep-water quay was advertised at Dent's Hole two miles east of Newcastle but, as a sign of changed demand, the site's owners were now promoting it as 'a proper place to build a factory'.[58] Meanwhile, just across the river at South Shore in Gateshead, the speculative nature of much small-scale keel- and ship-building is exampled by the case of Jonathan Brown (d.1836). To satisfy his creditors in 1819–21, Brown sought to auction off a 118-ton coaster 'on the Stocks, all finished but the cabin' together with 'a new strong built COAL KEEL, now ready for launching; likewise a new one and an old one, in good condition, at present in employ'.[59] The opportunistic nature of Brown's keel-building is further highlighted by the fact that within a few years he was adaptably back in business again as a small 'steam packet' (tug) builder and timber merchant.

However, since colliery owners, coal fitters and shippers all depended upon continuity in the river-borne supply chain – a dependence demonstrated by their vociferous reaction every time the keelmen threatened to strike – it seems likely that the principal demand for new keels was met by craft built to specific order rather than by casual acquisition from speculative builders. A collective policy of pre-ordered replacements would seem to have been necessary to maintain the Tyne's fleet of several hundred keels, where the annual wastage rate was probably 5 to 10 percent.[60][61] If so, this implies a general renewal rate of some 20 to 40 new keels per annum, though with even higher figures than that during periods of increased colliery output.

The supposition that commissioned, rather than speculatively built, keels comprised the greater part of the fleet's renewals and enlargements is reinforced by the observation that only one in ten of the 353 keels advertised for sale between 1712 and 1855 were new-builds, and a fifth of those newly-built keels were the result of forced sales occasioned by business failure or decease. Though sales advertisements

TABLE 2.7 The occupational status of vendors of keels advertised for sale, 1712–1855 (%).

		1712–1739	*1740–1799*	*1800–1855*	*1712–1855*
Coal Interests	Hoastmen	6	4		
	Fitters	18	7		
	Collieries		21	47	
		25	**32**	**47**	**34**
Mercantile	Merchants	66	4	24	
	Shipowners		8	5	
		66	**12**	**29**	**33**
Constructors	Shipwrights	9	19	5	
	Shipbuilders		22	11	
	Boat- & Keel-builders	9	9	3	
		9	**50**	**19**	**29**
Others			**6**	**5**	**4**

alone cannot yield a figure for the total number of new keels constructed (1712–1855), an occupational analysis of the vendors helps to define the marketplace sectors for them and shows that the balance changed over time (Table 2.7). This latter analysis also serves to reinforce the conclusions of Fewster and Wright that – as movable property – keels were considered a valuable source of rental income and similarly supports the view that, throughout the period concerned, keel builders often retained an ongoing financial interest in their products.[62][63] Representative of such men was Newcastle's William Robson (d. 1824, aged 80 years) at the Ouseburn, a tributary inlet serviced by keels and wherries. Robson appears to have practiced ship- and keel-building there in a small way from at least 1790 onward and during that period also gained the management of a sizable fleet of keels belonging to the Heddon and Willington collieries of Messrs. Bell and Brown, some of which he had probably built.[64]

Speculatively, it seems probable that the practice of a keel builder retaining a financial interest in a keel's ownership or management may have acted as a factor in maintaining construction standards. It seems unlikely that a builder who anticipated rental income would have tolerated inadequacies of design or durability.

That said, as with all wooden shipbuilding activities some poor-quality craft may well have been passed off to unwary third parties.

Layout

By the late eighteenth- and early nineteenth-century keel builders and users seem to have developed a uniform, functional layout for their craft that reflected its role both as a coal carrier and a working platform, and which had acquired a distinctive terminology to match (Fig. 2.12). At the core of this standardized layout was a shallow hold (cargo space) amidships abutted by triangular areas of deck fore and aft which, in turn, were connected by narrow, exposed walkways running along the hull sides. Owing to the hold's relatively small size, around 12 feet by 16 feet,

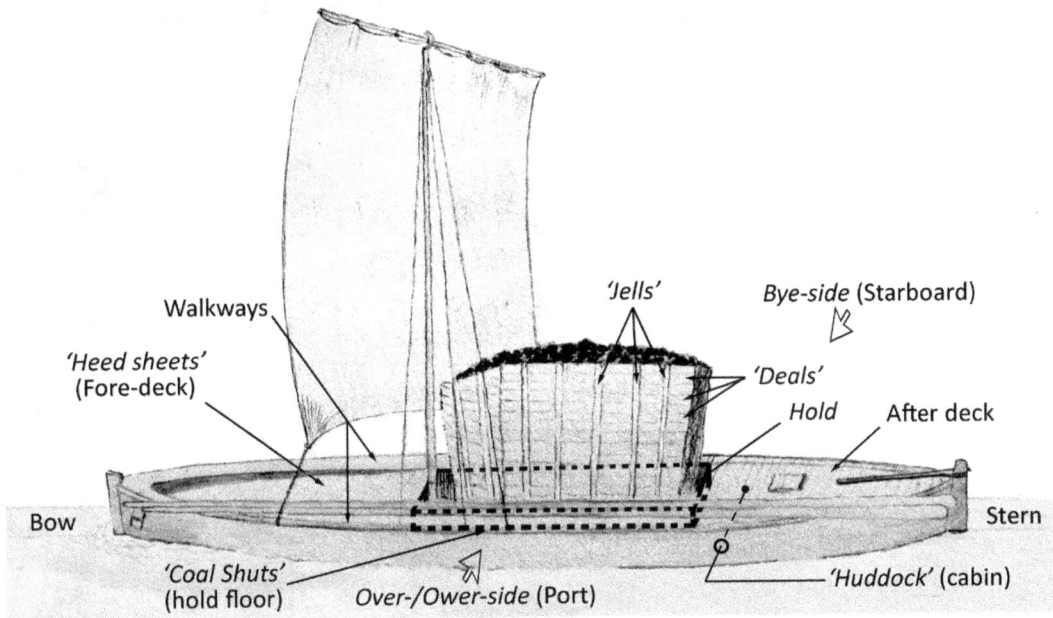

FIGURE 2.12 The basic layout and terminology of an early nineteenth-century keel's hull, with dialect terms italicized, as noted by R O Heslop (from a drawing in John Bell's compilation volume: *Keelmen,* c.1830).

it was necessary to heap up the cargo from its recessed floor ('shuts') to a height of 5- or 6-feet above deck level to accommodate the volume of rough-hewn coals – approximately 1,000 cubic feet – that made up the vessel's statutory load of 21.2 tons. But a heap of that height could not be made without restraint.[65]

Containment was usually achieved by the erection of a simple, temporary, box-like timber structure around the hold which is often depicted in contemporary illustrations. The practical details, however, are unclear though it reputedly comprised a frame of close-spaced, vertical posts ('jells') stepped inside the edge of the hold recess, against which was progressively laid a loose internal covering of planks ('deals') resting horizontally, edge-to-edge up to the required heights on all four sides (Fig. 2.13). Though crude in appearance this was a low-cost, low

FIGURE 2.13 Coal containment by rough, box-like 'jells' and 'deals' as depicted by local artists: top, unknown, published by M Dunn, 1852; middle, T M Richardson, print, 1819; bottom, W J Palmer, book illustration, 1882.

technology solution that provided cargo stability, prevented spillage, and allowed for managed discharge by hand. Most importantly, it was easy to dismantle and stow away the components after the craft was discharged.

Nevertheless, a few textual comments combined with the evidence of the SANT model suggests that more sophisticated containment methods involving the use of purpose-made, removeable 'sideboards', 'stages', or 'coal boards' were also introduced, although the little surviving evidence there is suggests that these came relatively late in the keel era.[66] The provision of such dedicated fittings on keels is also implied by the fact that truncated coaming extensions ('greedy boards') of similar form and function were installed around the holds of Tyne cargo wherries in a later era.[67][68]

On the SANT model the use of these dedicated sideboards is associated with the adoption of an asymmetric cargo platform, a development which again has been suggested was late in date.[69] This asymmetry, which is also seen in the Marr model, shifted the load towards the discharge side ('bye-side') and not only eased the work of 'casting' (shovelling) the coals into the receiving ship by bringing the bulk of the pile closer to the 'shovel men' but, through the clever differentiation of the sideboard height, brought the peak of the heap of coal directly over the vessel's centre-line, thus improving the keel's transverse trim and stability. As seen on the SANT model, this sideboard structure formed a simple hopper whose low, angled sideboards (fore and aft) on the bye-side had cutaways at the base to feed the coals onto broad triangular platforms. This arrangement eased the work of the casters and facilitated the rate of discharge.[70] These efficiency gains must, however, have come at the expense of higher fitting out costs. To provide adequate support for the sideboards – themselves more costly than rough jells and deals – a pair of heavy longitudinal beams also had to be built into the hold recess on the port side ('ower-side') together with an additional transverse beam aft, and strong iron clasps were needed to retain some of the sideboard posts. Moreover, the hold space may have required removable flooring at deck-level to allow the first chaldrons of coal to be stowed in the hold recess below (Fig. 2.7 and Fig. 1.4).[71]

Both the conventional and asymmetric containment systems left a triangular space (the 'spencer') free in the forward, port-side corner of the hold (Fig. 2.14). Extending down to the vessel's bilge, this was separated off from the load-carrying area by a diagonally aligned 'shifting board', leaving a compartment with just sufficient room in which to step (place) and handle the keel's mast. As far as can be ascertained, the mast of a square-rigged keel was housed there with great simplicity. The heel of the 25-foot mast, weighing some two hundredweights, was fashioned to a conical point that rested in a matching socket cut into a heavy wooden block secured to the floors (or keelson) and fore-bulkhead.[72] A simple clasp of some kind at deck level may then have been used to hold the mast upright in the

FIGURE 2.14 The SANT model's triangular spencer compartment, mast housing, and heavy support beams for the port sideboards all forms a complex timber structure (see also Fig. 2.7).

acute angle between the shifting board and bulkhead, and its rigidity when sailing was maintained by two pairs of shrouds (stays).[73] However, when the more efficient and powerful spritsail rig was adopted in the 1830s the squaresail mast's archaic step gave way to a tabernacle that housed a pivoted, lowering mast – as indicated by Mitcalfe's illustrator.

Forward, the spencer abutted the foredeck, colloquially known as the 'heed sheets' (head sheets). This deck surface exhibited a unique design feature through being ramped sharply downward (1:8) towards the bow, leaving the extended side walkways upstanding by around a foot at the stem (Fig. 2.7, elevation). An 18-inch square scuttle provided access to a poky storage area below the deck and heavy, upstanding, wooden 'billet heads' (posts) of square section pierced the deck for mooring and towage purposes. Typically, one pair of these was situated immediately in front of the hold to port and starboard outboard, whilst another pair was closely spaced in the bow. The stern deck was of much the same pattern although its surface was conventionally flat fore and aft and presented no more than a slight, water-shedding camber athwartships.

The after-deck's planking merged flush with the walkways on each side, and a shallow moulded coaming (above the aft beam) marked the after boundary of the hold. Since the stern deck functioned as the keel's steering platform, it was left as uncluttered as possible. Characteristically, it bore no more than a pair of billet-heads forward and inboard, or just one amidships.[74] A low-lidded scuttle gave access to the keelmen's iconic accommodation space below deck, the 'huddock' or 'huddick', a cramped, wedge-shaped space barely 5 feet in height fitted with plain side benches and a small coal-burning stove (usually located abaft the hold bulkhead) that was used for frying and boiling. Secondary fittings on deck included two robust iron thole pins, one on the port side forward – in line with the aft edge of the head sheets – for the keel's massive main oar, and a similar one located right aft to starboard for the 'swape' (steering oar).

From stem to stern the outer margin of each walkway comprised the flat top of a robust, 6 inch by 6 inch, rubbing strake which provided the vessel's main permanent fendering. The SANT model alone shows three pairs of semicircular blocks immediately below the rubbing strakes; each pair (port and starboard) lies coincident with the ends of a deck-level beam and their historic significance is discussed later (chapter 6). The SANT model also shows that the keel's walkways and rubbing strake were pierced by several irregularly spaced holes that apparently functioned as fairleads or fastening points for the standing and running rigging (Fig. 2.7).[75] For good practical reasons the hull surface between the rubbing strake and external keel was left smooth and entire, exhibiting no fittings or projections that might have caused entanglement or have been susceptible to damage.

Common to all four of the extant models is the fact that, whilst their sternposts are relatively narrow and conventional in shape, their fore-stems extend – to a greater or lesser degree – into a pronounced forefoot at the base. This trait is particularly evident on the SANT model where the external stem is notably falcate in form, widening from merely 4 inches at the rubbing strake to 2 feet in breadth where it meets the keel – a feature which again merits later discussion.

Statutory Measurement

If the exact dimensions and form of a new keel were of interest only to the builder and its owner, exact measurement of its taxable carrying capacity was of concern to the Crown – via its regulatory authorities in Newcastle. Throughout most of the coal keel's recorded history this capacity was statutorily measured when afloat by recording its 'deadweight' displacement, i.e. the draught to which the vessel sank when laden with official weights (of iron or lead) totalling 'one keel', 21.2 tons.[76] To permanently record this, the stem and the sternpost of each keel was then individually marked by 'nailing' to show its draught, fore and aft, when loaded. By the second quarter of the nineteenth century at least, additional nails recorded the draughts when unladen and also at intermediate ladings per chaldron. This proscriptive process was described in considerable detail in the regulations of the 'Commission for weighing Coal Waggons and Keels at Newcastle and Sunderland' as presented to a Select Committee in 1829:[77]

> You shall carefully observe, when Keels and Boats come to the Place of measuring, that they and every of them be light, clean and unstored, and that they have no Water in them, or Weight on board them, as Lead, Iron, Stone or other ponderous Matter, or other Gear or Materials but such only as they carry when they go and row to cast on board Ships. You shall then proceed to drive the first or Stock Nail, indicating the Light Mark of the Keel, which Nail must be on an exact Square, and driven angularly, so that the Edge of the Water may be even with the Middle of the Nail, forming a Triangle clear of the Water. You shall then cause Fifty-three Hundred Weights to be placed in the Keel, and see that the Nails are fairly driven on each Side of the Stem and Stern Posts to mark the first Chaldron, and repeat this Operation until the whole Number of Chaldrons are in the Keel, when an oblong Plate is to be nailed above the last Nail, to secure it from Loss or Removal, and to indicate the Loading of the Keel . . . [you] shall see that he or they that prick or drive the nails do it fairly, with the Top or upper Side of each Nail swimming clear, and even with the Water.[78]

Unfortunately, even the carefully drafted clauses of the Commission's regulations allow for ambiguity of interpretation today and, quite surprisingly, no such measurement nails are depicted on surviving models or contemporary illustrations. But after careful consideration the author suggests the arrangement presented schematically here (Fig. 2.15), with the vertical intervals between the nails reducing progressively – from bottom to top – as the area of the hull's waterplane increases with each added chaldron weight of immersion.[79]

The opening sentence of this regulation guarded against keel owners providing illicit overmeasure, for weights hidden during admeasurement might be removed

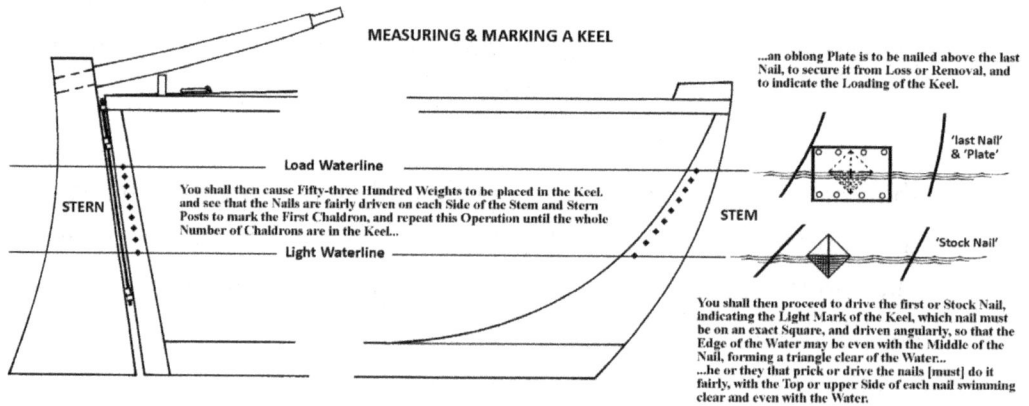

FIGURE 2.15 Schematic reconstruction of the stems of a keel measured and nailed according to the Coal Commission's regulations.

later to increase a keel's capacity. Conversely, weights added covertly whilst loading coals resulted in short measure. In 1655 for example, a London shipmaster complained that 'often the coal boat [keel], hath much water [bilgewater] which lies heavy, also great store of slates and other rubbish . . . a master is often deceived by the keelmen in the nayles'.[80] The Commission's regulatory precision also implies that earlier (pre-1775) marking systems had not been so thorough and allowed too much room for argument. For instance, a letter regarding an allegedly overloaded keel in 1768 referred to it being 'an inch over ye plate at the head and a quarter inch over the plate at the stern', although the accused keelmen argued that their vessel was correctly loaded to its regular marks: 'a half plate at the bow and under the nail at the stern'. Moreover, in waves and rough water the judgment of a keel's lading could prove especially contentious, as exemplified by the actions of skipper John Hymen whose unhappy experiences led him to proceed slightly under-laden (1768) 'when the roughness of the water prevents certainty [of measure]', rather than risk being fined by accusations of overloading.[81]

The Commission also remarked upon various methods of measurement evasion, including the need to take action against 'evil disposed persons' who:

Soon after admeasurement . . . lay [their] Keels on shore, upon Blocks under each End thereof, which causes those parts to rise, and the Midship parts to sink with their own weight, whereby the said Keels or Boats will carry more Coals than their just Burthen, and yet swim [float] remarkably short of their loading Marks or Nails, both at Head and Stern.[82]

Safeguards were also needed against nails being surreptitiously shifted during replacement work by '[Ship] Carpenters, Workmen or Other Persons', and particular warning was given to anyone who might 'screw or wedge up the Stem or Stern Post of any Keel or Boat' during repairs or use any other 'indirect or unlawful Ways or Means' to advantage a keel's operator.[83]

Further complications must also have arisen from a keel's displacement genuinely altering over time, as noted by Hostman's apprentice Ralph Jackson in May 1756: 'My Master told me to order Emmerson's [skipper] Keel to the Leadhill to be measured . . . In the morning Emmerson's Keel was measur'd she sunk about half an inch [below her nailed marks]'. Clearly, 'Emmerson's Keel' had increased its unladen displacement – perhaps through natural soakage – during the preceding year and, latterly, must have carried less than full measure when loaded to its nailed marks.[84] And Jackson not only notes another keel being measured 'with weights' at Newcastle Quay by the Customs House officers but comments, unfavourably, on Newcastle Corporation's imposition in October 1756 'of bail [a fee] for Keels being weigh'd [measured], which is first thing of its kind, (for a Keel) ever known'. Indeed, this charge upon keel owners remained thereafter, although 'the Crown' did bear the cost of supplying the weights used for the measurement process.[85]

Following measurement and nailing in accordance with the Commission's regulations, each keel was assigned a registration number and, from 1828 onwards, 'a brass plate with the [registration] number and measure' was then affixed on a beam or bulkhead inside.[86] However, there is no indication that keel owners ever complied with the aspirational provision in the government's earlier 'Register of Boats Act 1795' which stipulated that:

The true number of tons burthen of such vessels, and also the names of the owners thereof, and the place to which such vessel shall belong, are to be painted in large white capital figures, on a black ground, four inches in length at the least, and of a proportionable breadth, on the outside of the stern. . . .[87]

Indeed, the keelmen long resisted public and civic appeals for the distinctive marking of individual keels, much preferring to retain a collective anonymity amongst the frequently reported cases of collision, accident, thieving, and inter-crew disputes. That said, two of the four surviving contemporary models, together with Bell's sketch of a keel, c.1830, all exhibit large, plain, identifying ciphers (letters and numerals) of a style commonly seen in much later photographs of Tyne wherries.[88] The likelihood however is that these ciphers did not identify individual keels but represented group practice, perhaps indicating keels under common ownership or those in the 'fleet' of a particular fitter (colliery agent).

Materials and Structure

No contemporary texts or illustrations have yet come to light that describe either the constructional methods employed in building a coal keel, or the details of its internal structure. Nevertheless, some relevant issues can be investigated through analysis of the keel's external appearance and dimensions, the study of contemporary ship- and boat-building practices, and comparison with the internal structures of select, analogous British watercraft.

Only two published authors, and they are twentieth-century ones at that, specify the species of timber from which they believed keels were built – oak. In 1942 Viall wrote that the 'Planking consisted mainly of English oak, but elm was used in many cases below the waterline', but he gave no source for that statement.[89] Ten years earlier an anonymous writer averred that, 'They [keels] were wooden boats built of oak planks three or four inches thick', apparently rehearsing information acquired from J L Ridley of Newcastle Quayside who, it was averred, had 'twenty-five years of working acquaintance with the old keels'.[90] It is noticeable that neither author actually stated that oak was employed for the keel's main structural elements, although Viall perhaps inferred as much. But despite their evidence being late and loosely based there is little cause to challenge the popular belief that oak was the preferred material for keel construction. That interpretation is supported by contemporary newspaper advertisements in which the vendors of new built keels occasionally emphasized the use of oak throughout to indicate superior quality, as for example: 'FOR SALE. A New Keel built of the best Oak Timber and Plank', and: 'FOR SALE, a NEW KEEL, remarkably well built of the best English Oak Timber and Plank, launched, and ready for employment'.[91][92] But the fact that the majority of new builds were advertised without any such endorsement or, at best, gained generic descriptions like 'strong-built' or 'well and substantially built', suggests that construction in oak alone was probably the exception rather than the rule.

Nevertheless, the fact that oak was considered the timber of choice is highlighted by the number of early nineteenth-century advertisements that offered it in a keel building context, as in the auction of: 'A QUANTITY of ENGLISH OAK; Memel, African, and American TIMBER; Oak and Beech plank . . . with various other articles suitable for Ship and Keel Builders'; or the sale of '365 OAK KNEES and CROOKS, ex *Pursuit* from Rotterdam [i.e. imported], suitable for Ship Builders, Keel Building . . .'; and, 1844, 'A LARGE QUANTITY of SMALL ENGLISH OAK TIMBER, of good quality, suitable for building small Ships and Keels . . .'. [93][94][95] The likelihood is that much of the English oak used in keel building actually came from south coast suppliers via the coastal trade.[96][97] But occasional press advertisements show that local sources were also exploited, timber for example from the 3rd Duke of Northumberland's woodlands in Hulne Park (Alnwick), where 'A VALUABLE ASSORTMENT of WOOD, consisting of excellent Beech, of very Large and Long dimensions, fit for Keel- and Ship-Building; fine ASH, ELM, FIR, OAK . . . &c of superior quality' was auctioned (for cash-buyers only!) as late as 1841.[98][99]

In addition to native oak, keel builders almost certainly utilized a wide range of alternatives that became available in the early nineteenth century, selecting from amongst the wide assortment of 'oaks' imported from Russia and Prussia (via the Baltic), North America and even Sierra Leone in West Africa. These 'oaks' comprised a diverse range of timbers that were fully exploited by the North East's shipbuilding trade.[100] Although somewhat harder to detect in a keel-building context alone, hints of this shift to foreign 'oaks' can be detected in timber merchants' sales lists from at least 1820 onward; for example, the sale of 'SMALL ENGLISH OAK TIMBER' in 1844 cited above (note [95]) was accompanied by a quantity of short lengths of 3-inch thick 'AFRICAN OAK PLANK, of good quality' – planking which was almost certainly suited to keel building. Similarly, the mid-century Tyneside sale of a new, 75-ton 'FLAT BOTTOMED KEEL [lighter] built of English, African and Dantzic [Baltic] Oak', reflects the variety of hardwood supplies available to a builder of coal keels in the preceding decades.[101] That secondhand ships' timbers may have been re-cycled into cheaper, inferior keels seems possible too. For example, a sales advertisement of 1805 – when war had curtailed timber supplies – offered a newly built keel at Heworth accompanied by 'a Quantity of Old Ship Timber, Floors, Foot-Hooks, Knees etc. little worse than new' and, slightly suspiciously regards quality, the seller offered deferred payment terms too.[102]

Although the types of timbers employed over time may have changed, the dimensions of the raw materials needed would not, for the form of the keel stayed remarkably constant. That 'small' timber should be advertised as suitable for keel building is not surprising since, even from a small-scale shipbuilder's perspective, the common coal keel was at the lowest end of the range of tonnage built.[103] Some elements of the keel's structure would, however, have needed good quality, ship-size timbers, including the keel, keelson, main transverse beams, and hull planking. But excepting for the transverse beams, the lengths required would have been significantly shorter than usual, less even than those for a 50-ton coastal sloop. One late-Victorian commentator actually opined that 'the keel was usually built by shipyard apprentices, from the small timber left over from the building of large ships', and it is likely that this was sometimes – though not always – the case.[104] Large shipbuilding concerns, such as Hurry's and Smith's, could definitely have economized on materials and labour by doing so for they frequently built ships 'under [Lloyd's] survey' which resulted in an accumulation of timber rejected by the surveyors as being of inferior scantling or quality. And big yards employed large numbers of cheap apprentice staff who, unlike day-labourers and shipwrights, could not expeditiously be laid off during slack periods but might perhaps be diverted to speculative keel building. Nonetheless, from the mid-eighteenth-century onward writers regularly remarked upon the keel's unusually robust construction, with their descriptions ranging from Pennant's early observation of keels in 1769 as 'strong, clumsy and round', through Brockie's (perhaps derivative) late-Victorian 'heavy, clumsy and very strong', to Viall's valedictory assessment of 1942 as to their being 'extraordinarily strong'.

Though the construction sequence used in building a keel is unknown, it probably followed much the same pattern used locally in building small, wooden coasters.[105] [106] [107] But compared even to a basic single-masted coaster, the design processes required for laying down a coal keel and the fabrication of its components would have been uncomplicated (Fig. 2.16).

A building slip of around 50-60 feet in length, with 'keel blocks' at approximately 3-foot intervals would have been set out on an open foreshore. On this the 35-foot keel piece would have been laid down together with the fore and aft stems – thus completing the vessel's backbone. The next step would have been the erection of sufficient, prefabricated transverse frames and lengthwise ribbands to establish the hull shape, followed by the insertion of closely spaced intermediate frames. Having carefully 'faired' (bevelled) all these, the entire structure was locked together by a weighty, through-bolted, full length 'keelson' (upper keel) along the base.

This provided a rigid skeletal structure which could be clad with heavy, edge-to-edge laid planking fastened to the frames using hundreds of 'trenails' (stout wooden dowels) together with a judicious mix of metal bolts and spikes. Three heavy

FIGURE 2.16 Three keels (left) sail upstream past an almost completed coastal ship (right) and another only just recently begun – its skeletal floor frames and stern-frame just raised. Keels were built in commonplace riverside shipyards like this (engraving after J W Carmichael, c.1830).

thwartship beams, each perhaps 'lodging' (resting) on a substantial longitudinal 'shelf-piece' (stringer) each side, constituted the main transverse elements at deck level (see Fig. 2.7). [108] And, as depicted in the Mitcalfe model, these might be reinforced with heavy 'lodging knees', i.e. horizontal brackets (see Fig. 4.10). At the vessel's ends, lighter and more closely-spaced cross beams presumably carried the fore- and stern-deck planking which, on the evidence of the SANT model, was generally laid fore-and-aft in broad (approx. 1 foot) widths. Although around 1830 John Bell sketched narrow, crosswise deck planking (Fig. 2.12). Below deck level amidships, the 'shuts' (hold floor) likely required an underpinning of closely-spaced, full-width, hold beams strong enough to support the 21-ton coal cargo and the considerable weight of the hold coamings and side walkways. These latter appear to have been of solid, one-piece (not planked) construction, and were probably supported on the futtock heads and half-beams secured to the beam shelves, or with short hanging knees. [109]

Normally, cargo-carrying vessels would have received an interior cladding of relatively light 'ceiling' planking fastened to the inside faces of the frames but, for reasons of cost and function that may not have been the case with the keel, though it would have helped increase its structural strength.[110] On the evidence afforded by the Mitcalfe model and Heslop's notes, continued access to the keel's interior for purposes of inspection, cleaning – and maybe bilgewater bailing – was afforded by a large, approximately 2 feet 6 inch by 4 feet, scuttle at the after end of the hold.[111] No indication has yet come to light which suggests that a permanent lift-pump was fitted, perhaps because a pump was too prone to choke with coal sludge, and a scoop or bucket sufficed. However a drainage 'plug' (bung), which presumably could be drawn to relieve the keel of bilgewater or rainwater when it was dried out ashore, was certainly fitted.[112]

The remainder of the building process may have comprised little more than the secure installation of the billet-head timbers and the laying of deck planking, together with some basic joinery and light outfitting work, including: light bulkheads at the ends of the hold; plain bench seating and storage in the 'huddock'; two deck scuttles; a mast, yard, sweeps and rudder; and a few essential iron fittings, especially the rudder hangings. Finally, there would have been the application of protective coatings which, in the nineteenth century, were principally tar with a coat of (black) 'varnish' below the waterline, for 'no touches of any bright colour relieved the appearance' of a keel.[113] Earlier, in the mid-eighteenth century, it may just have been tar along with pitch to 'pay' (caulk) the plank seams, for on occasion the Hoastman's apprentice Ralph Jackson (1749–56) provided his master's keel crews with, for example, '3 gallons of Tar & 1½ stone of pitch'.[114]

Judging by later Tyneside practice for wooden craft of this size the launching of a keel was probably achieved by employing simple 'hill and hollow' launch ways.[115] These ways, lubricated by a liberal application of hot liquid tallow, would have sufficed to launch the vessel onto a chosen high tide.

Scantlings

Very few references survive that specify the actual scantlings (dimensions) of a keel's principal components as outlined above. From an examination (c.1942) of a local carvel-built lighter's hulk, Viall conjectured that a keel's frames were approximately 4 inches (sided) by 6 inches (moulded) and, from a source unknown, asserted that in the best quality keels 'the timbers [frames] of grown oak were so close that only the width of a man's fist would go between them. This space was a matter of price; the wider the space the cheaper the keel'.[116] He did however note that, as for many Tyne- and Wear-built ships, cheaper – but still durable – elm was sometimes used below the waterline.

Frames of around 4 inches thickness certainly sound credible and if spaced as closely as Viall indicates they would have lain at 8- or 9-inch centres, producing a structure in which the solid frames and the intervening spaces were roughly equal. Similar spacing is also suggested by close examination of the keel in a plate published in Brand's *History* (1789), where some twenty frames can be counted in its open hold. Frames of 4-inch siding with 6-inch gaps between them would both fit the hold's likely length, of some 16 to 18 feet, and match the artist's visual rendering (see Fig. 3.13).

In 1932 the anonymous author in the *Smith's Dock Journal*, quoted the keel's hull planking as 'three or four inches thick', that is, even thicker than that of an early nineteenth-century coastal sloop.[117] All nineteenth- and twentieth-century authors agreed that keels were 'carvel' or 'caulker' planked, the latter expression reflecting the fact that the planking's edge-to-edge butted seams were made watertight with an insert of oakum (teased out rope fibre) overlain with tar. Elsewhere in England the caulking of seams was generally regarded as the preserve of a separate shipbuilding trade, the 'Caulkers', but on the North East coast it was a task reserved for time-served shipwrights. With respect to the keel's planking, Mitcalfe alone noted that it was fastened to the frames with 'wooden pegs or "trinnels" [trenails]'.[118] These were probably 1 inch in diameter or, considering the thickness of the planking previously indicated, slightly more.

The layout of a keel's planking is known from the evidence of just two models and two contemporary sketches. On the SANT model the run of the 'strakes' and the butt joints of the individual planks which comprise them have been roughly inscribed by the maker onto the surface of its carved, block-built (solid wood) hull (Fig. 1.4). But there is an apparent discrepancy here, for the model's port side exhibits nine strakes whilst the starboard side shows only eight, a mismatch perhaps occasioned by the rather shaky delineation of the latter's three lower strakes. Although this model's garboard strakes are represented as composed of two, nominally 16-foot planks, most of the strakes above – including the sheer strakes – are made up of three or four planks, indicating the use of comparatively short components, some 5-11 feet in length.

By comparison, the planking runs on the Marr model are relatively evenly disposed and look more realistic. Each strake is formed of individually fashioned miniature planks butted (end joined) together and fastened onto the underlying block-built hull with tiny wooden pegs representing full-size treenails (see Fig. 2.4, bottom). Interestingly, once more there are nine strakes on the port side but only eight to starboard, a mismatch apparently resulting from the use of three relatively narrow lower strakes – strakes II to IV – on the port side (Fig. 2.17).[119] Again, the garboard strakes (strake I) comprise two, 16-foot planks each but, unlike the SANT model, the Marr model's sheer strakes – the longest strakes in the vessel – are formed of two planks only, whilst the intervening strakes (II-VII/VIII) comprise either three or two planks. This suggests that some keel builders employed relatively longer (more costly) planking components, ranging from 7 to around 23 feet in length and averaging some 10½ to 14 inches in finished breadth.

On close inspection, the sheerline of the Marr model also reveals an unexpected feature. At their ends, the sheer planks are left to sweep upwards in a natural curve that lets them run out across their full width on the line of the keel's deck. Conventionally, as in the SANT model, these sheer-plank ends would narrow and run parallel to the deck edge before being received in full on the stempost rabbets. This unusual constructional feature might be construed simply as a modelmaking

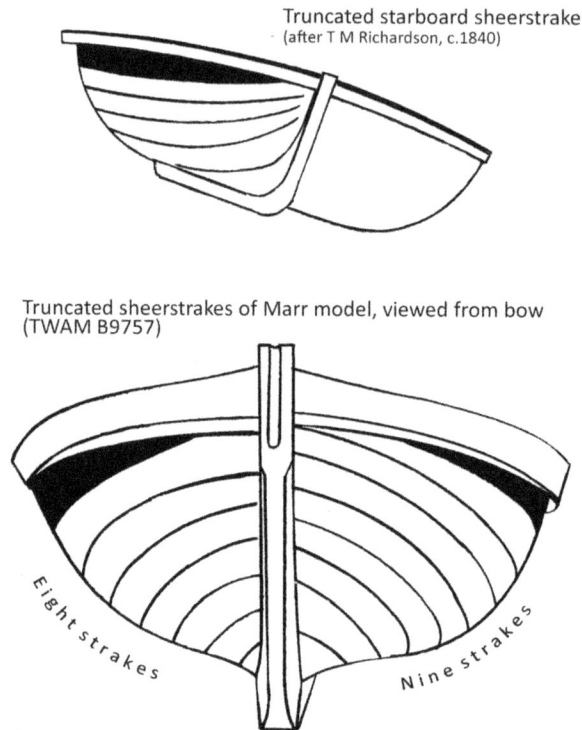

Truncated starboard sheerstrake
(after T M Richardson, c.1840)

Truncated sheerstrakes of Marr model, viewed from bow
(TWAM B9757)

Eight strakes

Nine strakes

FIGURE 2.17 The Marr model (bottom) has an unequal number of strakes to port and starboard, together with sheer strakes that terminate unconventionally on the topsides, not at the stem- and stern-posts.

expedient, but its utilization in full size keels is fully corroborated by a contemporary sketch of Thomas Richardson's which depicts a beached keel whose sheer plank ends certainly display this form (Fig. 2.17; see also, Chapter 6).

Keels, it would appear, could be built with either the conventional sheer strake arrangement, or this now more unfamiliar one. As will be elaborated later, this less familiar arrangement has been recorded in different historical and geographic settings. Common to both models' plank layouts, however, is the suggestion that keels were planked with butts (end joints) that were 'shifted' (staggered) by no more than 2½ to 4 feet in adjacent planks. This was much closer than normal shipyard practice, but still allowed positioning with the two or three strakes recommended 'between every two butts upon the same timber [frame].'[120]

On balance it seems that the scantlings of the timber required to build a nineteenth-century keel will have varied little from that commonly used in constructing, for instance, a small coastal vessel (Table 2.8). In some instances at least, keel building may well – as was suggested retrospectively– have enabled shipbuilders to put materials that were of insufficient size for use in larger vessels to good economic use.

TABLE 2.8 Dimensions and scantlings of a Tyne Keel and three comparable Inland and Coastal Craft.

PART	TYNE KEEL [38 × 15 × 6] Keel length: 35 ft Strakes: 8-9, carvel Frames: @ 8- to 9- inch centres, min.		BROADS WHERRY [57 × 14 × 6] Keel length: 56 ft Strakes: c.12, clinker Frames: @ 10- to 16- inch centres		60-TON SLOOP [56 × 16.3 × 9.7] Keel length: 44.5 ft Strakes: c.20, carvel Frames: 18 of, @ c.24-inch centres & 11 ft max. length		HAMBURG- BUILT SHIP, 1856 [40-50 ft waterline]	
	S. (in)	M. (in)	S. (in)	M. (in)	S. (in)	M. (in)	S. (in)	M. (in)
Keel	8	10	8-10	5-7	7-10	10	6.5	11
Keelson			3	12	9	9	9.5	11
Stempost	8	8>c.24	8	12	10	12	6.5	
Sternpost	8	c.12	8	12	10	11	6.5	
Floors			4	4	8-9.5	#6.5	6	8.5
Frames	4	6	4	4	7.5-6.5	#5	6	5.5-4
Main Beams	6	12	9	9	6		5	8.5
Beam Shelf			2	10	3	11	4.5	8.5
Inner Bm Sh.			3	3.5				
Plank (hull)	3-4		1-1.5, 2		2-3		2-3	
Plank (deck)			(oak) 2		(o/d'l) 2		2	
'Plankway'			(oak) 2	16 > 20				

Sources: column 2, author; column 3, Fuller M; column 4, Steel D; column 5, Steinhaus C F. Scantlings, rows 7-19. Key: Siding = thickness, &, mould'g (moulding) = width.

NOTES

1. For instance, the contemporary formula-derived 'register tonnage' used as an official measure to indicate the size of seagoing ships (and to calculate their dues) is inappropriate in the context of the keel.

2. Excepting for Warrington Smyth, all the authors listed in the table worked on Tyneside and the anonymous contributor to *Smith's Dock Journal* attributed much to an informant, 'Mr J Ridley of the [Newcastle] Quayside . . . his experience of them [keels] extending over twenty-five years'; this was probably the senior partner in shipbrokers 'J. Ridley, Son & Tully' (est. c.1860). Curiously, Smyth's dimensions (1929) are incorrectly attributed to another source, but nevertheless match those in Heslop's unpublished final manuscript!

3. The author's extensive field-research into vernacular boats informs this last statement. It is generally boatbuilders, not users, who are the repositories of exact dimensional data.

4. Clavering E. and Rounding A, 'A Map and its Meaning', in *Archaeologia Aeliana*, fifth series, v. XL (2011), 251.

5. D/CG 7/662, Lease agreement between: Sir James Clavering, Bt.; John Goodchild; and Thomas Clavering, dated 28-29 March 1740.

    TWAM, DT.BEL/2/31, Untitled plan depicting four separate areas of Swalwell and Derwenthaugh with various closes and keel births on the river Derwent highlighted, nd. c.1780, scale 4 chains to 1 inch (1:3168).

6. Dodd, *Report on the First Part of the Line of Inland Navigation*, 11; although Dodd (c.1756–1822) has rightly been described as a man whose numerous ideas rarely came to fruition, he was also a north easterner with a direct knowledge of the Tyne's topography and river trade.

7. On the first page of his Ms. 'Notes' Heslop sketched the plan view of a keel which included a rudder and the annotation '41 or 42 ft × 22' beam, 5' load'. In his final text he settled on 42 feet for length and amended the earlier (excessive) figure for beam.

8. Heslop, 'Notes', 5.

9. Mitcalfe, 'The History of the Keelmen', 5; Mitcalfe's figure accords well with evidence indicating that keels would require a 20-feet-wide channel for working access between a mooring tier and a quay wall (Tidal Harbours Commission Report, 1846, 347).

[10] TWAM B9779: this figured model was donated to the former Museum of Science and Industry (Newcastle) in the same month, September 1935, that Mitcalfe read his paper to the Society of Antiquaries of Newcastle upon Tyne.

[11] TWAM, B9780: this is the smallest, roughest and possibly the oldest, of the four surviving models. These limitations, together with the near absence of an external keel member, probably accounts for the anomalous figure of 59%, nor was it possible to establish this model's 'length of keel'.

[12] McKee, *Working Boats*, 107, 113, 123.

[13] Pomey, in *Principals of Shipbuilding*, 25-26.

[14] The model's eventual donor, Henry Carr of Heaton, cited his grandfather, 'Robson Caverhill' of the Keelman's Hospital, as the maker. A 'mariner' (seaman) of that name lived in the Keelman's Hospital from September 1845 until his death in January 1886 and would seem the most likely match, although a 'waterman' named Henry Robson Caverhill, d.1867, was also a resident there in mid-century (TWAM, CH.KH/5, Keelmen's Hospital Register). Variously spelt, Caverhill was a common surname in the river Tyne's water trades.

[15] North of England Institute of Mining and Mechanical Engineers, ZD-71-2.

[16] By the year 1902 Bertram was employed as a full time 'Assistant' at the Durham College of Science and Art (Newcastle) and had a reputation for illustrating local books with great veracity.

[17] To maintain the deck's structural strength and enhance security these hatches were relatively small. Those on a well dimensioned shipyard plan of a 48-foot, late nineteenth- century Tyne wherry measure a mere 1foot 4 inches square (this unique plan, acquired by H R Viall, is now in the Coastal Craft Collection of the National Museums Greenwich, note [19]).

[18] Heslop, *Northumberland Words*, vol. I, 138.

[19] Mannering, *Chatham Directory*, 48.

[20] Heslop, 'Keels and Keelmen', 4.

[21] 1810, a 'Coal Keel' stolen from Blyth was described as 'of the Blyth and Sunderland build, flat bottomed to draw little water' (*Newcastle Courant*, 27 January 1810); 1831, Wear keels described as of 22 feet beam and only 2½ feet draught (*Durham Chronicle*, 11 June 1831); and, in 1850, especial note was made of 'four flat-bottomed keels' being built on the River Wear where, owing to reduced demand, 'it was upward of twenty years' since any had been constructed. (*Newcastle Journal*, 31 August 1850).

22 Stammers, *Sailing Barges*, 7-23.

23 McKee, *Working Boats*, 31-32, 37.

24 Smiles, *George and Robert Stephenson*, 10-11.

25 Lambert, *Pictures of Tyneside*, plate 12.

26 National Museums Greenwich, PAD 9067.

27 www.watercolourworld, Thos. Richardson Snr., 'Forth Banks', Guy Peppiat Fine Art Gallery (accessed, 21/09/2021).

28 McKee, *Working Boats*, 78-83, 233-249.

29 Although differing slightly in scaled-up dimensions to the SANT model, the Marr and Mitcalfe models possess identical 'Profiles' and 'Boat Shapes' together with closely matched hull ratios: Marr model, L/B 2.6 and B/D 2.6; Mitcalfe model, L/B 2.6 and B/D 2.4.

30 McKee, *Working Boats*, 93, 239.

31 McKee, *Working Boats*, 239; McKee's calculations for the 'Tyne Keel' were based on Viall's published figure (1942) of 19 feet beam and, to a lesser extent, assumptions regarding length and draft; qualitatively though, the author agrees with his tabular collection of qualitative terms describing 'Boatshape'.

32 Galloway, *Annals of Coal Mining*, 47-48, 50, 68, 139, 146-47.

33 A degree of overloading and evasion (for owners' gain) was never eliminated, and long remained a source of dispute between coal shippers and the keelmen.

34 Where a structural centre-beam was present (see SANT and Mitcalfe models) it lay exactly at the vessel's longitudinal mid-point.

35 The calculations and basic hydrodynamic analysis which follow were made in accordance with established practices laid down in: Phillips-Birt, *Sailing Yacht Design*, 35-43, 64-65; and Kinney, *Skene's Elements of Yacht Design*, 39-47.

36 *Newcastle Courant*, 23 August 1828; report of legal case, The King v. Russell and Others, evidence of William Hume: 'Three feet or three feet one inch is the draught of a light keel, and four feet ten inches or five feet is the draught of a loaded keel. Some of the old light keels drew only two feet eight inches.' A couple of less experienced (or more biased) witnesses offered different figures, but in summing up for the defendants (15 August 1828) Sir James Scarlett effectively endorsed Hume's evidence by giving '4 ft 11in' as the draft of a loaded keel. That the basic parameters changed little is suggested by a report nearly 30 years later that a 'light keel's' draught was 2 feet 10 inches (*Shields Gazette* 18 February 1865).

[37] Bell, *Keelmen*, Keelman's annual bond (Ouston Colliery), 1819, para.7; when completing a sailing collier's cargo, a keel was allowed to carry nine chaldrons (23.85 tons), which would have increased the draught by a few inches.

[38] Speeds calculated from contemporary accounts of trip times.

[39] The analogy of a modern racing 'eight' is a useful one; the round-bottom provides minimum resistance under oars but – like a bicycle – requires its crew to maintain strict vertical balance to avoid capsize!

[40] Paradoxically, the VCG of the 21.2 tons of coal cargo can be calculated with a reasonable degree of confidence, it was positioned some 3 feet 6 inches above the load waterline.

[41] *English Reports Decisions*, 16 May 1801, Ex parte Robert Softley, 182. Although it was in his interests to make a case that keelmen were well suited for impressment as 'seamen', the naval officer concerned presented a largely objective appraisal of their well-regarded watermanship and abilities.

[42] *Newcastle Weekly Chronicle*, 1893; Letter No. 13,189 from 'Tyne, Morpeth'.

[43] Rowe, *Company of Shipwrights*.

[44] Rowe, *Company of Shipwrights*, 26-33.

[45] Clarke, *Building Ships*, 7-18, 26-30.

[46] Jackson, Diary F.

[47] *Newcastle Courant* 8 November 1755, 7 November 1767; in both cases Trewhitt's keels were 'in the employ of others' (i.e. leased out) at the time of sale.

[48] Parliamentary Printed Papers, 'Papers and Accounts Respecting Ships of War', 1805 (152. 192. 193. 205.).

[49] F&T Hurry for example, advertised 'several' – presumably used – keels for sale in January 1780, whilst in the nineteenth century T&W Smith of St Peter's reputedly 'had at one time 30 keels, hired out by the week'.

[50] *Newcastle Courant* 5 February 1807.

[51] *Newcastle Courant* 4 February 1826; Alexander Petrie had auctioned a 'coal keel, nearly new' just a few months previously, but his business did not resume after the fire.

[52] Manders, *Gateshead*, 81; Clarke, *Building Ships*, 16-17.

[53] In July 1757, George Boult handled the sale of four keels owned by a deceased fellow boatbuilder, Bartholomew Spain (*Newcastle Courant* 30 July 1757).

[54] W White's, *History Directory & Gazetteer of Durham & Northumberland, 1827*, 74, 123.

[55] *Newcastle Courant* 8 May 1819.

56 Their partnership as keel owners was dissolved in August 1854, maybe suggesting that the demand for keel hire was declining (*Newcastle Journal* 26 August 1854).

57 For example, Richardson in the *Parish of Wallsend*, 464, notes a small yard near the east end of the Keelmen's Row (Willington) where keels could be repaired and built.

58 *Tyne Mercury* 25 November 1817.

59 *Newcastle Courant* 28 August 1819, 5 February 1820; *Tyne Mercury* 24 April 1821.

60 No exact figures for the size of the keel fleet exist, but the numbers have been variously reported in the literature as: 320 in 1655; 338 in 1709 (Flinn); 400 in 1725; 688 in 1736 (Bourne); c.450 in 1772 (Pennant); approaching 320 in 1822; then reducing rapidly (if arguably) through the impact of mechanical loading to around 228 in 1827. Using a theoretical method based on total coal shipments, Wright (Thesis, Table 2.2) calculated: 450-480 in the early eighteenth-century; and 650-680 in mid eighteenth-century.

61 Keels were extremely hard worked and suffered rough usage so, although arbitrary, a depletion rate near to that experienced by the coastal and near seas merchant fleet in the mid-nineteenth century seems possible (Osler, 'Shipping Deployments', 131-34).

62 Fewster, *The Keelmen*, 152-53, 161-62.

63 Wright, Thesis, 107-110, concludes that in the seventeenth and early eighteenth century keel ownership was concentrated in the hands of hoastmen and shipwrights, with 27 of the latter holding 119 keels between them; merchants and others were much less involved.

64 Mackenzie, *Descriptive and Historical Account*, 379. The 'Wm. Robson' of Robson & Gray, shipbuilders, Salt Meadows (Gateshead) c.1811–1830 was probably William's son and, interestingly, that partnership's assets upon bankruptcy included 'an excellent coal keel' (*Newcastle Courant*, 29 May 1830). I am grateful to Michael Greatbatch for assistance in clarifying the Robson story.

65 Without any kind of containment, the coal's natural 'angle of repose' (35-40°) would have allowed a heaped height of merely 4 feet on this floorplan.

66 Nicholson, 'Keels and Keelmen', 1889; Leifchild, *Our Coal and Coal Pits*, 71; *Durham Chronicle* 14 November 1851.

67 These boards are frequently seen in turn-of-century and later photographs of Tyne wherries, for example: Beamish Museum, Photo No.164699 (reproduced in Taylor and Williams, Fig.14); Ouseburn Heritage information sheet No.5, 1999. The author is grateful to Michael Greatbatch for the colloquial wherry term, 'greedy boards'.

68 Intriguingly, Norfolk Broadland's cargo wherries used analogous coaming extensions known as 'lifting/moving uprights'.

69 Viall, 'Tyne Keels', 161.

70 The conventional layout previously described gave the casters ('shovel men') only the 18-inch wide walkway to work from.

71 Compared to the conventional keel's layout this asymmetric design reduced the cargo-bearing area by around 30%, and calculations suggest that it would have been necessary to fill the recessed hold space to achieve full load capacity. Higher heaping of the coals – to at least 6 feet above deck level – may also have been required.

72 Plain conical mast steps of this nature were fitted in Northumbrian fishing cobles and Tyne foyboats (mooring boats) well into the twentieth century.

73 This certainly seems to be suggested in a naif sketch of a keel collected, but not drawn by, marine artist J W Carmichael (1799–1868): TWAM K16524 (Laing Art Gallery). However, the tabernacle gate and securing pin indicated in Viall's drawing (1942) of the SANT model does not, and never has, existed.

74 Curiously, the SANT model has no billet-heads at all, but its afterdeck is supplied with two heavy iron ringbolts and a large horned cleat; the removable top of the stovepipe passed through a circular hole in the deckhead.

75 In the author's experience, a hole in a piece of wood is the cheapest and simplest form of fairlead or cleat!

76 Relevant enactments included those of: Henry V, ninth year (1422); Charles II, thirteenth year (1667–78); William III & Mary, sixth and seventh years (1694); George II, eleventh year (1738); and George III, fifteenth year (1775), thirty-first year (1791), and fifty-fifth year (1815).

77 In essence, the Commission's remit and regulations appear to have resulted from a late eighteenth-century Act of Parliament: (15 Geo. III) Measurement of Coal Waggons Act etc., 1775, from which further legislation followed in the first quarter of the nineteenth century.

78 *Newcastle Courant* 31 October 1829: cited in evidence presented by Sir Cuthbert Sharp, Commissioner and Collector of Customs, Sunderland, to the Select Committee (House of Lords) on the State of the Coal Trade. See also: 'Coal Trade: Minutes of evidence, Appendix to 03 April 1830', in *Journal of the House of Lords: Volume 62, 1830.*

79 *Journal of the House of Lords: Volume 62, 1830*, 202-212, Commission for weighing Coal Wagons and Keels at Newcastle and Sunderland, Rule 7.

80 Gardiner, *England's Grievance*, 93-94, witness John Harrison of London. Harrison's descriptive term 'coal boat' later appears in probate inventories and in the catch-all phrase 'keels, coal boats and lighters' commonly used in newspaper advertisements and, consistently, in keelmen's annual bonds, i.e. employment contracts. Wright inclined to treat the term as a later discarded synonym for keel, finding no evidence that it represented a separate boat type, and in this the author tends to agree (Wright, thesis, 103). Possibly the term's specific meaning degenerated overtime and came to be employed for any coal-carrying craft of keel-like character before, eventually, becoming obsolete. Heslop, for example, did not record it.

81 Fewster, *The Keelmen*, 111-12; citing documents in TWA 349/29.

82 *Journal of the House of Lords: Volume 62, 1830*, 202-212, Commission for weighing Coal Wagons and Keels at Newcastle and Sunderland, Rule 16.

83 Ibid., Rule 14.

84 Jackson, Diary F, 8 & 10 May 1756.

85 Ibid., 11 October 1756.

86 *Journal of the House of Lords: Volume 62, 1830*, 202-212, Commission for weighing Coal Wagons and Keels at Newcastle and Sunderland, Rule 21 ('Lastly').

87 Maxwell, *Marine Law*, 39.

88 TWAM, B9779: '14 (stern), C (bow)'; TWAM H5441: 'K' (bow and stern); TWCMS 2018.614, 'H' (bow).

89 Viall, 'Tyne Keels', 161.

90 Anon., 'The Tyne Keels', 66.

91 *Tyne Mercury* 27 July 1802.

92 *Newcastle Journal* 26 October1839.

93 *Newcastle Courant* 29 October 1825.

94 *Newcastle Journal* 22 October 1836.

95 *Newcastle Journal* 7 September 1844.

96 Osler, 'Goods to Newcastle', 163-65.

97 *Tyne Mercury* 5 October 1815; advertisement 'To SHIP & KEEL BUILDERS etc., New Sussex Oak Timber & Plank . . . from Newhaven'.

98 Shrimpton, *Alnwick Parks*, 23-25, 31; this indicates that Hulne Park had been largely despoiled of its ancient oaks in the sixteenth century, although significant stands remained in the Duke's domains at nearby Cawledge and Shilbottle.

99 *Newcastle Journal* 10 April 1841.

100 Clarke, *Building Ships*, 50-54; using primary sources, Joe Clarke's account of the timbers used by the region's shipbuilders is both comprehensive and definitive.

101 *Newcastle Journal* 3 March 1855.

102 *Newcastle Courant* 2 February 1805.

103 Coastal sloops of 50-60 register tons, capable of carrying some three to four 'keels' (by measure) of coal, were the smallest seagoing vessels such builders regularly constructed.

104 *Newcastle Weekly Chronicle*, 1893; Letter No. 13,189 from 'Tyne, Morpeth'.

105 Clarke, *Building Ships*, 46-49.

106 Barrow and Osler, *Tall Ships*, 46-51.

107 Alternative construction scenarios do remain possible, but these would have been associated with much earlier building techniques or vessel typology, so their discussion is left to chapter Six, 'The Historical Perspective'.

108 TWAM 1475/74; local maritime 'terms' collected by shipowner C Willan, 1945. Well known Tyne wherry builder and repairer Mr Lindsay of St. Anthony's indicated that with respect to a wherry or keel's frames the: 'top timber [was fitted] with bearers to take the shuts [i.e. hold floor]'. The 'top timber' clearly equates to the topmost futtock (i.e. top part of the frame) but leaves the form of the 'bearers' supporting the 'shuts' uncertain, his use of the plural perhaps suggesting that each hold beam was individually attached to its respective frame – rather than being lodged on a continuous beam shelf.

109 Fuller M, *Norfolk Wherry*, 20-21. There are close structural and functional parallels between the Tyne keel's 'walkways' and the Norfolk wherry's 'plankways'; the latter comprised '25-foot lengths of 2 inch oak about 20 inches wide [amidships] . . . the ends scarfed about 9 inches full width [i.e. to the bow and stern extensions]', and all fashioned to 'the outside shape of the hull'.

110 Since the 'shuts' carried the keel's cargo the vessel's interior below that level would have required no protective ceiling planking, and this would have saved a minor building cost. In service, an un-ceiled interior might well have helped the crew keep the keel's bilges clean and dry. This was desirable since accumulations of detritus or bilge water would have adversely affected its displacement by reducing the carrying capacity as marked.

111 Mitcalfe, 'The History of', 4-5. Also unsigned typescript notes dated: 25th September 1935, held by the Science Museum, London; these typescript notes were almost certainly compiled by Mitcalfe. They were enclosed in a letter from B W Bathe (Science Museum, London) to A G Osler (Newcastle Museum of Science and Industry), 19

January 1976. The reputed Caverhill-built models both depict hold scuttles (TWAM: B9779 and B9780).

[112] Bell, *Keelmen*; handbill on behalf of keel owners at Dunston dated 12th November 1822 offering 50 guineas reward for information leading to the conviction of 'some Evil-disposed person or persons [who] DREW THE PLUGS, and thereby sunk twelve Keels at Pontop Staith, and three Keels at Southmoor Staith'.

[113] Anon., 'The Tyne Keels', 66; 'varnish' almost certainly referred to glossy, black, bituminous varnish.

[114] Jackson, *Journal B*, 28 March 1751.

[115] For example, as seen in a photograph of the launch of the 55-foot Tyne Wherry *Elswick No.2* in 1939 (Newcastle University, from the collection of the former 'Adult Education Department'), published in *The Last Tyne Wherry – Elswick No.2* (Tyne & Wear County Council Museum Service information sheet, c.1981).

[116] Viall, 'Tyne Keels', 161.

[117] Anon., 'The Tyne Keels', 66.

[118] Mitcalfe, 'The History of', 4.

[119] The fact that the least number of strakes (eight) lie on the keel's loading and discharge side (i.e. to starboard) in both models may, or may not, be coincidence.

[120] Steel, *Naval Architecture*, supplementary tables; even in 1805 Steel remarked that the placing of butts so close was allowed only owing 'to the scarcity of Oak Plank' of sufficient length.

THREE

ENVIRONS AND PROPULSION

A FACT THAT IS OFTEN TAKEN FOR GRANTED, or overlooked, is that the lower River Tyne provided 15 miles of tidal waterway that was well suited to the seaward transport of what became the region's principal economic asset – coal. It was the coincidence of some key topographic and geological features that resulted in this advantageous situation.

Luckily, the earliest locations for exploiting shallow-mined coal coincided not only with the limit of the river's tidal flow at Hedwin Streams but also with the presence of two navigable tributaries, the Derwent and Team. True, the river's upper- and mid-sections contained extensive shifting shallows, but these were an inconvenience rather than a deterrent to experienced watermen. Furthermore, as mining spread eastward to penetrate the coalfield's deeper reserves, much of the resultant output could be routed via the river's mid-section below Newcastle, providing a much shorter passage by keel to the seagoing 'colliers' that lay in the deep-water channel downriver or at Shields Harbour. Although in gradient terms the lower Tyne represented an 'old' river, its navigation was relatively free of the awkward and unstable meanders that this description usually implies. Furthermore, only one natural feature, Bill Point, together with the potentially dangerous, man-made obstacle of Newcastle Bridge posed serious navigational hazards. But there were a few less predictable dangers, especially those occasioned by the gales and ice of harsh winters and the flooding caused by heavy rain or meltwater, all of which could sink keels or break them adrift. Taken overall, however, the fluvial regime was favourable to the year-round operation of keels. Fortuitously too, the valley's west to east alignment allowed a useful degree of complement between tide and weather (Map 2).

As a broad generalization, loaded keels travelling downriver gained the benefit not only of a tidal regime that featured a longer duration of ebb than flood tide, but frequently found opportunity to run under sail before the prevailing westerlies too. And, provided it stopped short of a damaging flood, the passage downstream was occasionally augmented by a fast-running, rain-induced 'fresh'. An appreciation of these physical aspects of the local environment does much to help explain the apparently conservative 'antiquity' of the practices by which a keel was propelled and managed, practices that were often regarded by travellers and laymen as archaic or old-fashioned. In truth, the successful operation of keels lay not in adopting specialized (or more modern) modes of propulsion, but upon applying an amalgam of five long-established complementary techniques: 'driving' (drifting); rowing; 'puoying' (poling); 'tracking' (hauling); and sailing.

None of these five techniques was particularly fast or efficient alone, but when utilized by an experienced crew they could amount to significantly more than the sum of their parts, thus facilitating fast passages. Effective passage-making decisions consequently relied upon the skipper's acumen and experience allied to the hard manual labour of his near inexhaustible crew of three – two 'shovel men' and a 'pee-dee' (boy). Smartness of loading, speed of passage and expedient turnarounds were essential elements in making a living because keelmen were remunerated not for the actual time taken when making a delivery, or for the 21.2 tons of coals carried, but by the 'tide': a notional round trip from the loading staith to a ship downriver and back upriver (unladen) to the staith again. The payments for such a 'long tide' or 'ship tide' were made in accordance with an agreed sliding scale

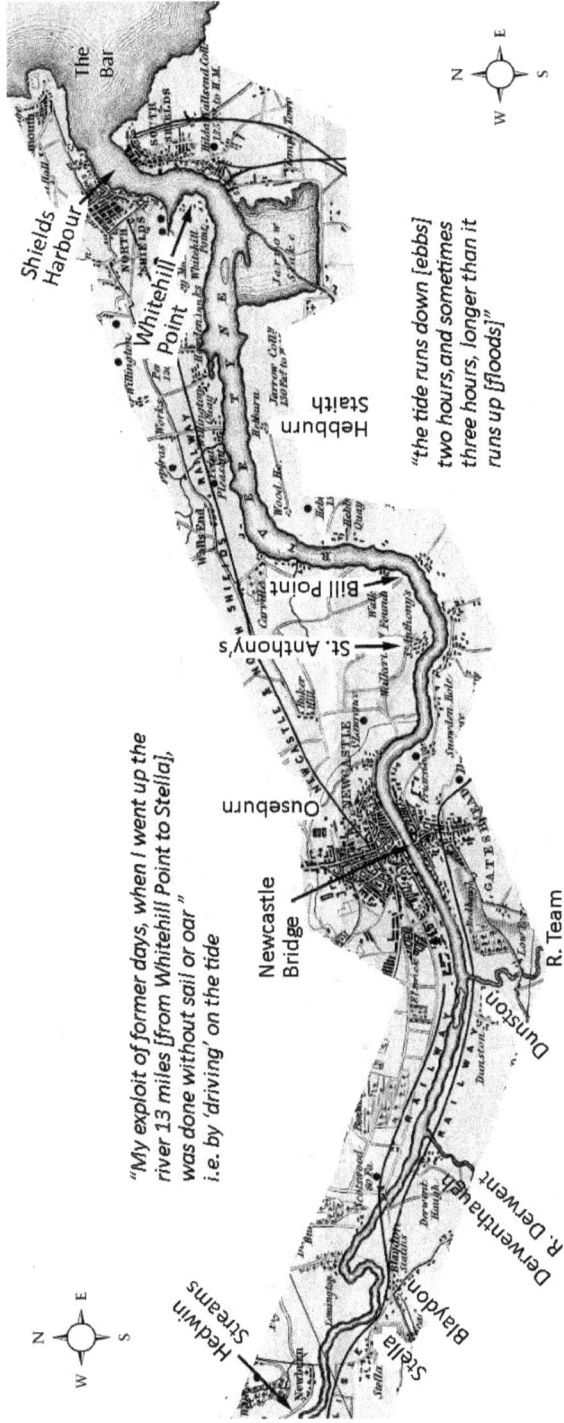

The Bar

Shields Harbour

Whitehill Point

Hebburn Staith

"the tide runs down [ebbs]
two hours, and sometimes
three hours, longer than it
runs up [floods]"

Bill Point

St. Anthony's

Ouseburn

Newcastle Bridge

R. Team

Dunston

Derwenthaugh
R. Derwent

"My exploit of former days, when I went up the
river 13 miles [from Whitehill Point to Stella],
was done without sail or oar"
i.e. by 'driving' on the tide

Blaydon

Stella

Hedwin Streams

MAP 2 The lower River Tyne c.1838 from the tidal limit at Hedwin Streams, to Tynemouth 'Bar' off Shields. The distance by river from Shields to Newcastle Bridge was approximately nine-and-a-half miles, and to Stella fifteen-and-a-half (note: only select intermediate locations are shown).

based upon the mileage between the staith and the ship, as also were the lower rates for shorter 'bye tide' trips from, for example, a staith to a riverside manufactory. The keel's main freight charge was generally paid by the shipper whilst the coal owner contributed long-established: 'Ship Dues; Owners Wages; Bread; and Beer' monies (Fig. 3.1).[1 2]

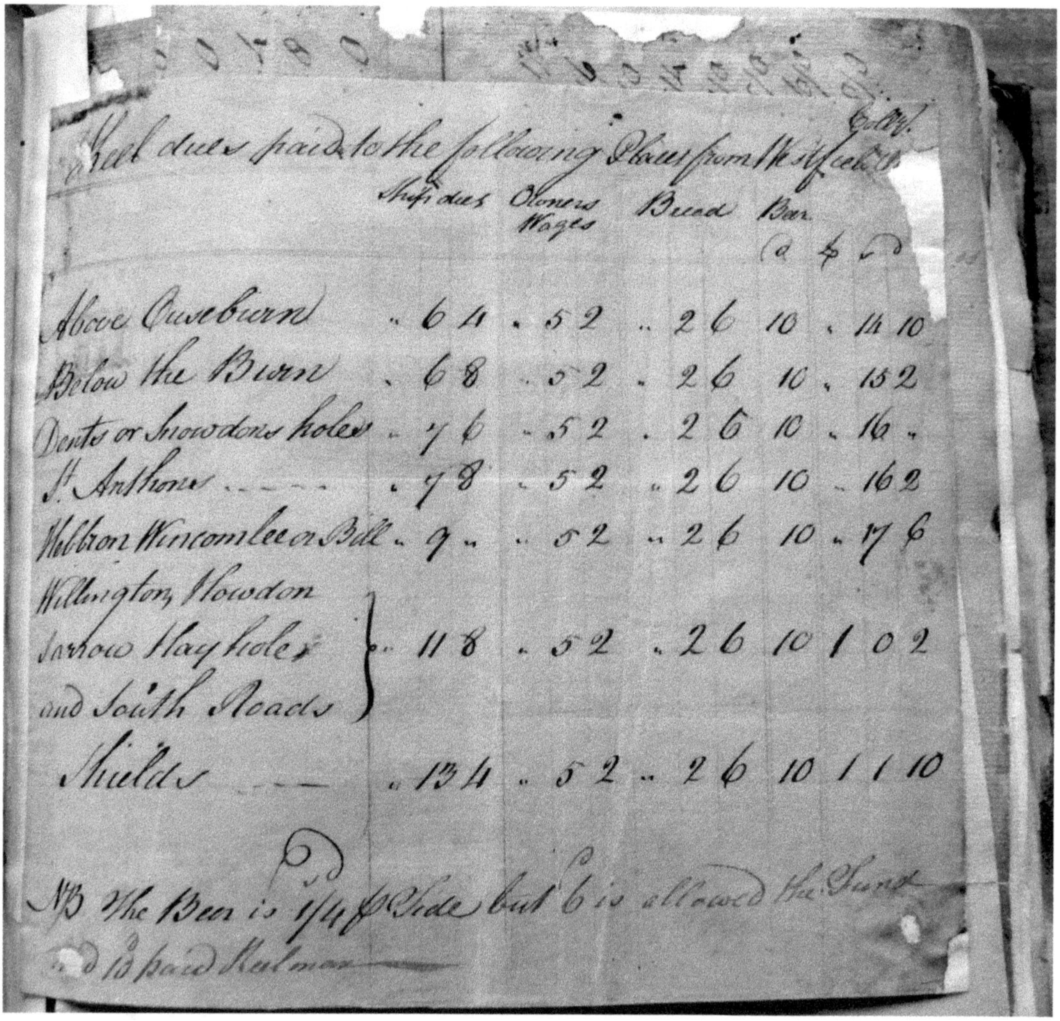
Keel dues paid to the following Places from the Staith

	Ship dues	Owners Wages	Bread	Beer	£ s d
Above Ouseburn	6 4	5 2	2 6	10	14 10
Below the Burn	6 8	5 2	2 6	10	15 2
Dents or Snowdons holes	7 6	5 2	2 6	10	16 .
St Anthons	7 8	5 2	2 6	10	16 2
Wellbron Wincomlee or Bill	9 ..	5 2	2 6	10	17 6
Willington, Howdon Jarrow Hay hole and South Roads	11 8	5 2	2 6	10	1 0 2
Shields	13 4	5 2	2 6	10	1 1 10

NB The Beer is 1/4 p Tide but 6 is allowed the Fund and 10 paid Keelmen

FIGURE 3.1 Account book entry listing the payments offered by an upriver colliery to keel crews for delivery to various point on the river, from 'Above Ouseburn' to 'Shields', c.1822 (from John Bell's compilation volume: *Keelmen*).

TIDE AND OAR

The Tidal Regime and Waterway

The one constant factor affecting the speed of passage up and down the river was the tidal regime, a dependence that is implicit in the historic term noted above by which the Tyne's keelmen were remunerated: 'the tide'. No keel skipper, waterman or pilot could have prospered without a well learned, if empirical, knowledge of the river's tidal regime as it altered throughout the four-week lunar cycle. He had to intuitively know the times of high and low water at 'full and change' of the moon, their approximate 50-minute progression on successive days in between, the varying strengths of the tidal stream and height of tide between 'springs' (at full and new moon) and 'neaps' (at quarter moon), together with the diurnal cycle of two high- and two low-waters which provided a daily tidal conveyor belt that, theoretically, reversed its direction every six hours.

In practice however this six-hour reversal was only a guide, for the nature of the North Sea's tidal basin and the conformation of the lower Tyne resulted in a significant difference between the duration of the flood (incoming) and ebb (outgoing) tides. As formally described by the distinguished engineer John Rennie in 1816, '[the tide] continues to run upwards for about five hours, and ebbs about seven hours; but if there is a strong fresh in the river, it is frequently half an hour later, and then it does not run upwards more than four hours' (Map 2).[3] In more colloquial terms, this characteristic of the tidal regime was rehearsed a few years later by a Tyne pilot, Henry Young: 'the tide runs down [ebbs] two hours, and sometime three, longer than it runs up [floods].'[4] Whilst the pattern of the flood and ebb was not in dispute the question of the speed of tidal flow was, since any changes that were detected over time signalled the improvement – or deterioration – of the river's navigable channel. And the state of that channel was a contentious issue because its maintenance was entirely in the hands of Newcastle Corporation, the beneficiary of all the major port dues and sole arbiter of riparian expenditure.[5]

The surviving evidence on tidal flow is thus found in adversarial and subjective sources but, in summary, these suggest that at its greatest rate – at half spring tide flood – the tidal flow within the river ran at between 3 to 4 knots, although there are intimations that this rate declined during the first half of the nineteenth century.[6]

By mid-century even the adherents of Newcastle Corporation claimed no real improvements. In 1849, pilot John Hutchinson's claim that the tide had decreased from 4 to 3 knots at Shields harbour where, 'Three men can now row a coble [against the tide] which used to require from four or five men' has the ring of practical authenticity.[7] Indeed, during the second quarter of the nineteenth century there were frequent complaints that the river's navigable waterway was increasingly being impeded by shifting shoals, projecting (coal drop) staiths, badly built training walls, and poorly-maintained ballast shores. This situation was trenchantly summed up by the Inspector, Captain John Washington R.N., who, in February 1849, convened Parliament's 'Preliminary Inquiry' into the proposed River Tyne Conservancy Bill:

> . . . [it] must be manifest that the several duties usually attached to the conservancy of a harbour have not been attended to [by Newcastle Corporation] on the Tyne; that the most ordinary duties of river engineering, such as regulating and deepening the channel, cutting off projecting points, dredging away or otherwise removing the shoals, so as to produce a uniform bed of the river, have all but been entirely omitted . . .[8]

One undisputed gauge of a river channel's constraints was afforded by the speed with which its 'tide wave' (high water time) travelled upriver. Unfortunately, the speed of propagation of the Tyne's tide wave proved to be far inferior to that of Britain's other large commercial rivers.[9] It was less than half that achieved in the Clyde or the Thames, averaging only 8 mph against their 20 mph. Correspondingly, and of particular importance for the keelmen, was the delay in appearance of the 'first flood' (observable tidal flow). This arrived at Newcastle Bridge fully 2 hours 12 minutes after it first passed the harbour bar at Shields – barely 10 miles distant. Added to this, there was a loss of 'four to five feet rise [height] of tide' between the bar and Newcastle, multiplying the difficulties of navigating the shoals in the river below Newcastle Bridge. From a keel skipper's practical point of view, the dilatory progression of the tide wave meant that before his present tide fell to low water at Stella – the loading place farthest upriver – the next high water would already have arrived on the bar at Shields. He thus had to make constant forward calculations as to the depth of water and tidal stream likely to be encountered at any critical juncture between his points of lading and discharge. Taking all this, and much more, into account Washington bluntly reported that the Tyne's situation was one in which, 'It is hardly possible to imagine a worse condition of a navigable river.'[10]

Driving

Whatever other means of propulsion might be employed, a keel skipper's ability to make best use of the tidal flow underwrote the speed of a successful passage. Using the tide came as readily and instinctively to a keelman as drinking a 'can' of ale. At its simplest the crew did little more than allow the keel to 'drive' on the most favourable stage of the tidal flow, a technique that was outlined by keelman Samuel Bell at the Admiralty Inquiry of 1849:

> I have been 46 years on the river. I was first on board a keel as a boy, and used to be a skipper . . . I have gone as a boy, 42 years ago [c.1807], in a keel in a spring-tide on a summer's morning, and she has driven all the way to Stella Dyke [staith] in one tide . . . we dropped up with the tide only. We [only] put our strength on [used the oar] at Ouseburn to get through Newcastle Bridge.

A verbally engaging witness, Bell then digressed into a near bucolic summer scene, elaborating on the keelmen's talent for driving on the tide alone as circumstances permitted (Map 2):

> My exploit of former days, when I went up the river 13 miles in one tide, was done without sail or oar. I have done it several times, and many keelmen have done the same thing. We never used our oars but in pulling through Newcastle Bridge. There was no wind; it was a calm summer's day. I was in the regular habit of driving from Shields to Stella. The time it took me to go up depended on the tide. We could not do it on a neap tide . . .[11]

Long passages by driving were clearly practicable only on and around spring tides when, as Bell estimated, the tide ran at some 4 knots in the mid-river section. And the validity of his comment 'that many keelmen have done the same [trips]' was borne out by other witnesses at the same Inquiry.

Matthew Charlton, a keelman for 40 years, averred that, 'I have adopted the practice of driving up both man and boy', recounting his 10-mile passage in an unladen keel 30 years ago (c.1819) when: 'We have laid down our oars at Whitehill Point, and driven up to Dunstan Dykes [Dunston staith], two miles above Newcastle Bridge, in one tide. We could have gone a long way farther . . . We could drive our keels without oar and sail formerly'.[12] His last remark highlighted the belief – one that was shared by many other watermen – that the Tyne's navigable channel and tidal flow had deteriorated within their generation. In corroboration, John Fulthorp, a former 'coal keelman' with over 50 years' experience, described the length of passage formerly achieved (c.1800) by driving alone, 'Both when a lad and a man I have driven within the tide in a keel from Whitehill Point to Dunstan [Dunston], a distance of 10 miles; if there had been call we could have driven to Lemington, 2½ miles farther, an hour or an hour and a half before high water.' Another such commonplace passage was immediately related by long-time ballast keelman William Ford who remembered 'driving a keel up in a spring-tide [c.1820] from Whitehill Point to Blaydon [13½ miles], just keeping her head straight'. Implicit in Ford's final phrase was the fact that the keel required no propulsive force other than the tidal flow, merely steerage by 'swape' (steering oar).[13] Charlton, when questioned, also contributed the interesting observation that 'derived from [his] practical experience' a keel would 'drive better loaded than light [unladen]'; a result, presumably, of the increased tidal pressure on a laden keel's larger underwater area and draught. Indeed, Bell's statement that 'it took six hours to run [drive] down when loaded' and less than half that (2½ hours) 'to row', seems to support Charlton's observation, though he added rather pointedly: 'but I never tried myself to row it in two and a half hours.' Driving, rather than rowing, undoubtedly had the great advantage of conserving the crew's energy for the arduous, end-of-passage task of discharging the keel's 21-ton cargo.

As recounted later by John McKay (1889), skippers loading at Stella Shore – the head of navigation – often found it expedient to make a two-stage, tidal trip downriver (Map 2):

As Stella Staith is upwards of fourteen miles from Shields Harbour, where most of the ships lay to receive their coals . . . It was customary for the keels, after loading, to be taken either over Blaydon Ford or to Derwenthaugh [1 mile and 2¾ miles downriver respectively], to await the next tide. This was necessary to get a good start. If the keels were not favoured by wind they had to be "set down" [poled] against the [flood] tide . . . After the tide ebbed the oars were generally put out, and the keel was rowed or drifted down to where the ship was lying. It generally took four or five hours to get to Shields.[14]

The same writer also volunteered the fact that a 'lang tide' (round trip) from Stella commonly occupied 15 to 17 hours overall.[15]

Interestingly, several first hand, nineteenth-century accounts – like Charlton's – tend to imply that keelmen considered rowing a technique to be used more for manouevring the keel advantageously within the tideway, or for passing obstructions, rather than as a primary means of propulsion. Nevertheless, it was the latter idea, that of the animated 'Keel Row', which became fixed in the popular imagination, although it was a perception that owed far more to the cultural impact of popular songsters, versifiers and eighteenth- and nineteenth-century illustrators than it ever did to objective, everyday observation.[16] In short, the sight of a keelman rowing a keel was a visible and praiseworthy manly working-class task that might be celebrated in song and print, whilst 'driving' with the tide was an arcane practice that could well be construed as idleness.

Rowing: words and pictures

The fact that Tyne keels were rowed in an unusual fashion, one that was unique in Britain, has long encouraged the idea that rowing was the keelman's preferred mode of propulsion. Indeed, the keelmens' rowing technique aroused the curiosity both of pioneer leisure travellers and several more specialized writers who later came north to investigate the commercial activities and history of the Great Northern Coalfield. More locally it was also a subject that occasionally received attention in print from local antiquarians, historians, and illustrators, together with representation in the works of marine and genre artists. Printed textual interest thus spanned more than 200 years, from the published *Itinerary* of the antiquarian traveller William Stukeley in 1726 to an anonymous article in the *Smith's Dock Journal* of 1932, and between times it included the writings of a local, turn-of-the-nineteenth century antiquarian and dialect scholar: R Oliver Heslop. Though varying in their degree of detail and of style, it is remarkable that all these writers consistently describe the same rowing technique, collectively confirming that it remained unchanged from at least the early eighteenth century to the time of the keel's final decline, i.e. the third quarter of the nineteenth century. This attests not only to the method's longevity but also to its optimization for local needs.

76

Although impressed by the quality and variety of the Roman relics he found when visiting Newcastle around 1725, William Stukeley (1687–1765) was distinctly unimpressed by its inhabitants who, he later reported, 'speak very broad; so that . . . one can scarce understand the common people, but are apt to fancy one's self in a foreign country'. Nevertheless, he did take time to observe and publish a description of a singular working practice employed by these 'common people':

> The manner of rowing their great barges here is also very particular, and not unworthy of remark: four men manage the whole; three to a great long oar, that push it forward; and one to another such a-stern, that assists the other motion, but at the same time steers the keel, and corrects the bias the other gives it.'[17]

Although mention of the Tyne's 'great barges' fitted neatly into Stukeley's resume of the district's mines and coal trade, his particular focus on the 'manner of rowing' might seem a little unnecessary. But as a polymath he had a theory to pursue. Earlier in the *Itinerary*, whilst on the south coast, he had deprecated the fact that, 'Though the mariners have much mathematics on board . . . I had occasion to observing a gross error that has not been thought on, in the shape of their oars'. At great length he subsequently explained that the shape of an oar blade should follow the example of nature where, in similarly functioning appendages, 'the extremity is always pointed, and the broadest part is nearest the joint [fulcrum] where the power lies', whereas he noted that in the oars commonly used by sailors and watermen 'the extremity of that fan-like part, which opposes the water in rowing, is broadest.'[18] If, further north, he observed that the blade of a Tyne keel's 'great long oar' was narrow and relatively parallel-sided – a configuration it shared with large, eighteenth-century ship's 'sweeps' – and was thus shaped somewhat more to his way of thinking, he failed to record it!

Stukeley's description of rowing keels, from the 1720s, was later endorsed by the noted Newcastle historian the Reverend John Brand (1744–1806), who quoted that traveller's posthumously published text (1776) verbatim in his *History* of

Newcastle of 1789, though with the addendum that, 'They [keelmen] call the great oar, used as a kind of rudder at the stern of this vessel, the swape. Swappe, to strike or fling down with violence, occurs in Chaucer'. And wishing to impress readers with his grasp of all the textual authorities, Brand then cited in slightly abridged form that 'curious traveller', Thomas Pennant's (1726–1798) most recent published description of the keel (1776), a description presumably based upon observations made during his 'tour' in 1772:

> These boats are strong, clumsy, and oval, and carry twenty tons apiece. About four hundred and fifty are constantly employed: they are sometimes navigated with a square sail, but generally by two very large oars, one on the side, plied by a man and a boy; the other at the stern, by a single man, serving both as oar and rudder. Most of these keels go down to *Shields*, a port near the mouth of the river, about ten miles from *Newcastle*, where the large ships lie . . .[19]

Intriguingly, in a slightly earlier 'tour' publication (1771), Pennant had not chosen to focus on the keel's movement under oars at all, but had sketchily indicated that, 'sometimes they [keels] are navigated with a square sail, but generally are pushed along with large poles.'[20] Propulsion by poling was, however, a topic that Brand had reserved for himself – as is elaborated later.[21]

Regrettably, even this scant measure of interest in the rowing of keels did not extend into the first half of the nineteenth century, an absence which is quite surprising since the keelmen's occupation was then in full public view through reportage of their numerous strikes, court cases, and appearances before government-initiated inquiries. In like context, several newly published works appeared which dealt with the history and activities of the Great Northern Coalfield, including the role of coal transport by keels. For example, in 1835 John Holland's comprehensive new book, *The History and Description of Fossil Fuel, The Collieries, and Coal Trade of Great Britain,* used an illustration of a keel under oars on its title page, but for his textual description of the keel's usage he was content to simply quote from the old writers

A Reproduction of an interesting old Print which illustrates the Manner in which the Capacity of the Keel was often increased

FIGURE 3.2 This illustration, which was variously published for almost two centuries, rather simplistically depicts the keel crew's three-man rowing technique (*Smith's Dock Journal*, 1932; *The History and Description of Fossil Fuel* by J Holland, 1835).

– Stukeley, Pennant and Brand. By and large, published accounts from the latter half of the nineteenth century continued to be derivative, and Holland's simplistic illustration of a keel under oars was, and still is, reproduced without question or comment (see Fig. 3.2).

No further significant published observations on rowing keels seem to have been made until the 1930s, when W S Mitcalfe made passing mention in a historical paper and, nearly 20 years later, an anonymous contributor to the *Smith's Dock Journal* (a company magazine) detailed the twin-oar method of keel and wherry rowing adopted during the late nineteenth century. Confusingly, Mitcalfe's text described the traditional three-man, single oar method but, maybe unwittingly, his main illustration (after Hedley) depicted this much later twin-oar technique![22]

Meanwhile, R O Heslop's far more precise description of the three-person technique lay unnoticed for over a hundred years before eventually being quoted in print, in part at least, by Fewster in 2011:[23]

The chief method of propulsion was by the means of one large oar worked by two men and a boy, this was usually rowed upon the port or ower-side, of the vessel from a sloping platform on the heed-sheets. To make a stroke the keelmen bore upon the loom of the great oar until its blade cleared the water. Then, walking in a stooping posture in the direction of the stern, they swung the oar on its rowlock and on reaching the summit of their stage suddenly dipped the wash into the water. All then kicked back their right legs, making a strong pull, which they continued as they walked backward in step to the end of the stroke. On reaching this they immediately bore down and swung the oar for another stroke as before. A second and shorter oar, called "the swape", was simultaneously worked over the stern by one man, who pulled stroke for stroke with the great oar and held the course or steered the keel at will. The "swape" was always in the hands of the "skipper", who with the two men and the boy beforementioned, four hands in all, formed the crew.[24]

Rowing: the technique

Despite Heslop's thoroughness, his description still leaves several practical questions unanswered. What, for instance, was the length of the rowing oar, where and how was its pivot point located, and why was there a 'sloping platform on the heed-sheets' (fore deck)? More generally, especially given the dearth of textual evidence, can the examination of contemporary illustrations help provide answers?

Nowhere, it seems, are the actual lengths of a keel's propulsive ('great') and steering ('swape') oars quoted, although contemporary graphic representations emphasise their size. For example, Bell's technical sketch, c.1830, of a keel under sail indicates that one of the two stowed oars was barely shorter than the keel itself and the other, presumably the 'swape', was a little under that (see, Fig. 2.12). These lengths accord well with the oars carried on board a keel detailed in a well-known painting of the same period by J W Carmichael.[25][26] Although later in date (1882), Palmer's engraving of *A Keel of the Old Type* shows the washes (blades) of the stowed oars protruding some 5 feet past the sternpost to port, with the handles

80

presumably lodged forward on the heed sheets or walkway.[27] Correspondingly, a naive, late eighteenth-century rendering of ice-bound keels indicates oars whose blades extend some 8 feet (equal to the after deck length) over the stern, with their handles seemingly butted up to the hold bulkhead forward.[28] These few graphic evidences may be considered slender but they are corroborative, suggesting an oar length of around 35 feet. For all practical purposes, this equates to the length, i.e. 36 feet, of the shortest naval 'ship's sweep' cited in shipbuilding texts of the early nineteenth century.[29]

In form, the keel's main oar is generally shown as having a long, narrow blade and Bell's sketch – the best depiction available – suggests that it was fairly parallel-sided, merging into an undifferentiated shaft and loom that terminated in a slightly tapered handle. Standard naval practice indicates a maximum blade breadth of 9 inches for a 36-foot sweep, with a shaft and loom diameter of a little under 5 inches. Overall, Bell's blade appears rather narrower than that, although the shaft and loom diameters look comparable. Scandinavian 'Fir' (Norway Spruce, *Picea abies*) imported from places such as Porsgrund and Eastrice in Norway and Christiansand in Sweden, was the preferred material for keel oars and swapes. From the mid-eighteenth century onwards local merchants not infrequently sold timber specifically for this purpose. For example, an advertisement in the summer of 1763 offered 'a large quantity of fir timber from 20 to 45 feet, fit for . . . keel masts, swapes, oars, or yards for ships, &c.', whilst in 1794 another vendor offered 'fir spars' of 25 to 50 feet in length as timber suitable for 'Keel Oars, Scaffolding' and other purposes.[30] In a maritime context, terms such as 'fir spars' and 'rough spars' indicated small unworked tree trunks, raw material from which a coal keel's large, single-piece oar could be readily and cheaply fashioned by local craftsmen, although ready-made oars appear to have been imported too.[31] For instance, late in 1787 'a Parcel [quantity] of Oars and Keel Sets [puoys]' arrived in a cargo from 'Christiansand and Norway', and two years later 'Keel Oars' were amongst the cargo of 'exceedingly good Norwegian timber' salved from a Scandinavian ship stranded at the mouth of the Tyne.[32] Practically, it would seem that good quality 'Fir' offered relatively light weight against adequate stiffness when made into keel oars and swapes, but even so a keel oar must have weighed somewhere around 1-1½ hundredweight (112-168 pounds) and will have required considerable experience and strength to deploy and retrieve.[33]

Given that the pivot point of a 36-foot oar was located on the edge of the deck in line with the keel's forward transverse beam – as shown by the thole pin on the SANT model – then the 10 feet of loom and handle remaining inboard would have provided quite enough length for the grasp of two men and a boy (Fig. 3.3). However, the resultant crude gearing (i.e. velocity ratio) of 1:2.6 appears high and tiring, especially when compared with the 1:1.25 to 1:1.50 commonly employed by standing rowers on British cargo boats elsewhere, although the sweeps of their craft were generally single-manned and shorter, under 30 feet.[34]

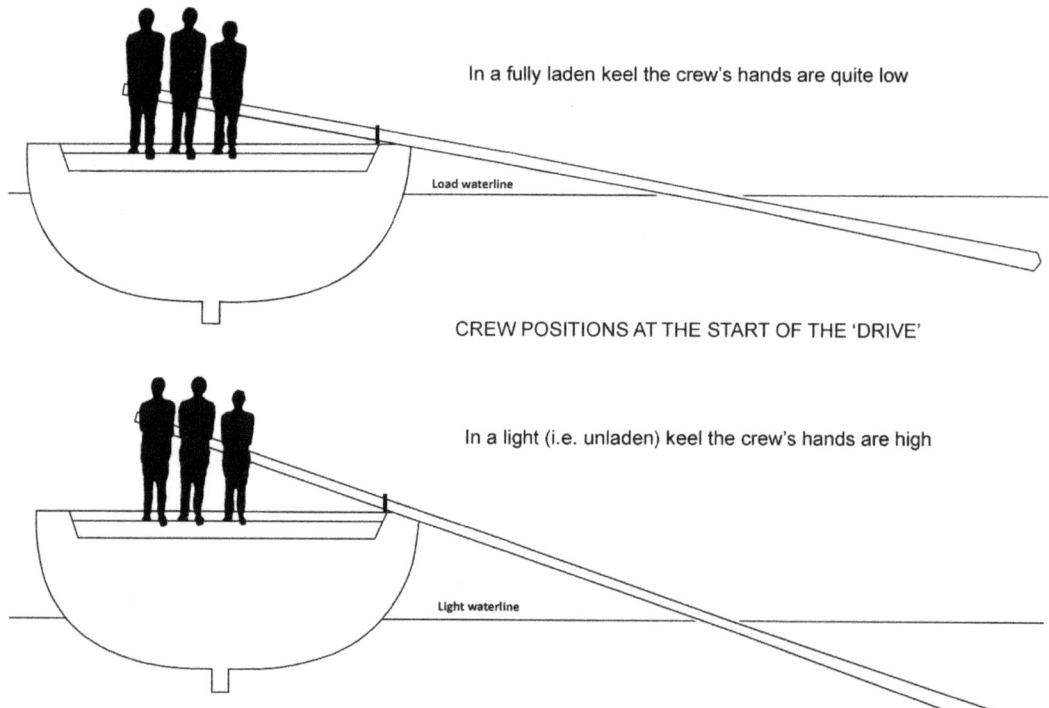

In a fully laden keel the crew's hands are quite low

Load waterline

CREW POSITIONS AT THE START OF THE 'DRIVE'

In a light (i.e. unladen) keel the crew's hands are high

Light waterline

FIGURE 3.3 Top, crew positions and oar angle when rowing a fully loaded keel; bottom, crew positions and oar angle when rowing an empty unladen keel (based on SANT model measurements).

With regard to the pivot position of the keel's oar, it must be stressed that those nineteenth-century illustrations of keels which show this halfway along the foredeck, e.g. Holland, 1835, and Taylor, 1858, should not be taken literally. The keel's fore deck at that halfway point was under 6 feet wide and tapered rapidly to the bow, so anyone walking vigorously backwards from there would have fallen overboard![35] Regrettably, not one textual source details the nature of the oar pivot used on late eighteenth- or early nineteenth-century keels. Fortunately however, the SANT model's simple, heavy —and presumably solidly embedded – single iron thole pin, with just sufficient height to provide a bearing for the oar, demonstrates a convincingly rugged and practical low-cost solution. Again, there is no textual mention of the method employed to retain the oar against the thole, though the use of a tough, removeable rope grommet slipped round the oar's loom and the thole seems most likely. As a cheap and effective oar-retaining solution, grommets of different kinds were used both locally and elsewhere in Britain and Northern Europe.[36 37]

The practical function of the 'sloping platform' or 'stage' referred to by Heslop (descriptively referred to hereafter as a 'ramp') is an open question (Fig. 3.4). No other author even mentions it. But a variety of contemporary illustrations attest to the fact that it was once an integral feature of the keel's fore deck. Three visual examples that span a hundred years suffice: 1789, the keel in the foreground of John Brand's bookplate, the 'Ruins of the Bridge'; John Bell's detailed sketch of a keel, c.1828; and 1882, W J Palmer's book vignette, 'Keel'.[38 39 40] Furthermore, a ramp features on three out of the four extant, authentic models of keels.[41] But an explanation of the ramp's ubiquity emerges only through a detailed understanding of the keelmen's rowing technique.

Insight into the unusual technique employed in rowing keels can be achieved through close study of the few reliable descriptive texts that survive, aided by a rigorous assessment of the constraints imposed by the vessel's layout and size. In this way a measure of reconstruction can be achieved which marries a modern understanding of the four successive phases of a rowing stroke with, most particularly, Heslop's textual descriptions (c.1902) quoted below (Fig. 3.5):[42]

FIGURE 3.4 The foredeck's 'sloping platform' (ramp) as evidenced by: top, Brand's illustrator, 1789; middle, John Bell c.1828; bottom, the maker of the SANT model.

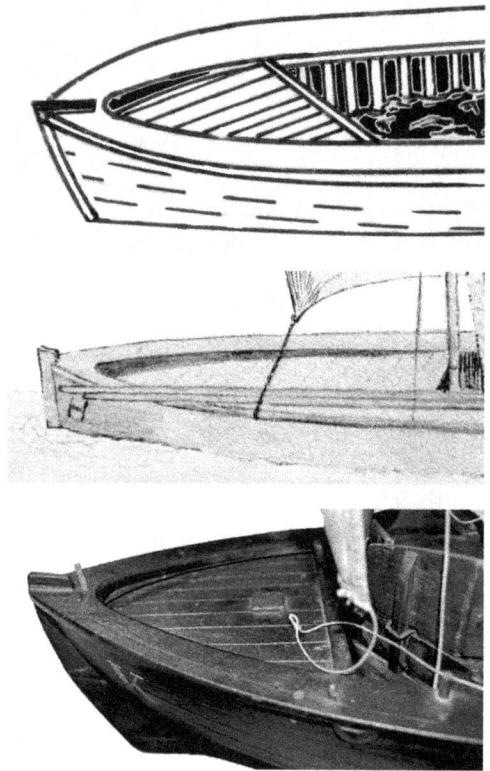

Catch (Rowing Phases: 2-3), '. . . on reaching the summit of their stage [ramp] they suddenly dipped the wash [oar blade] into the water.'

Drive (Rowing Phases: 3, 4-8), 'All then kicked back their right legs, making a strong pull, which they continued as they walked backward together until they traversed the platform [ramp] to the end of the stroke.'

Extraction/Release (Rowing Phases: 9-10), '. . . on reaching this [the bottom of the ramp] they immediately bore down on the great oar until its blade cleared the water.'

Recovery (Rowing Phases: 10-12), 'Then walking in stooping posture in the direction of the stern [i.e., back up the ramp], they swung the oar on its rowlock [thole] and on reaching the summit of their stage . . .' they began the stroke again.

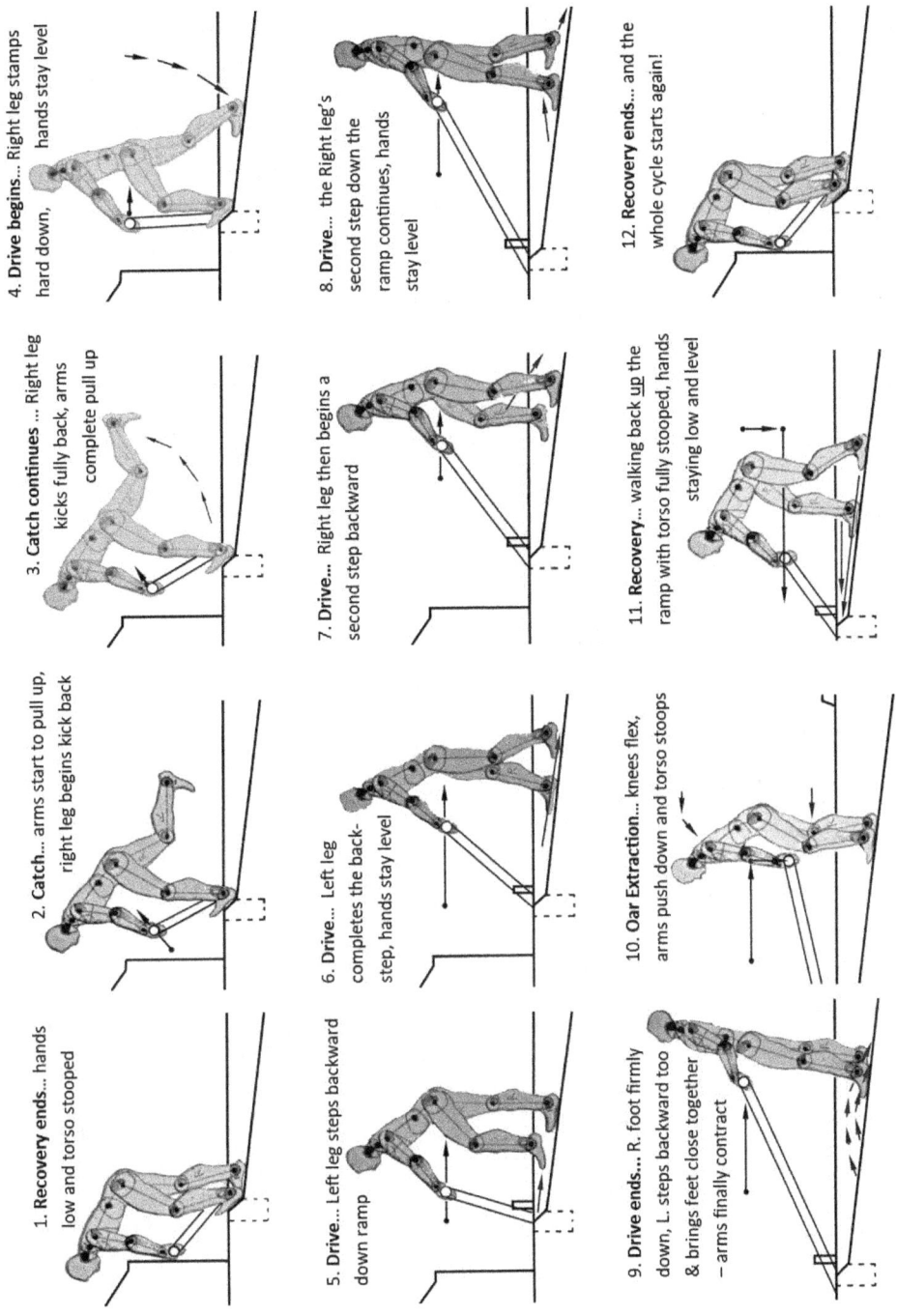

1. **Recovery ends...** hands low and torso stooped

2. **Catch...** arms start to pull up, right leg begins kick back

3. **Catch continues ...** Right leg kicks fully back, arms complete pull up

4. **Drive begins...** Right leg stamps hard down, hands stay level

5. **Drive...** Left leg steps backward down ramp

6. **Drive...** Left leg completes the back-step, hands stay level

7. **Drive...** Right leg then begins a second step backward

8. **Drive...** the Right leg's second step down the ramp continues, hands stay level

9. **Drive ends...** R. foot firmly down, L. steps backward too & brings feet close together – arms finally contract

10. **Oar Extraction...** knees flex, arms push down and torso stoops

11. **Recovery...** walking back up the ramp with torso fully stooped, hands staying low and level

12. **Recovery ends...** and the whole cycle starts again!

FIGURE 3.5 The phases of the rowing cycle: 1, pre-catch; 2–3, catch; drive, 4–8; extraction/release, 9–10; and recovery, 10–12 (note: only one oarsman shown).

This rowing action must have required not only remarkable coordination on the part of the three crew members, who were working tightly shoulder-to-shoulder, but also exceptional strength in each of the individual's back and upper torso to deal with the repeated demands of moving from a heavily stooped but mobile posture (recovery) to full extension under load (catch and drive). Furthermore, the power stroke, i.e. the drive, had to be achieved in what by most rowing standards was a limited compass, a swept angle of merely 35°, although owing to the oar's great length this still meant that the tip of blade had to be pulled through an arc of some 17 feet.[43] Unusually for a British working boat the major part of the stroke's drive was accomplished aft of the pivot point (thole), for in a keel the men's forward reach was strictly limited by the edge of the hold or by the upstanding coal boards when loaded. Furthermore, when fully laden not only had the crew to move the keel's greatly increased weight but, owing to the reduction in freeboard, had to

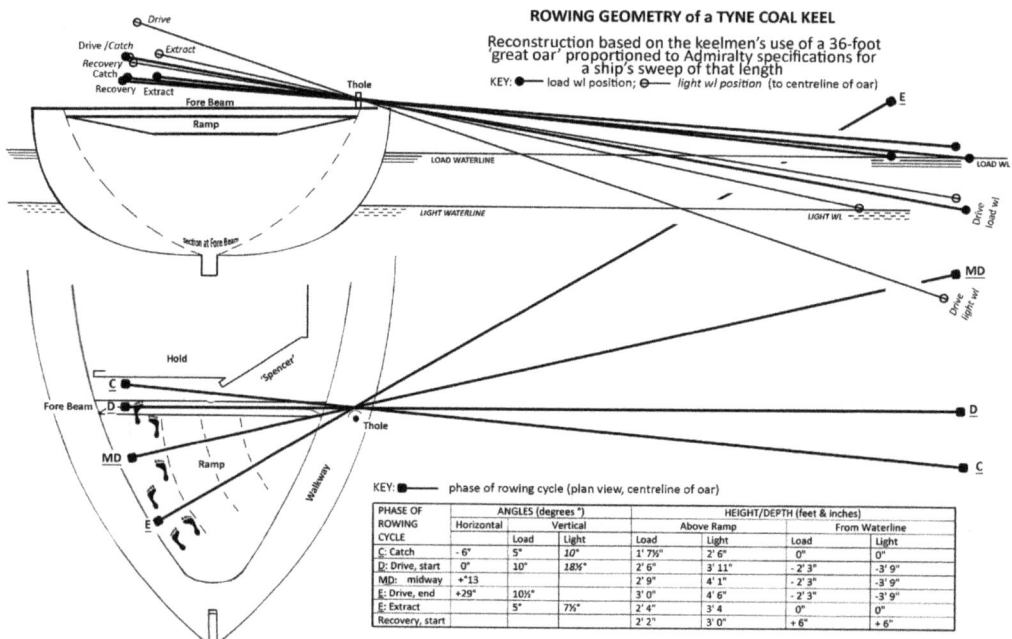

ROWING GEOMETRY of a TYNE COAL KEEL
Reconstruction based on the keelmen's use of a 36-foot 'great oar' proportioned to Admiralty specifications for a ship's sweep of that length
KEY: ● — load wl position; ⊖— light wl position (to centreline of oar)

KEY: ●— phase of rowing cycle (plan view, centreline of oar)

PHASE OF ROWING CYCLE	ANGLES (degrees °)			HEIGHT/DEPTH (feet & inches)			
	Horizontal	Vertical		Above Ramp		From Waterline	
	Load	Light		Load	Light	Load	Light
C: Catch	- 6°	5°	10°	1' 7½"	2' 6"	0"	0"
D: Drive, start	0°	10°	18½°	2' 6"	3' 11"	- 2' 3"	-3' 9"
MD: midway	+°13			2' 9"	4' 1"	- 2' 3"	-3' 9"
E: Drive, end	+29°	10½°		3' 0"	4' 6"	- 2' 3"	-3' 9"
E: Extract		5°	7½°	2' 4"	3' 4	0"	0"
Recovery, start				2' 2"	3' 0"	+ 6"	+ 6"

FIGURE 3.6 The basic rowing geometry of the keel in both an unladen and a loaded condition (evaluations based on measurements taken from the SANT model).

operate in a more uncomfortable and less efficient crouched or stooping stance (Fig. 3.6). For although the angle (≈18°) at which the oar met the water surface in an unladen keel was not dissimilar to that of comparable British working boats elsewhere, in the loaded condition the oar angle (≈10°) was considerably reduced from this widespread norm.[44]

Whether or not the keel's oar blade was feathered during the recovery phase is nowhere made explicit. But Heslop's emphasis both on 'suddenly' dipping the oar blade upon entry and 'immediately' bearing down on the handle to gain clearance at the end of the drive, is consistent with a non-feathering action, and this seems most likely. Indeed, the non-feathering technique was commonplace amongst British fishing craft and work boat crews where, in normal practice, the simplicity of a boat's gear and its ease of use often outweighed the marginal efficiencies gained through the more complex feathered stroke. Realistically, the large diameter handle of the keel's massive, multi-crewed oar seems likely to have posed a problem to grasp and rotate if feathering, and it may be noted that the largest naval ships' sweeps (40-50 feet) of the era were fitted with separate side handles for this reason and were worked non-feathered (note [29]). Blade windage during the non-feathered recovery phase seems unlikely to have been a problem in keels as all relevant contemporary accounts agree that propulsive rowing was employed only during settled weather.

Examination of the keel's rowing geometry suggests two reasons for the adoption of a ramped, rather than conventional, flat foredeck (heed sheets). Firstly, it gave useful gravitational (downhill) impetus during the catch and drive, enhancing the force applied to the oar under load and perhaps helping to combat crew fatigue. Secondly, and perhaps less obviously, the accrued vertical fall of some 6 inches decreased the level to which the hands had to drop in forcing the oar handle down when extracting the blade from the water at the end of the drive.[45] This not only eased the degree an individual had to bend, but also provided a bigger margin of safety when extracting the blade from the water, for with such a large oar 'catching a crab', i.e. failing to get the blade out of the water, could have resulted in injury or even death (Fig. 3.7).

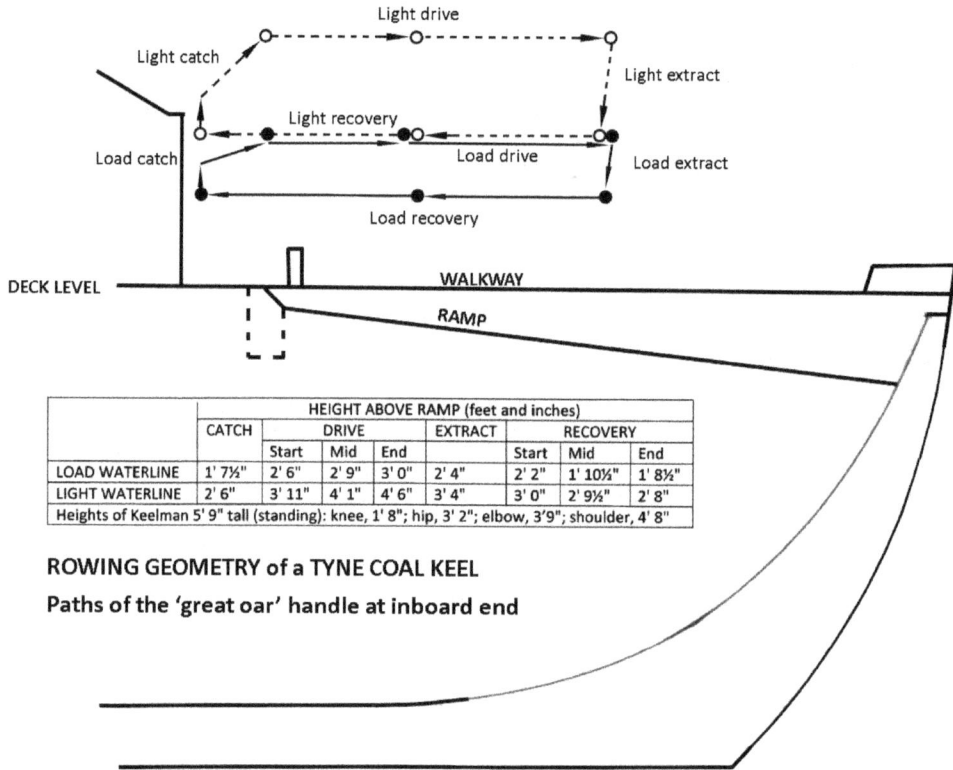

	HEIGHT ABOVE RAMP (feet and inches)							
	CATCH	DRIVE			EXTRACT	RECOVERY		
		Start	Mid	End		Start	Mid	End
LOAD WATERLINE	1' 7½"	2' 6"	2' 9"	3' 0"	2' 4"	2' 2"	1' 10½"	1' 8½"
LIGHT WATERLINE	2' 6"	3' 11"	4' 1"	4' 6"	3' 4"	3' 0"	2' 9½"	2' 8"
Heights of Keelman 5' 9" tall (standing): knee, 1' 8"; hip, 3' 2"; elbow, 3'9"; shoulder, 4' 8"								

ROWING GEOMETRY of a TYNE COAL KEEL

Paths of the 'great oar' handle at inboard end

FIGURE 3.7 Viewed in profile, and seen in relation to the oar handle paths, the ramp's role in enhancing rowing efficiency becomes more apparent.

One feature of keel rowing that some contemporary observers commented upon was the peculiar kick-back at the beginning of the rowing stroke, an action that is also occasionally shown – albeit naively – in paintings and published prints (Fig. 3.2; Plate 3). Although the connection is not self-evident, this seemingly odd bodily action may have been associated with the use of the foredeck ramp, as is evidenced by the SANT model. On this model the face of the fore beam at the head of the ramp has been purposely chamfered to act as a solid foothold for the start of the rowers' kick-back, functioning as the 'stretcher' did for seated rowers (Fig. 3.4, bottom). All of this argues that the ramp and associated kick-back action aided rowing efficiency, although it would require an authentic reconstruction of a keel and specific trials to confirm that supposition.

Rowing: the elusive swape

If a level of uncertainty remains over some aspects of the main oar's use, then the role of the keel skipper's distinctive 'swape' is less certain still. Two things are obvious, however: the swape was somewhat shorter than the principal oar; and it was used in a different manner. But by how much it was shorter, and what exactly was its function, is open to interpretation. Two references, from the opposite ends of the chronological spectrum, seem to afford useful corroborative insight, namely: Pennant (1776) noted that 'the other [oar] at the stern, [worked] by a single man, serving both as oar and rudder'; and Heslop (c.1902) wrote, 'At the same time [as the three crew rowed] a second and shorter oar called the Swape was worked over the stern on the opposite side [sic] bye-side (starboard) by one man, who timed his [sic] pulled stroke for stroke with the great oar and thus held the course or steered the vessel at will'. [46] In their different ways both authors agree that the swape was used both for propulsion and for steering, but exactly how? By analogy the latter function, that of steering, is relatively simple to explain. The manoeuvrability afforded by a long stern oar was well known on Tyneside, and was practised, for example, by the crews of whaleboats in the Tyne's prominent Arctic whaling fleet and, closer to home, in the successful 'Shields Pattern' rowing lifeboats. However, simple passive, directional steering with the starboard-side swape seems unlikely to have kept a keel on a straight course, for the bias imparted by the great leverage of the port-side rowing oar will have veered the vessel's head to starboard with every stroke. Hence, perhaps Heslop's comment that the steersman (i.e. skipper) 'pulled stroke for stroke' with the oarsmen, thus counteracting the keel's constant tendency to yaw to starboard.

Quite how the skipper 'pulled' is another matter, for the position of the swape's thole pin, at the extremity of the after deck (to starboard), would have precluded a conventional, sideways rowing stroke. Most likely he employed a modified single-oar, stern sculling stroke, in which the application of maximum power to the blade on the inward (starboard-to-port) sweep was followed by a corresponding degree of reduced drive by feathering on the outward (port-to-starboard) one. In experienced hands, an asymmetric action of this kind would have provided a useful amount of forward propulsion in addition to steerage. And this hypothesis also provides an explanation of Stukeley's insight (c.1725) that: 'another such [oar/ swape] a-stern . . . assists the other [main oar's] motion, but at the same time steers the keel, and corrects the bias the other gives it', an astute observation by a knowledgeable observer that is supported by Pennant's later (c.1772) succinct eyewitness observation that the swape 'served both as oar and rudder'. Viewed more broadly, stern oar techniques of a similar kind seem to have been practised by lightermen elsewhere in Britain, as on the Thames, but have rarely gained mention in print.[47]

In the absence of textual evidence as to the actual length of the swape, the best guide is afforded by estimates based on the dimensional constraints of the keel itself. Measured from the deck-mounted thole pin to a man's chest (or shoulder) height at the front of the afterdeck, the swape's inboard length was little more than 8 feet at best. Calculated at the same gearing ratio as the main oar, this would suggest a total length of around 29 feet, although the gearing of a sculling oar is generally lower than that employed for rowing.[48][49] A figure of 29 feet is also supported by the simple geometric calculation required to establish the minimum length of swape that would achieve blade immersion in an unladen keel. Consequently, a nominal length of 30 feet seems reasonable, corresponding with generalized statements that the swape was shorter than the main rowing oar. Nevertheless, Bell's sketch and other – admittedly more impressionistic – depictions hint at lengths somewhat greater than that.

In particular, Brand's illustrator (1789) includes a unique structure from which the swape is being operated: a below-deck-level gangway across the after end of the hold (Fig. 3.8). Not only would this have allowed a longer inboard loom, but through lowering the body position of the user it would have decreased the angle at which the swape met the water, resulting in greater outboard length as well.[50] Perhaps the simple answer is that the exact length of a swape depended upon an

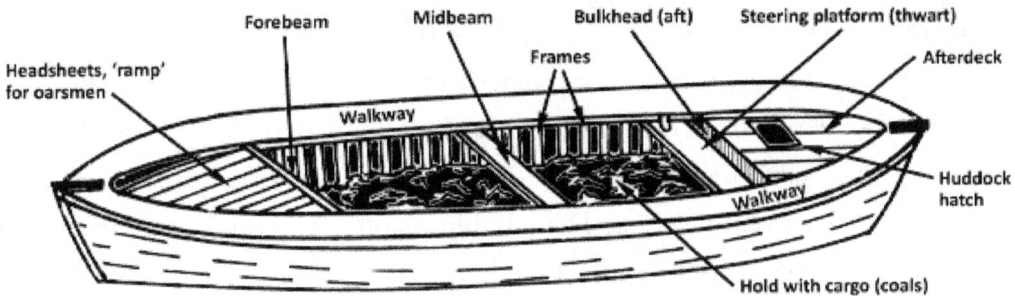

FIGURE 3.8 Top (right), the skipper of a keel working his swape from a broad thwart or steering platform located at the after end of the hold (from Brand, 1789); bottom, the principal deck-level features of a late-eighteenth century keel of this type.

individual skipper's preferences – or pocket.[51] That the swape also functioned as a steering device under sail is left for later discussion.

Rowing: the final era

Sketchy as it is, the evidence points towards the introduction of a new, more convenient system of rowing shortly before the mid-nineteenth century, at which point the keel's long-established three-man oar fell into disuse. Two factors may have occasioned this change. Firstly, the widespread adoption in the 1840s of fore-and-aft sailing rigs that used permanent, deck-stepped masts whose presence likely precluded the use of the traditional three-man oar. Secondly, the keel owners' increased desire to drive down their cost levels, a move which eventually resulted in three-man crews. For instance, from at least 1849 onwards the dozen or so keels of Stella Colliery were rarely manned by more than three men, whereas previously a young boy (the 'pee-dee') was always carried in addition.[52][53] The exact nature and timing of this shift away from rowing with the customary three-man oar remains uncertain, but it is significant that two witnesses at the *Admiralty Inquiry* of 1849 referred to the use of the 'lang oar' in the past tense, hinting at changes in the 1830s–40s.

Overall, it seems reasonable to conclude that use of the three-man oar had declined by the mid-century, to be replaced by systems that employed two men rowing independently from the fore deck. Each of these 'pair oar' rowers, deployed to port and starboard respectively, used a much shorter, captive oar worked on some form of removeable pivot. Detachable pivots were essential, for the side walkways had to remain clear and unobstructed when – as was frequently the case in the shoaly river – it was necessary to propel the keel by poling. Although dating from a later era, Newcastle artist Ralph Hedley's genre painting of 1905, *Weel May the Keel Row*, provides useful detail from which to reconstruct at least one type of pair oar system. Hedley depicts two (i.e. port and starboard) demountable, folding outriggers each carrying a captive, non-feathering oar worked by a standing crewman who has sufficient space to take two or three steps when completing a stroke (Fig. 3.9).

In practice, this kind of iron outrigger had several clear advantages. It allowed the thole (pivot point) to be positioned further forward than previously, but at the same time it maintained the original transverse distance from the keel's centreline. Consequently, not only was the three-man oar's gearing maintained, or even improved, but the swept arc of the stroke was increased by some 10° since the oarsman could make his 'catch' farther ahead than the old thole position allowed. Moreover, there was an added advantage in that the thole of the outrigger was higher, its position above deck level allowing the oar handle to lay more comfortably and effectively in the oarsman's grasp (Fig. 3.10).

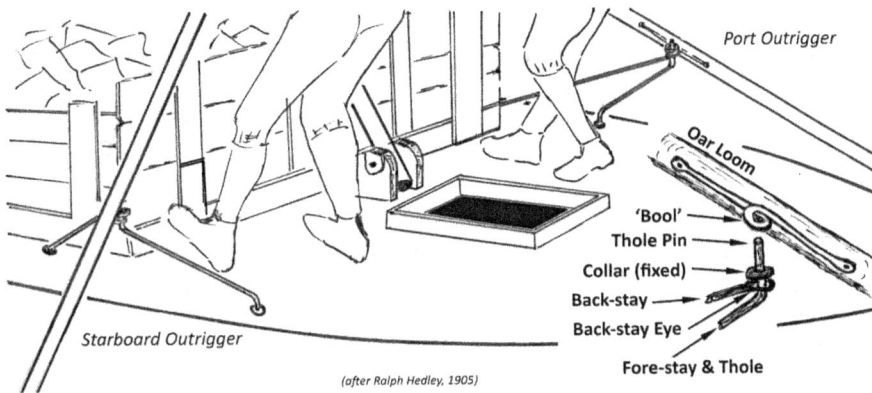

Port Outrigger

Oar Loom

'Bool'
Thole Pin
Collar (fixed)
Back-stay
Back-stay Eye
Fore-stay & Thole

Starboard Outrigger

(after Ralph Hedley, 1905)

FIGURE 3.9 Reconstruction of the equipment used in the pair oar rowing of a keel (or Tyne wherry) as evidenced in Ralph Hedley's oil painting *Weel May the Keel Row*, 1905.

ROWING GEOMETRY WITH PAIRED OARS:

Using appr. 22-foot oars, each fitted with a 'bool' (forged eyeplate) working on the single tholes of demountable hinged iron outriggers
(after R Hedley, 1905)

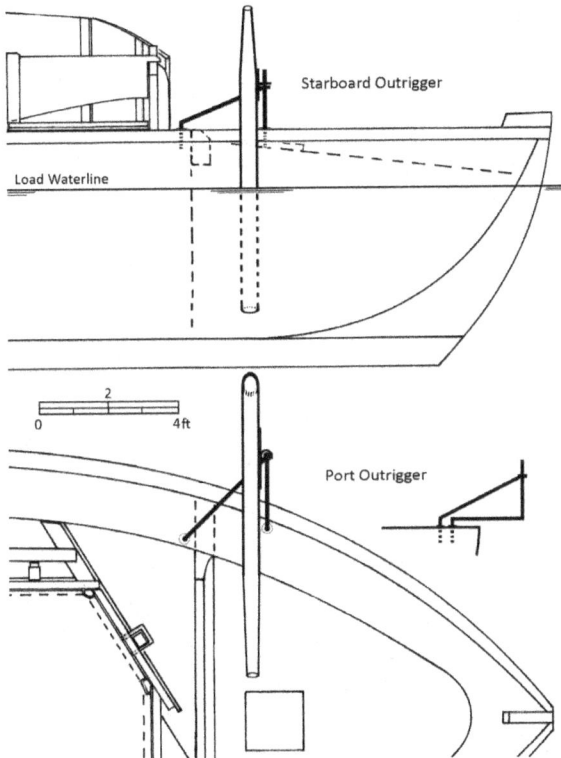

Starboard Outrigger

Load Waterline

2

0   4ft

Port Outrigger

FIGURE 3.10 Rowing geometry of a pair oared keel using the demountable outriggers depicted in Hedley's painting of 1905.

These coal keel, and Tyne wherry, outriggers seem likely to owe their origin to the pioneering devices fitted to early nineteenth-century Tyne racing skiffs. The first outrigger made from iron actually appeared in 1830, but it was not until this innovatory approach was refined by the famous Clasper family in the 1840s that it became recognized as an essential racing boat fitting.[54] That the principle of the iron outrigger might be transferred to the racing boats' working counterparts is not surprising, for not only were the technical advantages obvious, but racing and working boats shared the same waterway and their occupants frequented the same pubs, whilst some professional oarsmen began their working lives in the river's water or waterside trades. Naturally, the keel or wherry outrigger was far more robustly constructed than that of the racing boat and, critically, it was not a permanent fixture but had to be easily set up and detached as required. The pattern shown by Hedley was probably just one amongst many variants, all of which could be cheaply if roughly fabricated in wrought iron rod by a ship-smith or blacksmith, and all of which could readily be stowed away after use. And simplicity was the key. Hedley's outrigger comprises just two triangulated stays: an after stay, which rotated by means of a forged eye upon the upright element of the forward stay, so both could fold flat – like a fisherman anchor – when not in use; and a forward stay whose upper portion formed a thole with an attached (presumably welded) collar that provided support for the oar. In use, flanged spigots at the base of each of stay fitted into suitably positioned deck sockets. As to the oar itself, the shaft was fitted with a cleverly fashioned 'bool' (oar plate) forged from a single length of iron rod that was turned full circle in the centre, forming a ring to fit over the thole, whilst its ends were spread and flattened to take the fastenings that secured it to the loom (see Fig. 3.9, detail).[55][56]

A later, rather vague, piece of published evidence (1932) clearly outlines a different pair oar arrangement for keels, one that did not involve outriggers:

On the gunwale of the keel standing rowlocks were fitted. They were supported in a chock and were stayed by an iron bar. The lower end of this bar had a hook which slipped into an eyebolt on the gunwale when the rowlocks were in use. In this way the rowlocks were always braced against the stresses set up by the working oar. They could easily be unshipped if necessary, by slipping the hook from the eyebolt . . . [the oars] worked in the rowlock by means of a thimble and eyebolt. The oars were about 22 ft. long and straight-bladed. At the grip they were of modest dimensions to enable them to be handled as easily as possible, but at the rowlock they were about 7 in. in diameter, and at the blade end were as much as 9 in.[57]

The inference is that, although a tension stay was used (as with an outrigger), the actual oar pivot was positioned at the deck edge. Again, the use of some form of captive oar is implied, although the description is so technically vague and ambiguous as to leave the exact form and action of the 'rowlock', or thole pin, unclear. One possible interpretation is shown here, but others are clearly possible (Fig. 3.11).

That a single tholepin pivot might be described as a 'standing rowlock' is unsurprising, for the rather disparaging term 'pitman's rollick [rowlock]' was used for the single thole and bool arrangement of the small rowing boats hired out locally at the seaside and on park lakes – it provided an easy method for inexperienced rowers to use and reduced the risk of losing an oar overboard. Whether such a standing rowlock was a permanent fixture or not is unclear, 'standing' may simply refer to its being upstanding in use. However, the use of a hook-and-eye for securing the tension stay suggests that, like an outrigger, the entire fitting (other than the supporting chock) was removeable. Restricted by the deck edge pivot, the oar's inboard length could have been little more than 5 feet, leaving 17 feet of length and weight outside. Consequently, the adoption of oars no less than 7 inches in diameter 'at the rowlock' suggests that this was to satisfy the oarsman's commonly felt need for counterbalance weight, rather than to give shaft strength alone.

Nevertheless, when working oars of such weight and length singlehanded, the keelmen of this era were no doubt just as dexterous and skilled as their counterparts

ROWING GEOMETRY PAIRED OARS:

'Standing Rowlocks' - reconstructed from the
description in *Smith's Dock Journal*, April 1932
(other interpretations are possible)

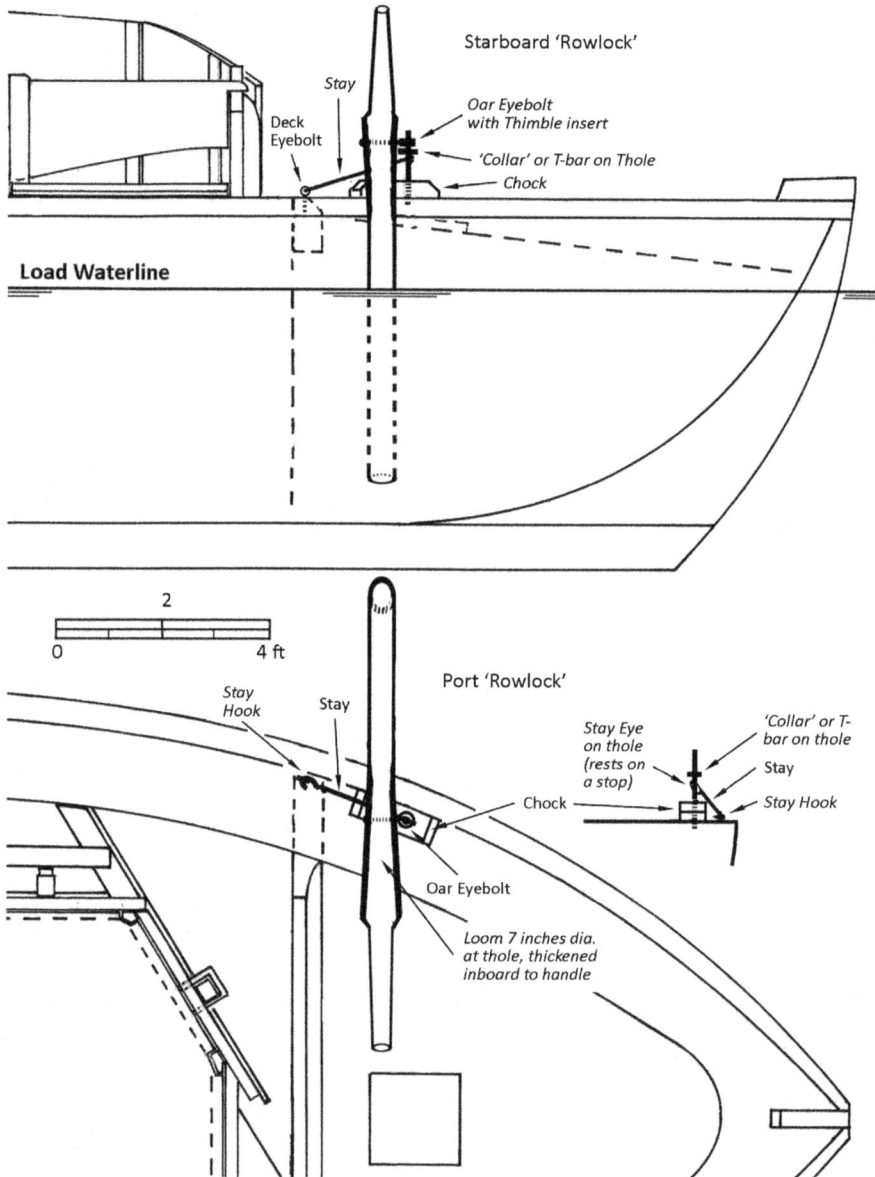

Starboard 'Rowlock'

Stay

Deck
Eyebolt

*Oar Eyebolt
with Thimble insert*

'Collar' or T-bar on Thole

Chock

Load Waterline

2

0   4 ft

Stay
Hook

Stay

Port 'Rowlock'

*Stay Eye
on thole
(rests on
a stop)*

*'Collar' or T-
bar on thole*

Stay

Chock

Stay Hook

Oar Eyebolt

*Loom 7 inches dia.
at thole, thickened
inboard to handle*

FIGURE 3.11 Reconstruction of the pair oar equipment described in an article in the *Smith's Dock Journal*, 1932; other interpretations are possible.

on the 'London River' (Thames). There, for instance, when moving fore or aft a Thames lighterman allowed the water to do the work by trailing his oar alongside and, by knowing his oar's exact centre of balance, he could take advantage of any convenient fulcrums afforded by his vessel's superstructure and deck fittings in deploying and lifting it.[58]

POLING AND HAULING

Apart from rowing, the two other methods of manual propulsion employed on a Tyne coal keel were poling and hauling, although neither could be entertained except in specific circumstances. Poling could be practiced only along the shallow-water sections of the river – typically in depths of 15 feet and under – but this gave considerable scope for progress since many of the natural shoals were longstanding and extensive, and they remained so throughout the keel era. Hauling could be resorted to only where a sufficient interval of waterside was accessible, unobstructed and had sufficient depth of water alongside to float a keel, a combination that became increasingly hard to find. Despite the limitations of each, these two methods of propulsion were greatly valued for their capacity to move a keel, albeit slowly, against moderately adverse conditions of wind, tide, or stream. But to engage in them was not welcome, for they demanded the expenditure of much manual effort.

Poling: to 'set', 'put' or 'puoy'?

Through the popularity of its attractive catchy tune and repetitive rhyming lyric, people in late Victorian drawing rooms nationwide came to know adaptations of the Tyneside anthem: 'The Keel Row'. In one version of this song (1812) a keelman's wife extols the virtues of her chosen man, Johnny, the 'Breet star o' Heaton' (Bright star of Heaton), but probably only local folk appreciated the colloquial point that, as she expressed it, Johnny could not only 'row' his keel 'so tightly' (smartly) but he could equally well 'set' (pole) it too.[59]

Heslop's definition of this latter action in his *Northumbrian Words* (1892) – 'To propel a keel with a powey is called to put or to set' – is not only concise but, in the context of keel usage, confirms the lesser-known dialect use of the more generic term, 'put'. And it was Heslop who later took the trouble to describe the now obsolete, but once commonplace, 'settin' (poling) or 'puttin' process (Fig. 3.12, right):

In the shallows it was usual to propel the keel by the process called "settin". This work was done by the skipper and bullies, each of whom thrust with his shoulder against a "puoy". The puoy, or pooey, was a slender pole of about 18 feet length shod with a horn-shaped fork of iron. To "set" the keel the crew stood at the bows and faced the stern, each man holding a puoy in one hand. The puoys were quickly shot forward [i.e., astern] and downward until their forked ends touched the riverbed. In this sloping position of the puoy each man laid his shoulder against its upper end and leaning forward, pressed with his whole weight against it. As the keel moved under him he stepped along its side platform [walkway], gripping the deck with his toes as he went and continuing to exert his full strength in this way until the quarter was reached. As each man recovered an erect position he instantly plucked his puoy from its "had" [hold] in the riverbed. A quick right-about turn was made, accompanied by a kick up of the right leg and each man stepped briskly forward, trailing his puoy with one hand until the bow of the keel was reached. Here a face-about movement was made, the puoy again shot down, and another "set" made, the process being continued exactly as before. It was all done with the smartness of a drill exercise; with the movements timed and in unison, and the bullies not infrequently matched themselves against other crews at aquatic festivals, when a "settin" match afforded an example of the speed attainable in a race between keels thus propelled.[60]

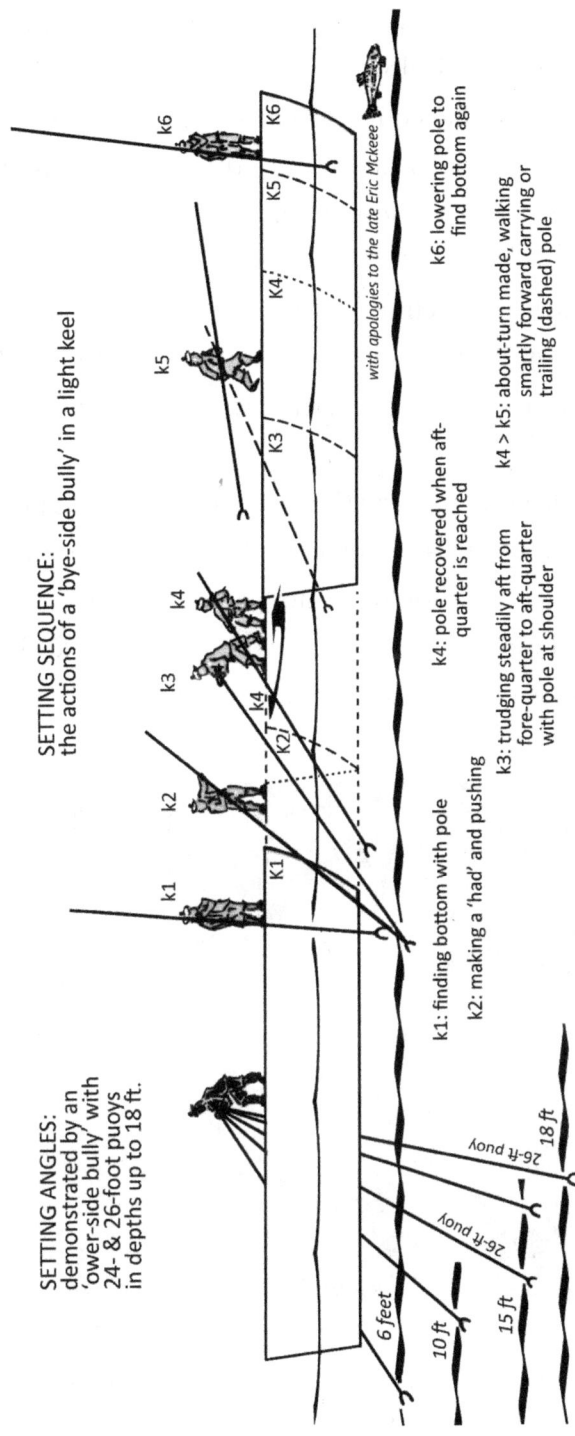

SETTING ANGLES:
demonstrated by an
'ower-side bully' with
24- & 26-foot puoys
in depths up to 18 ft.

SETTING SEQUENCE:
the actions of a 'bye-side bully' in a light keel

k1: finding bottom with pole

k2: making a 'had' and pushing

k3: trudging steadily aft from
fore-quarter to aft-quarter
with pole at shoulder

k4: pole recovered when aft-
quarter is reached

k4 > k5: about-turn made, walking
smartly forward carrying or
trailing (dashed) pole

k6: lowering pole to
find bottom again

with apologies to the late Eric Mckeee

6 feet

10 ft

15 ft

18 ft

26-ft puoy

26-ft puoy

FIGURE 3.12 Right: Setting Sequence – the continuous sequence of actions, K1 to K6, employed by a keelman when poling a keel along in shallow water. Left: Setting Angles – the diminishing component of forward gain experienced by a keelman as the water depth increased.

Luckily, this account leaves few queries as to the bodily process of poling a keel and, as with its rowing, Heslop emphasizes the physicality and discipline involved. Similarly, his textual account matches – and reflects – the only explicit contemporary depiction of the process, Brand's bookplate of 1789 (Fig. 3.13) together with that author's description of poling:

> The poles with which the keelmen on certain occasions navigate their vessels are called puys . . . With these puys [poles] our keelmen push on their keels in shallow water in the following manner, when it is inconvenient to use sails or oars.
>
> One on each side going toward the prow puts down his pole to the bottom, in a position inclined towards the head of the keel; at the same time thrusting against it forcibly with his shoulder, and walking down the gangway towards the stern, as the keel moves under him; by this means the keel gains a tolerably quick and even course on the water; having walked the full length of the vessel,

FIGURE 3.13 Two keel crew and the 'peedee' (boy) pole a keel upriver through the shallows off Gateshead shore whilst the skipper plies his swape. The remains of the medieval bridge devastated by the 'Great Flood' of 1771 is in the background (Brand, 1789).

they pluck up the puys, return hastily to the prow, put them down again, and thrust as before.[61]

Both Brand and Heslop speculate, inconclusively, on the origin of the word 'puy' and its dialect variants: pooey; puoy; powey; and poy.[62] But of more practical concern is the fact that neither author elaborates on the specific size(s) or form of the pole and pole-end used, although Heslop's termination in a 'horn shaped fork of iron' suggests a pair of prongs facing downward. Functionally, that would correspond well with analogous forms such as the pitchfork-like iron 'grains' fitted to the bottom of the 'stowers' (poles) used aboard the Humber's – much larger – sailing keels and sloops, and the rather simpler downward facing wooden wedge which enhanced the grip of the Norfolk wherry's 'quant' (pole) on the riverbed (Fig. 3.14, top). [63][64]

More regionally significant, however, is the fact that the term 'poy' survived late into the twentieth century to describe the pole used for propelling and guiding cobles (open fishing boats) in the tidal shallows at the north Northumberland haven of Beadnell. As described by Katrina Porteous (2021), this poy was 'a blacksmith-made implement, a long pole with a shallow crescent shaped metal end'. Furthermore, she observes that: 'the word "puoy" was used as a verb as well as a noun with a pronunciation that was indistinguishable from the verb "to put"', as for example: '"Puoy it ower there" meant put it over there'; whilst '"Puoy her ont' the dry" meant 'push the boat on to the sand'.[65] The correlation of recent dialect usage in Beadnell with Heslop's Tyneside-based definition of 1892 is striking, but there would seem to be no easy explanation for the apparent absence of the term elsewhere along the Northumberland coast.

Contemporary graphic evidence from Tyneside as to the physical form of the keel's puoy is sparse and ambiguous. For example, Taylor's iconic engraving (1858) 'Old Coal Staith – Keels Loading' shows a long pole, which terminates in an inverted pair of upward facing 'horns' on either side of a central spike, projecting over the bow of a keel (Fig. 3.14, bottom). This is much the form of the once common double-headed boathook, whose twin hooks were used for catching hold

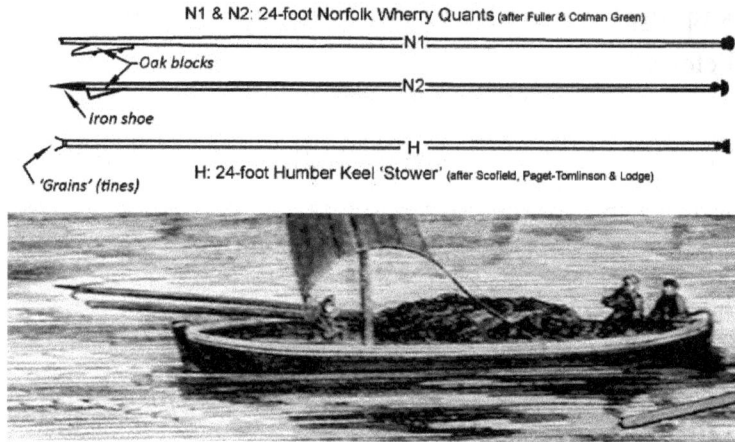

FIGURE 3.14 Top, two Norfolk wherry quants and a Humber Keel's stower (after: Fuller & Colman Green; and, Schofield, Paget-Tomlinson & Lodge); bottom, a coal laden Tyne keel of eighteenth-century pattern departs a staith under sail with the huik (or a puoy) and an oar stowed right forward, projecting well beyond the bow (from Taylor, 1858).

of ropes or protrusions whilst the spike was deployed for fending off. This is an interpretation that certainly fits a later statement that, 'Every keel carried two boat-hooks and two "puoys" – the latter were setting poles about 30 ft. long', though whether the pole depicted alongside the presumed boathook in Taylor's illustration is a puoy, or an oar, must remain uncertain.[66]

Further confusion on the puoy and boathook issue results from the ambiguity of contemporary dialect writings which describe a keel as being poled not with a puoy but by means of a 'huik' (hook), a lack of clarity typified in the sardonically amusing keelman's tale of *The Flay Craw* [Scare-crow]:

But good luck niver hes much last:
The Meedis Hoose they'd just gone past,
When round aboot, te thor dismay,
The wind it crept – then slunk away . . .
'Twas noo pitch dark; an' still thor lay
Two gud lang mile to gan: so they

A' lowered huik wi' little glee,
An' myed the Peé Dee tyek one, tee.
But suen, poor soul! His huik got fast
(Mind, game he was – ay, te the last);
He pulled an' twisted, till the keel
Left huik behint – an' lad as weel![67]

Because the success of a humorous verse story like this relied upon an audience's shared experience, it is informative of everyday practice. Firstly, the story's hearers or readers recognized that if the wind became adverse or fell calm when sailing then, provided the water was sufficiently shallow, poling rather than rowing was the keelman's preferred option. Nevertheless, it was natural that the crew still 'swore, And cursed' when it became inevitable, indicating that poling was considered hard work and they were reluctant to engage in it. But since they were anxious to get home that night, even the keel's boy (the 'Pee Dee') was rudely ordered into poling service, a decision which implies that poling was normally considered the work of the skipper and his two 'bullies' (crewmen) alone. Nevertheless, the crew did not consider the distance to be covered – from 'Meedis Hoose' (the pub on King's Meadow island, above Dunston) to 'Leminton' (Lemington) – at all unusual, although it meant more than 2 miles of upriver poling (Map 2). Neither was it thought strange that an individual might get dragged overboard if his huik became 'fast' (stuck) in the riverbed, although understandably the storyteller gives the event a risible, rather than an all too common, tragic ending.

With only ambiguous textual rather than clear-cut iconographic or artefact evidence to hand, it is impossible to clarify whether the terms 'puoy' and 'huik' were simply interchangeable in the vernacular vocabulary, or whether a keel's boathook had the dual function of poling – though this latter seems less likely. It could even be the case that, on Tyneside at least, the presumed archaic terms puoy and puoying eventually translated themselves into the accepted, received words for a keelman's pole and the action of poling.

By all accounts, the terms puoy and puoying generally appeared in newspaper articles and advertisements and are also found in the texts of lawsuits, official reports, and published inquiries. And, without doubt, they were the terms favoured by antiquarians. Heslop, for instance, cites nothing other than 'puoy' (and its variants) as the word for the keelman's pole, reserving 'hyuk' for objects of hook-shaped form – as in a corn sickle or a 'hyuk-nebbed' [hook-nosed] man – and makes no mention of any marine usage.[68] Nevertheless, the use of huik for a keelman's pole appears in vernacular writings (like *The Flay Craw* above) with which Heslop was familiar. And, intriguingly, it occurs several times in Thomas and George Allan's popular local collection, *Tyneside Songs* (1891), for which Heslop was the dedicatee, whereas puoy is entirely absent from the unpretentious dialect verses published therein.

Perhaps, paradoxically, it was antiquarian interest that saw puoy become the accepted dialect word for a keelman's pole, whilst huik, which long outlasted it in everyday speech on the river, was perceived as no more than general Tyneside slang.[69]

Poling: the practice

Whatever the terms employed, several more pertinent and practical questions remain today: what length of pole was required, in what depth of water could poling be used, whereabouts on the Tyne was poling generally employed, and how long for?

Contemporary opinion on the length of pole varied, with Heslop's 'slender pole of about 18 feet' (note [60]) figuring right at the lower end of the scale. Indeed, elsewhere he actually suggested as much: 'On the Tyne, a very long pooey and a shorter one were used to suit the varying depth of water.'[70] Indeed, 'hooks and puoys' of various lengths were frequently cited as proxy depth gauges during discussions over the nature and extent of the river's shifting channels and shoals. With respect to the depths of water that a keel could reasonably be puoyed in, an expert witness in 1824 remarked that, 'A keel can be puoyed in 5 feet of water, and [if necessary] can be puoyed in 17 or 18 feet; but it is much more difficult and inconvenient in deep water, and in an ebb tide it is a stoppage [obstacle] altogether.'[71] A little over 20 years later, ex-keel skipper Samuel Bell attested that '10 or 11 years ago' (c.1838) it was normal to use a 24-foot puoy in the 11 feet of water on Jarrow Shoal, and his testimony was supported by that of long-time ballast keelman Thomas Marrison of Shields, who described the need for poles even longer than that when – in his early days – Shields Harbour had been deeper than it was 'now' (1849):

> As the water grows shoaler we get less [shorter] puoys. Formerly, keelmen never got a less puoy than 26 feet. Now, as the water grows shoaler, I do not think they are 22 feet long, and plenty of bottom with them. Before this time we could not find bottom at all, even with 26-foot puoys, in setting across from New Quay to the Middle Sand. Now we have 22-foot puoys, and we never lose bottom. We can go right across now [at dead low water] with puoying where we formerly rowed to get over 100 yards.[72]

Oral evidence thus suggests that pole lengths of between 18 and 26 feet were used at various times and in various places and, although a depth of up to 18 feet might occasionally be traversed, the accustomed operating zones lay in depths ranging from just above 3 feet – sufficient to float an unladen keel – to a dozen feet or so (Fig. 3.12, left). Poles of 'around 30 feet' (note [66]) would seem unlikely, or rare. Indeed, practice in heavy working craft elsewhere suggests that pole lengths of around 22 to 25 feet were optimal in respect of manhandling and reach; for example, Humber Keels carried two 'stowers' of 22 and 24 feet respectively, whilst the 'quants' of Norfolk wherries generally lay in the 20- to 24-foot range. These last provide a likely guide for the way in which a Tyne keel's pole was fabricated and formed: '[quants] are approximately twenty-three to twenty-four feet long, and are made from pine [spruce?] poles. They are de-barked, squared up and then rounded to approximately three inches [diameter] at six feet from the bottom end, two and a half inches at the bottom end, and one and three quarter inches at the top end.'[73] That is, for strength and balance the shaft of the Norfolk quant had a double taper with its greatest diameter lying where the maximum stress and bending moment occurred, between the waterline and the riverbed, whilst the upper shaft was reduced to a thickness easy to grasp and handle (Fig. 3.14, top). But, unlike its counterpart the Norfolk quant, there seems to have been no conical wooden 'butt' fitted over a Tyne puoy's upper end to provide bodily protection and grip. On the evidence of contemporary newspaper advertisements, the keel's puoy, like its oar and swape, was made from grown poles of Norway Spruce.

Regarding the places on the Tyne where poling was regularly carried out, various late-eighteenth and early-nineteenth century accounts suggest that it was widely employed wherever the depth and bottom conditions allowed. But it was especially useful in two areas, the 'above bridge' section from Newcastle to Lemington, and the mid-river stretch from Hebburn Quay to Jarrow Slake where the many, subtly shifting, shallows included: Walker Sand; Cockcrow Sand; Hebburn Shoal; Muckhouse Shoal; Killingworth Shoal; Jarrow Spouts Shoal; Hay-hole Shoal; and the Middle Sand (Map 3). But keels were poled equally well in more confined locations like the Mill Dam 'gut' at South Shields – which was accessible to keel traffic until 1816 – or in tributaries like the Ouseburn and, somewhat further back in time, even for 'setting' through the narrow, 27-foot, arches of Newcastle's old medieval Bridge.[74]

Hard physical labour though it was, the keelman's skills in setting also afforded him an opportunity to indulge his liking for leisure-time display and competition, engaging in events which might provide the chance of a cash prize and, no doubt, potential betting gains on the side. As intimated by Heslop, 'the bullies not infrequently matched themselves against other crews at aquatic festivals', and a single example from the Howdon Regatta of June 1857 will suffice:

A PUTTING MATCH for £2 10s, in keels used for the purpose of conveying coals; open to all; three men and a boy in each keel; entrance 2s; first keel £2, second keel 10s . . .

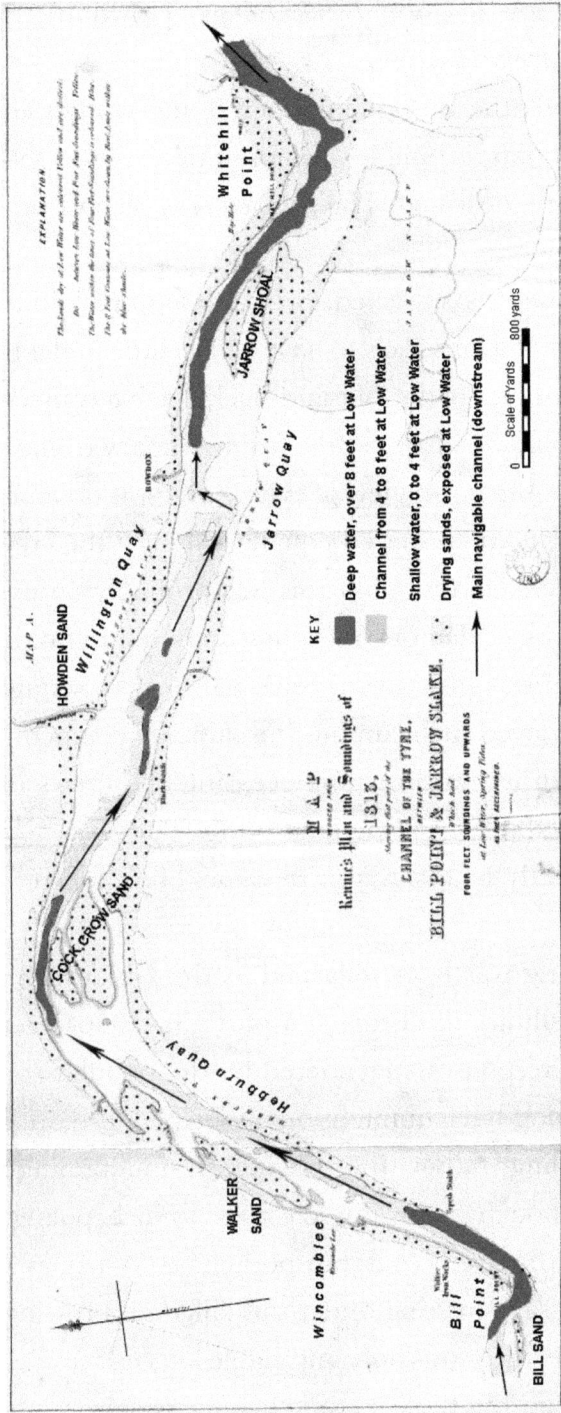

MAP 3   The tortuous section of the Tyne navigation between Bill Point's hazardous channel and Whitehill Point (near Shields) that had to be traversed by keelmen during the first half of the nineteenth century. A government report of 1846 highlighted the fact that 'upward of 80 acres of sandbank dry at low water . . . sharp angles increase the difficulty of navigation . . . and the width of the river remains extremely irregular'.

There were three entries, the *Blink Bonny* (Howdon), the *Champion* (Willington); and the *Jarrow* (Jarrow).

The *Blink Bonny* took the lead, maintained it and won easily. *Jarrow* and *Champion* got in close quarters, and it was not until a regular set-to with their "poweys" that they were separated. The *Jarrow* came second.[75]

Regrettably, the sporting paper concerned, *Bell's London Life*, did not report the actual race distance, though it seems likely to have been a little under three-quarters of a mile, that is, half the distance of the 'out-and-back' rowing course. For practical reasons, however, it took place in an area 'free from ordinary traffic up and down the river, and a full and unobstructed view of every contest is obtained'. The prize money may have been slight when shared equally amongst the crew – although one wonders if the boy received any – but this was probably outweighed by the opportunity for competitors to demonstrate their masculinity and muscularity, gain local acclaim and, in this instance, receive national reportage. Whatever, the riverside communities loved such rumbustious aquatic competitions amongst well-known local personalities, and on this occasion the crews of *Jarrow* and *Champion* obviously enjoyed a bout of puoy jousting! The *South Shields Gazette*'s subsequent report can clearly be taken at face value: 'This race created a great deal of amusement'.[76]

To summarize, if poling was later regarded as the Cinderella amongst the various methods of propelling a keel this can partly (perhaps even largely) be attributed to the cultural responses engendered by the popular song, the 'Keel Row', the reactions to which have unintentionally helped obscure the very real contribution made by poling, rather than rowing, in maintaining the passage-making abilities of keels. Though largely unrecognized as such, poling was a crucial factor in helping maintain the river's coal transport chain. When, as *The Flay Craw* so evocatively records, passage-making under sail failed and rowing would have been laboriously ineffective, there was only one viable alternative . . . Arguably, no other waterway in Britain saw this basic method of moving a watercraft prosecuted more routinely or more frequently over such a length of historic time, and to the same degree of national benefit as did the 'Coaly Tyne'.

Hauling

Least well recorded, and probably least practised, of all the methods of moving a keel on the Tyne was 'tracking', that is, man-hauling a keel towards its destination by means of a rope taken ashore. The author knows of only one vague graphic depiction, whilst the few textual references that occur are largely uninformative and, since it required no specialized equipment, it does not appear to have generated any dedicated dialect words or terminology (Fig. 3.15). The opposite in fact is the case, for keelmen seem to have used the word 'tracking' quite loosely for any kind of passage making as well as for the specific act of man-hauling.

Although Britain's burgeoning inland waterways and improved river navigations elsewhere were generally well provided with purpose-made towpaths for equine or manual hauling, that does not appear to have been the case on the Tyne – a direct consequence of complex historical, riparian, industrial, and topographical factors. In 1795, for example, the deficiency was highlighted by Ralph Dodd who, for sound practical reasons and to promote his own canalization scheme (between Newcastle and Carlisle), pointed out that even in the more rural section of the river above Newcastle Bridge:

> The want of a towing path is evidently to be seen . . . I have observed, from a little fresh [floodwater] descending with the stream, or from a smart westerly breeze of wind, that the keels with double crews on the shore, are obliged to be tracked against the wind or stream; whereas one single horse would perform their labour with one-fourth the expense to the proprietor.[77]

Not only that, but he further deplored the absence of such provisions along the river navigation between Newcastle and the sea, pointing out the advantages that a continuous towpath would provide in bringing up seagoing vessels and keels. And once more he emphasized that 'when there is any fresh in the river, not even the most laborious oar of the keelman can bring them [up] against the down-pouring current of the stream.' Admittedly, a permanent towpath would not be used by 'craft passing up or down, with the wind or tide in their favour', but it would confer important advantages on the river's numerous 'market or passage boats' by helping them to run to schedule. And such a 'path-way', he said, could be raised a little above flood level at the river margin where it would also serve as a low flood barrier, and might advantageously be constructed of the coal trade's abundant incoming 'ballast' (a revenue making requisite of Newcastle Corporation). More marginally, and as a pragmatic sentiment that would appeal to late-eighteenth century merchants and gentry, he further eulogized that the towpaths 'may in no small degree contribute to health and pleasure, forming a firm dry walk by the sides of streams, and presenting to the eye the varied scenery of land and water'. Or was Dodd simply environmentally ahead of his time?

Disingenuously, however, he minimized his proposed towpaths' many problems, including the presence of shoals and a lack of deep water along many parts of the shoreline, deficiencies which, in practice, could not simply be solved by his recommendation of 'a sufficient length of track-rope . . . with a watchful helm and proper steerage'. In similar fashion he skimmed over the solutions to 'another difficulty that may present itself, namely, the interference of the coal staiths' which supported the spouts (coal chutes) that, even in his time, were proliferating on some stretches of the river.[78] Like most of this mercurial engineer's creative plans, the proposed canalization scheme was never realized but, luckily, his works provide the best impression of the conditions for tracking keels on the Tyne that survive. For example, it is Dodd alone who indicates that hauling sometimes required co-operation between two Tyne keel crews to 'double-man' a towline. But, unlike the position on the Wear, there are no references to teams of human trackers (including women and children) being employed to haul 'strings' of several keels.

FIGURE 3.15 A rare, if indistinct, image of a keel being hauled strenuously upstream by three crewmen as loaded keels sail lazily past downriver. A beer house, inset, lies temptingly close nearby . . . (details from a print by Collard & Ross, 1841).

By the mid-1820s the tracking situation had deteriorated even further, for counsel and witness testimony in the Keelmen's celebrated lawsuit (1828) against the owners of Wallsend Staith indicate that although keels had formerly been able to 'track down along shore . . . by ropes, dragged by horses or men', it was now impossible to do so past the 'gears' (coal staith) in contention.[79] And elsewhere, no less than ten similar 'gears' had been erected in just four years. As a method of moving a keel, tracking was clearly becoming less and less viable and may effectively have disappeared by the mid-century. Unlike poling, there is no reference to it as an issue in the comprehensive *Admiralty Inquiry* of 1849, and all sources concur in describing the substantial increase in barriers to free passage along the riverside occasioned by: the construction of new coal drops; a proliferation of riverside port industries; the spread of urban dwellings; a significant expansion of ballast heaps and ballast quays; the revetment and enclosure of river frontages; Newcastle's systematic insertion of groynes etc.; the list goes on. Although, perhaps to suit his own argument, Dodd had inferred (1795) that horses were not employed for keel haulage on the Tyne the witness statement cited above (1828) clearly contradicts that opinion, but unfortunately elaborates no further. Indeed, considering the number of horses employed on the many wagonways that delivered coal to the riverside, it would have been surprising if a horse was not occasionally harnessed up to a keel.

Overall, tracking soon became a nostalgic memory, as retailed in McKay's reminiscence of 1889: 'At the King's Meadows [island] a line was sometimes passed ashore with loops on the end. The keelmen then went ashore and hauled the keel down, the "Pee Dee" being left on board to steer and keep the keel off the shore'.[80] Whether the 'loops on the [line's] end' were permanent or just temporarily thrown in – a double bowline would have sufficed – is an open question, and there are no reports for the Tyne that suggest the use of the purpose-made human harnesses that were donned by haulers, both male and female, on inland navigations elsewhere.[81] Technically, there is little more to explain regarding tracking technique, although McKay's description above illustrates one important requirement, the ability to prevent the keel either veering outward into mid-channel or running into the bank. Steering by means of the rudder or swape was of limited use, if applied too heavily such steerage would simply act as a brake, much to the detriment – and expletive-making annoyance – of the haulers. Efficient tracking thus demanded that the towline ran from the correct balance point on the longitudinal axis of the vessel (its centre of lateral resistance) which was no doubt found by trial and error, and maybe differed according to a keel's draught and windage at any point in time. But retrospective determination of such niceties is now beyond reach. Experience on waterways elsewhere also teaches the advantage of carrying the inboard end of a towline high up, on a short temporary mast or spar, thus helping to avoid surface obstructions.[82]

This was a technique that was either unknown to, or not used by, the family of 'a young man of the name of Snowden' who, in September 1796, tragically drowned when: 'He was on board a keel, which his father and uncle were hauling up the River, against the wind; the rope got entangled in some bushes, and in slackening it too suddenly, he fell overboard and perished in the presence of his relations, who could afford him no assistance'.[83] Even the apparently simple business of tracking had its dangers.

NOTES

1 Fewster, *The Keelmen*, 120, n.[4].

2 Heslop, 'Keels and Keelmen', 51; Heslop generalizes that 'in latter days' 25 shillings (£1.25) was paid for a 'lang [long] tide' occupying15-17 hours, and around 16 shillings (£0.80) for a 'bye [short] tide, and that 'four to six lang and short tides were the ordinary work of a Keel in busy times'. The example shown in Figure 3.1 totals £1-1s-10d (£1.09) for a 'lang tide' from the colliery to Shields, comprising: ship dues, 13s 4d; owner's wages, 5s 2d; bread, 2s 6d; and beer, 10d.

3 PP. Tidal Harbours Commission. Second Report of the Commissioners, 1846, 330-31, App. B, No.187; copy of John Rennie's report for Newcastle Corporation, 1816.

4 Evidence of Henry Young in the case of: the *King v. Russell and Others*, 1824 (as reported in the *Durham Chronicle* 14 August 1824); a similar disparity between flood and ebb was also found at the coal trade's main coasting destination, 'the London River' – Thames.

5 Rennison, thesis, 189-199.

6 *Admiralty inquiry 1849*, witnesses including: Samuel Bell; Robert Donkin; Merton Weldon; William Boyle; William Nelson; and John Minto.

7 John Hutchinson, sea pilot, witness before 'The Select Committee to whom the Tyne Conservancy Bill is Referred, 1849', as reported in the *Newcastle Journal*, 19 May 1849.

8 Washington, *Report of the Admiralty Inspectors*.

9 This speed was ascertained practically by recording the time lag between high water at successive points from Shields Harbour to the head of navigation, Hedwin Streams.

10 Washington, *Report of the Admiralty Inspectors*, 13.

11 *Admiralty Inquiry 1849*, 12-13.

12 *Admiralty Inquiry 1849*, 13-14.

13 *Admiralty Inquiry 1849*, 17.

14 McKay, 'Keels and Keelmen'; although writing in 1889, John McKay recounted practices and personalities of the 1840s.

15 McKay may also have been the source for Heslop's account that, when loading at Stella, it was usual 'to work the Keel round to Lemington Point, there to lie in readiness so as to make a good start upon the next returning tide . . . With the ebb of the tide the actual voyage began' (Heslop, 'Keels and Keelmen', 49).

16 Variously titled and notated, the song became a 'local anthem' in the nineteenth century before spreading farther afield and finally achieving recognition as a concert item and

school songbook piece: http://www.farnearchive.com; https://en.wikipedia.org/wiki/The_Keel_Row; https://tunearch.org/wiki/Annotation:Keel_Row_(The) (accessed 11/12/2020).

17 Stukeley, *Itinerary*, vol. 2 (2nd edition, 1776), 68.

18 Stukeley, *Itinerary*, vol. 1, (2nd edition, 1776), 130.

19 Pennant T, *A Tour in Scotland and Voyage*, 311-12.

20 Pennant T, *A Tour in Scotland 1769*, 29; in this account Pennant uses the adjective 'round' rather than 'oval' to indicate the keel's form and overestimates the carrying capacity at 'twenty five tuns'.

21 Brand, *The History and Antiquities*, 261.

22 Painting *Weel may the Keel Row* by William Hedley c.1905; sold by Anderson & Garland (Newcastle), 18/06/2019.

23 Fewster, *The Keelmen*, 2.

24 Heslop: 'Keels and Keelmen', 7-8; Heslop, 'Notes on Keels', 5-6.

25 Bell, *Keelmen*.

26 Carmichael J W, *The Mayor's Barge on the Tyne*, c.1826-30, TWCMS: B6661; in the foreground a ship is receiving a new bowsprit from a keel employed as a lighter. One of this keel's oars is slightly greater in length than its deck and the other a little shorter.

27 Palmer, *The Tyne*, 156; this again suggests an oar length close to the deck length.

28 *The Tyne Bridge - The Great Frost*, 1784, TWCMS: H18496 (Laing Art Gallery)

29 Steel, *The Art of Making Masts etc*, 'Oar Making' appendix and tables.

30 *Newcastle Courant* 25 June 1763; 23 August 1794.

31 It seems unlikely that keel owners would have paid as much for an oar as the £1-19s cited by Steel for a 36-foot Admiralty pattern sweep (endnote 29). A complete 'new' working keel of the early eighteenth century was valued at around £40 (Wright, Thesis, 107-109).

32 *Newcastle Courant* 24 November 1787; 18 April 1789.

33 Local lifeboatmen also preferred fir oars over the (heavier and more pliable) 'rove ash oars' in common use.

34 McKee, *Working Boats*, 139.

35 The visually misleading position of the pivot point may well have arisen from these illustrators' desire to simplify and dramatize the scene, at the expense – or ignorance of – the rules of perspective.

36 Steel, *Elements and Practice*, 35, 51, 183, Pl. XXXI; describes: (a) the practice in the famed Tyne lifeboats, introduced in 1789, of rowing with 'an oar slung over an iron

thole, with a grommet (as provided)'; (b) defines [thole] pins as 'pins of iron or wood, fixed along the gunwales of some boats . . . whose oars are confined by grommets'; and (c), describes 'Grommets for Boats. Wreaths of rope which confine the oars to the pins in the gunwale'.

37 Osler A, *Mr Greathead's Lifeboats* (Newcastle 1990), 77; the 'large and elegant print of the Life-Boat invented by Mr Greathead' (engraved by Elmes after Atkinson, 1802) depicts, if somewhat imperfectly, grommet retained oars worked on single iron tholes.

38 Brand, *The History and Antiquities*, 48ff.

39 Bell, 'Keelmen'; also, John Scott's oil painting, *Tyne Wherry at the Mill Dam*, 1850, TWCMS G4024.

40 Palmer, *The Tyne*, 260.

41 TWCMS H5441; TWCMS B9779; and TWCMS B9780.

42 Heslop's two manuscript texts vary slightly and the quotations given comprise elements of both.

43 Information on the swept angle of working boats is sparse but, for example, includes archeological reconstructions of: the Gokstad Faering, 54° (McKee, 1974); and an Athenian Trireme, 46° (Rankov et al., 2012). These suggest swept angles that are somewhat larger than the keel's, though still modest by modern standards, a modern sweep-oared racing shell achieves around 90° (Kleshnev, 2006).

44 McKee, *The Sea Trials*, 32.

45 Heslop, 'Notes on Keels', 6.

46 Ibid.

47 Harris, *Under Oars*, 12, 16; in his memoirs, master Thames lighterman Harry Harris, records his actions as a youngster when lining up to shoot a bridge as rapidly 'throwing the [28-foot] oar into position against the stern post . . . In this position the barge is steered and helped ahead and slightly sideways if desired', remarking later that apprentices were commonly sent 'aft to steer and, at the same time, by laying the oar well round the stern, help the headway'.

48 Assuming, in both cases, a blade length of some 10 feet (blades were typically one-third of a sweep's length overall) and double-handed operation of the handle at around chest level.

49 Although its authenticity is not proven, a model oar (as figured by Viall, 1942) that accompanies the SANT model scales at 28 feet, giving just under 9 feet inboard and a gearing of 1:3.2.

50 A calculation based on this illustration suggests a swape of some 32 feet may have been required.

51 Fewster, *The Keelmen*, 118-19; in the late eighteenth century some owners paid skippers a small cash allowance known as 'steerage money' (4d per tide) for 'finding geer' for their keels, but this payment became the subject of grievance and dispute.

52 Fewster, *The Keelmen*, 183.

53 McKay, 'Keels and Keelmen'.

54 Whitehead, *The Sporting Tyne*, 5-6.

55 Heslop, *Northumberland Words*, 547; 'BOOL', an iron plate attached to the oars of keels and wherries. The *bool* has a round eye in its centre, and through this the thole pin passes.'

56 Griffiths, *Fishing and Folk*, 87; notes the same term for comparable oar fittings on cobles employed in the region's sail fishery.

57 Anon., *Smith's Dock Journal*, 66.

58 Harris, *Under Oars*, 20.

59 Allan's *Tyneside Songs*, 45-46.

60 Heslop, 'Keels and Keelmen', 10-12; Heslop's manuscript footnote actually draws its quotation: "He'll <u>Set</u> or row se [sic] tightly", from an extended version titled *The New Keel Row* (originally published by Bell in 1812) and popularized in Allan's *Tyneside Songs*, 1891, 45-46.

61 Brand, *The History and Antiquities*, 261.

62 Both Brand and Heslop speculate, indecisively, on the origin of the word 'puy'. The former author suggests: 'Poy, appoyo, Spanish'; and 'Appuy, of appuyer, to support, is a pole used by rope dancers to poise themselves with.' And the latter writer cites *Cotgrave's Dictionary*, 1632: 'Appuy, a stay, buttresse, prop, rest, or thing to leane on; also as Appuye, Appuyer. To stay, support, sustaine, underprop, hold, or beare up'.

In his book *Northumbrian Words* (1892) Heslop also notes the use elsewhere of a 'bang' (pole) for 'guiding or propelling a boat', and a 'kent' for the same purpose; although the present author suspects these last were principally words of the border rivers.

63 Schofield, *Humber Keels*, 23, 270, 276-77.

64 Colman Green, *The Norfolk Wherry*, 5, 43.

65 Katrina Porteous, personal comm., 26-27 February 2021; I am extremely grateful to Katrina for bringing this unexpected survival of 'poy' to my attention, and her valuable

insights into the associated dialect usage; the term is also cited in an extensive lexicon she provided for Bill Griffith's *Fishing and Folk*, 217-246.

66 Anon., *Smith's Dock Journal*, 66.

67 Allan, *Tyneside Songs*, 'The Flay Craw; or, Pee Dee's Mishap' (Taylor ms., 1872), 509-11.

68 Heslop, *Northumberland Words*, 397, 547.

69 The term remained current in river parlance until at least the late twentieth century, most notably in the form of the Tyne foyboatman's (mooring operative's) heavy, long-shafted boarding 'hook' which was skilfully deployed when making fast to moving ships in order to tow back alongside.

70 Heslop, *Northumberland Words*, 547.

71 *Durham Chronicle* 14 August 1824; evidence of sea pilot Henry Young in the case of: The King v. Russell and others.

72 *Admiralty inquiry 1849*, 10, 13, 84.

73 Fuller M, *Norfolk Wherry*, 42.

74 *Newcastle Courant*, 10 November 1764; accident report.

75 *Supplement to Bell's Life in London*, 7 June 1857; the author is grateful to Ian Whitehead for drawing this informative report to his attention.

76 *Shields Daily Gazette*, 3 June 1857.

77 Dodd, *Report on the First Part*, 7; Dodd excoriated the nearby Wearside practice of using teams of poor women 'yoked like quadrupeds' to haul keels upriver, and pointedly praised the substitution of horsepower for manpower on the upper Thames.

78 Dodd, *Report on the First Part*, 7, 21, 27.

79 *Newcastle Courant*, 23 August 1828; report of *The King v. Russell & Others*.

80 McKay, 'Keels and Keelmen'; on the nearby River Wear the several 'hailers' simply put a long rope over their shoulders and grasped it with their hands.

81 For example, leather straps 'braced around their bodies' were used by the teams of full time 'bow haulers' employed on the upper Severn until the mid-century (Trinder, *Barges and Bargemen*, 29-30, 67-68).

82 McKee, *Working Boats*, 131-33.

83 *Newcastle Courant*, 17 September 1796.

FOUR

SAIL AND STEAM

IN THE INTRODUCTION TO HIS wide-ranging work on British sailing barges Michael Stammers remarked that, 'The most common sail was the single square sail. Often this sail was something that was set only when the wind was fair, and was often used in combination with towing [by horse- or man-power] . . . or with large oars known as sweeps'.[1] This observation reinforces Eric McKee's earlier suggestion that although the use of square sails in cargo-carrying barges might originally be 'no more than an improvisation to take advantage of a following wind', it was always an improvisation that might become established practice, especially if the prevailing wind set along the line of a waterway's course. Furthermore, McKee noted that if greater sail-power or windward performance became desirable – perhaps through increased competition – the adoption of fore-and-aft rig with corresponding hull improvements often resulted.[2]

Beyond that point lay not evolution but technological revolution, a revolution in which the latent chemical energy of a fossil fuel (coal) replaced that supplied by wind and muscle power. Although a variety of rivercraft demonstrated steam power's practical application afloat during the first quarter of the nineteenth century, steam's penetration of Britain's bulk-carrying inland water trades proved tardy and erratic. Over time, however, the shift from sail to steam (or motor) became irreversible.

The Tyne was no exception to these changes but, as in much else, keel users followed their own distinct trajectory.

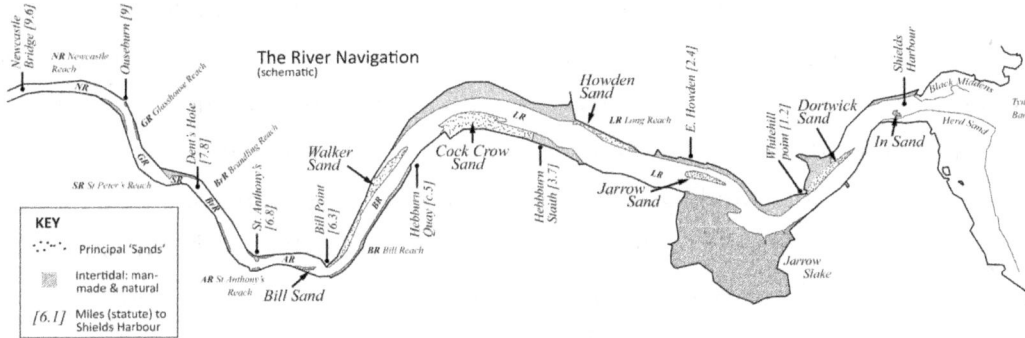

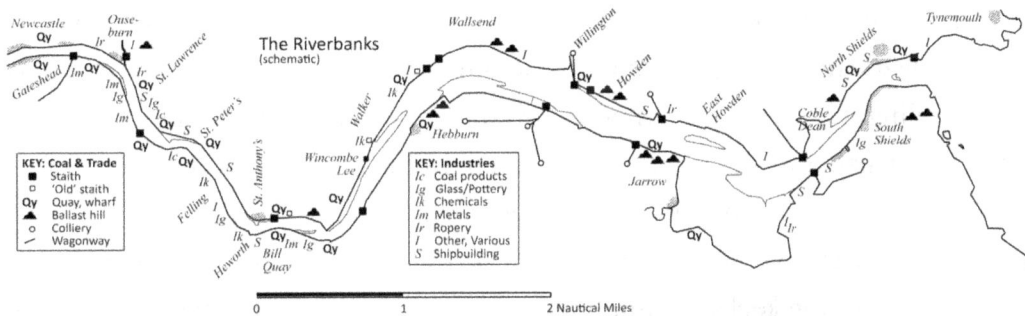

MAP 4 Top, the major features of the Tyne navigation between Newcastle and the sea as known by early-nineteenth century keelmen; bottom, the principal riverside industries, quays, staiths and shore facilities serviced by coal keels and other rivercraft.

SAIL

Squaresail Rig

For local artists and illustrators of the late eighteenth and early nineteenth century the square sail of the keel was a signifier of the River Tyne and its commerce, and their depictions range from the minutely engraved monochrome specks in the background of Thomas Bewick's magnificent 'Oak Tree' vignette to John Wilson Carmichael's black-sailed keel drifting languidly past the colorful panorama of Newcastle Quay.[34] For the historian of watercraft, however, these portrayals of the keel's squaresail fall short. True, many of them confirm the uniformity of the keel's singularly squat rig whose plain rectilinear sail was spread on a yard that was invariably hoist to the top of a stumpy mast with a curiously fashioned cap. Beyond that, barely a handful of representations contain useful technical detail.

Any greater understanding of this rig relies upon little more than three visual sources: the SANT model; a drawing (c.1830) by John Bell of Newcastle; and an anonymous, naïve pencil sketch found amongst some otherwise professional sketches of watercraft made by marine artist J W Carmichael that are now in the collections of the Laing Art Gallery.[5] Unfortunately, the first source (the SANT model) is of limited value since the present arrangement of its standing and running rigging is clearly not as original, but the outcome of long forgotten damage or lack of understanding (Fig. 4.1). Nevertheless, this model offers the only reliable evidence for the exact size and shape of a keel's squaresail together with the dimensions, form, and housing of its uniquely fashioned mast.

Although attractive and well observed, Bell's contemporaneous drawing lacks working detail of the keel's sail and rig (see Fig. 2.12). But that deficiency is partly offset by the third source, the anonymous, childlike, bird's-eye view sketch that shows a minuscule crew of 'matchstick men' handling a thoughtfully drafted and annotated squaresail rig above a crudely outlined hull (Fig. 4.4). This naïve but informative piece seems to have been made – likely by a keelman – to satisfy Carmichael's need for accurate preparatory information.

Though the single squaresail was not uncommon on river barges and lighters elsewhere, even the limited evidence available shows that the rig of the Tyne keel displayed singular features (Fig. 4.2) The two side stays that supported the mast were attached to the mast below the point to which the yard was hoist, as distinct from the common practice elsewhere of attaching stays to the masthead above. Consequently, the keel could carry no forestay to complete the normal triangle of

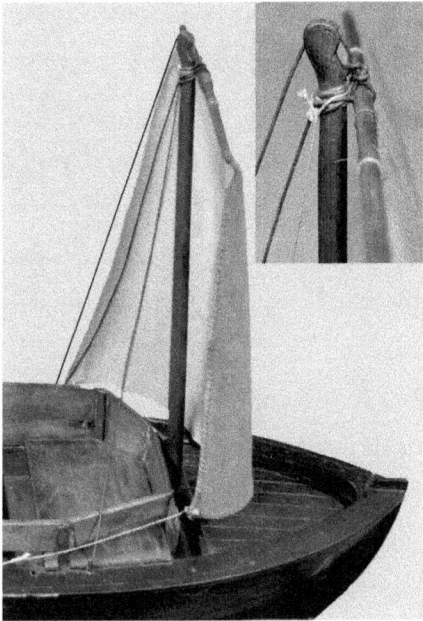

FIGURE 4.1 Though the fabric of the SANT model's squaresail is well preserved, the original rigging has suffered from damage, loss, and casual replacement over time. At least three generations of cordage can be traced in the masthead rigging alone (inset).

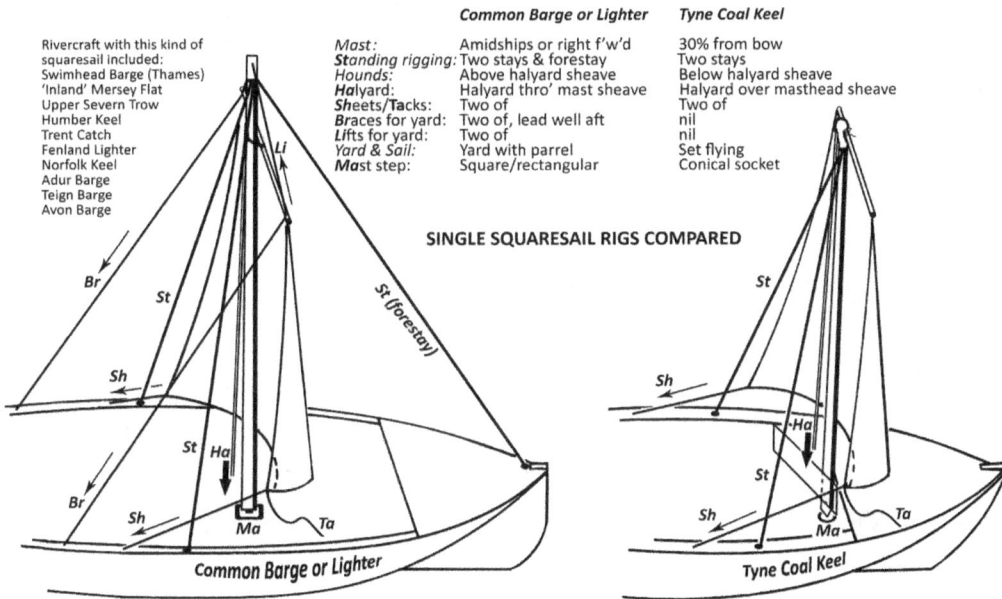

	Common Barge or Lighter	Tyne Coal Keel
Mast:	Amidships or right f'w'd	30% from bow
Standing rigging:	Two stays & forestay	Two stays
Hounds:	Above halyard sheave	Below halyard sheave
Halyard:	Halyard thro' mast sheave	Halyard over masthead sheave
Sheets/Tacks:	Two of	Two of
Braces for yard:	Two of, lead well aft	nil
Lifts for yard:	Two of	nil
Yard & Sail:	Yard with parrel	Set flying
Mast step:	Square/rectangular	Conical socket

Rivercraft with this kind of squaresail included:
Swimhead Barge (Thames)
'Inland' Mersey Flat
Upper Severn Trow
Humber Keel
Trent Catch
Fenland Lighter
Norfolk Keel
Adur Barge
Teign Barge
Avon Barge

SINGLE SQUARESAIL RIGS COMPARED

FIGURE 4.2 Though superficially similar in appearance, the Tyne keel's single squaresail rig (right) displayed significant differences from the comparable rigs generally employed by British barges and lighters elsewhere (left).

standing rigging support. Similarly, the keel employed no lifts or braces to support and swing its squaresail yard, for the lines controlling the sail were reduced to a bare minimum of sheets and tacks alone.

The run of the keel's halyard to the yard also followed an unusual path, carried *via* a dumb sheave over a purpose-fashioned mast cap rather, than as was conventional, through a sheaved aperture cut through the upper mast. No parrel was used to constrain the keel's yard to the mast, but when fully hoist it lay secure in a concavity cut in the mast cap's forward face (Figs. 4.1 and 4.3). Though of commonplace taper and diameter, the 25-foot-long mast possessed two notable features. Firstly, the foot and the receiving step were cut to a conical (not rectangular) form and would appear to have allowed the whole mast to be rotated if required. Secondly, as numerous contemporary depictions show, the top 18 inches or so of the mast (i.e. the masthead) possessed a curious, asymmetrical, query-mark-shaped profile. Termed the 'heughn', this oddly fashioned masthead appears to have been a simple, cheap, and ingenious solution to the problem of finding the shortest (and effectively lightest) mast that might accommodate the amount of sail required.[6] Essentially, the upper face provided an open dumb sheave of large diameter for the passage of the halyard, whilst the concavity cut into its forward face provided a snug rest for the yard when at full hoist. These features were cleverly aligned. The centre of the dumb sheave lay around 1 foot above the stays and was aligned with the after face of the mast, the overhang thus created carrying the fall of the halyard clear of the mast aft. Correspondingly, the geometric centre of the hollow which received the yard was aligned with the mast's forward face, thus locating the yard securely within the body of the mast itself – not outside it (Fig. 4.3).

The late-Victorian Newcastle historian R J Charleton commented retrospectively on this masthead arrangement: ' There was no pulley then on the top of the mast by means of which to hoist the sail; but the rope ran through a notch which was kept well greased, and a keelman of the old school would have scorned the idea of a block or a pulley, as being an innovation and a piece of laziness'.[7] What Charleton

SQUARESAIL KEEL: Spar and Sailplan

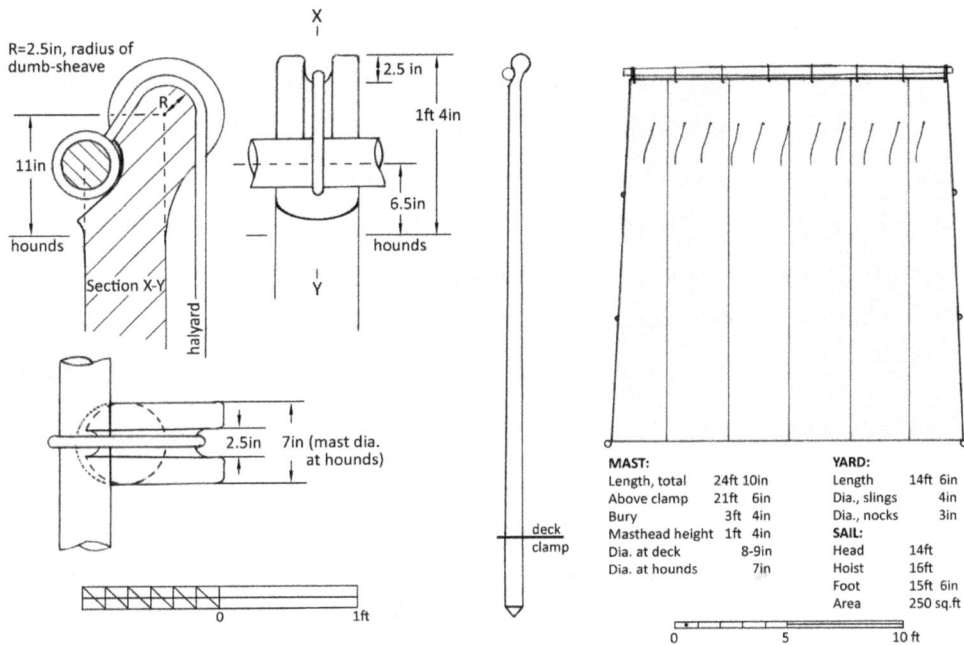

FIGURE 4.3 Dimensions of the sail and spars of a squaresail-rigged Tyne coal keel together with details of its unique masthead sheave, the 'heughn' (derived from the SANT model and contemporary illustrations).

did not mention was that, according to the creator of the keelman's sketch (Fig. 4.4), this 'rope' – technically a halyard tye – was operated with a simple purchase at its lower end that provided a useful 2:1 mechanical advantage in raising a sail and yard whose combined weight will have been considerable. Again, this purchase may originally have been fitted with a perforated wooden 'bullseye' or 'heart' rather than a conventional block containing a rotating pulley (sheave), although the keelman's drawing does seem to indicate a pulley. Correspondingly, the sketch suggests that the hauling and standing parts of this purchase led not, as would be conventional, to a cleat on the mast, but to-and-from a fixture in the spencer compartment. This piece of graphic evidence seemingly explains the function of the downward-facing iron nail driven into the forward face of the SANT model's spencer just below the fore beam – it represents a fixed belaying pin.

Furthermore, the sketch depicts the hoisting process, with one 'bully' hauling down the fall of the purchase from the security of the spencer whilst his companion swigs it taut from the port walkway above. And this same hoisting technique is suggested by the disposition of crew in a keel making sail in Robert Havell's engraving (after T M Richardson) of Newcastle *From The Rope Walk, Gateshead*, 1819 (Fig 4.4, inset). From the set of the sail in the keelman's sketch the vessel he depicts is sailing on a starboard reach, and the leeward (i.e. port) shroud has been deliberately shifted to the gunwale well forward of the mast to act, in effect, as a forestay. Unfortunately, the sketch-maker left the leads of the bowlines incomplete.

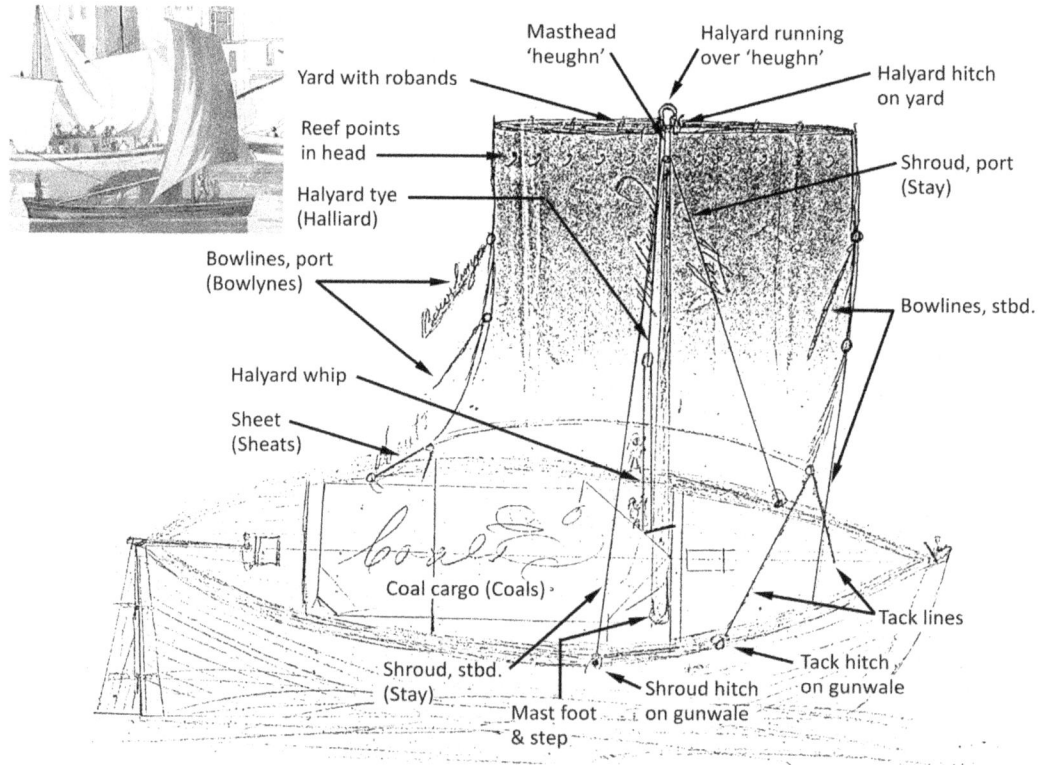

FIGURE 4.4 A worn, undated, naif sketch – probably by a keelman – affords significant evidence about the standing and running rigging of a squaresail-rigged Tyne keel (redrawn and annotated by author from the original). Inset: two crew hauling home a keel's halyard (engraving by R Havell, 1819).

But, though now faded, the lower windward bowline appears to have led down to the gunwale at the fore-bow, and it looks as if all four bowlines may have been employed on this point of sailing – stiffening both leeches.

As evidenced by the SANT model, the slightly trapezoidal sail appears to have been proportioned to the keel's hull size (Fig. 4.3). The foot (bottom) and hoist (depth) alike approximated the keel's maximum beam but were gored, i.e. tapered, some 9 inches on each leech (side) to narrow to around 14 feet at the head, which was secured to the yard with six or seven separate robands (ties) together with earings (corner ties).[8] Some original ties of thin, perhaps hempen, line that represent the robands and both earings survive on the SANT model and they are well shown on the keelman's sketch too, though the latter portrays a yard with a more distinct taper than its three-dimensional counterpart. Regrettably, the model's plain fabric sail gives no clue as to a full-size sail's construction. But naïve as it is, the keelman's sketch fortunately shows more, clearly delineating a sail that comprises:

- six cloths cut vertically
- a row of reef points situated close (around one-sixth of the hoist) below the head
- cringles at the clews (bottom corners) for sheets and tacks
- and two – roughly equidistant – cringles for 'Bowlynes' (bowlines) along each leech.

It may reasonably be assumed that this sail's production followed standard sail-making practice of the period including hemp roping all round, flat seaming and the turning in of rope cringles, and was perhaps fashioned from flax canvas equivalent in weight (i.e. thickness) to Royal Navy No.7 or 8, although employing one of the broader, cheaper (30 to 36-inch) merchant service widths.[9] Finally, the much remarked upon black-sailed appearance of the working keel clearly resulted from a combination of one of the commonly applied treatments used for sail preservation in vernacular craft together with the coatings of coal dust that inevitably accreted over time.[10]

Judging from local newspaper advertisements, keel sails were made and retailed largely, and understandably, by suppliers close to Newcastle Quayside. For example, early in 1753 Matthew Scafe, a general merchant selling high quality foodstuffs, dry goods, fish, spirits, and even 'Battle Gunpowder', included 'Flax; Lint; and Harn for Keel Sails or Sacks' in his list of goods 'Just Arrived' for sale.[11] Correspondingly, in 1777, mention of the same cloth appears in a felony notice regarding George Hay, a 'Weaver, at Wallknolls [sic]', who reported the theft of various trade goods including, at the head of the tally: 'a web of Harn or Keel Sail Cloth, a Web of Sack Cloth . . . four Hanks of boiled Lint Yarn for sail cloth', together with 'one Keel's Sail Gear, one Sacking Gear'.[12] Significantly, 'Harn', which was defined by Heslop (1893–94) as 'a coarse hempen cloth', is associated in both these accounts with sack making and was obviously an inferior material for making sails, whilst George Hay's account emphasizes the distinction between hempen cloth, meant only for keel sails, and the superior flax (Lint) yarn intended for weaving ship-quality 'Sail Cloth'. Whether this distinction remained throughout the era of the squaresail is uncertain but advertised inventories of products and bankruptcy reports continue to associate the making of keel sails with the production of tarpaulins and sacking, though all fell within the general remit of sail making. In 1782 for instance, the forced sale of Paxton and Hodgson's 'Sail Cloth Manufactory' at Wall Knolls, included: 100 Bolts of Canvass, from No. 1 to No. 8; Tarpaulins; Keel Sails; Harns; Sackings; and Port Sails.[13] And over 20 years later, in October 1806, the entrepreneurial Richardson and Co. (of Ouseburn) took over from Thomas Kidd of Wall Knoll, informing the public of their intention to 'carry on the Manufacturing of SAIL CLOTH, KEEL SAILS, and SACKING'.[14] Indeed, the Wall Knoll site appears to have been associated with the making of such sails right to the end of the squaresail era, for in April 1830 the forced disposal of Robert Belt's assets at the Wall Knoll Canvas Manufactory listed '17 pieces Keel Sails; 43 tarpaulins' and, in 1835, his eventual successor, John Reed, promised the ongoing manufacture of 'all Kinds of Tarpaulins, Port Sails, Keel Sails, Parcelling, Harns, Sacking . . . etc.'[15] [16]

Occasionally keel sails were sold by auction, a fact which reinforces the idea that they were a generic, rather than a vessel specific, product.[17] But, if regarded as a commonplace article of rather low quality, keel sails had a recognized value amongst the keel-using fraternity, and thefts were not unknown. A particularly malicious incident was reported in 1781 when 'Two Breadths (cloths) of a new sail of the Keel No. 46 . . . then lying at anchor off the Sandgate were feloniously cut out and taken away', most likely the action of an individual needing to repair his own sail. Presumably, the substantial 5 guineas reward that was offered marked not only this new sail's cash value but a policy of deterrence toward intra-community theft.[18] More cheekily, in October 1807 the sail of Newcastle Corporation's own keel, lying at the Quayside, was 'feloniously stolen and carried away', a slender reward of 1 guinea being offered for the culprit's apprehension – perhaps there was little expectation of an informer![19] Such miscreants were occasionally apprehended, however, including the Wallsend Colliery miner Henry Martin, who imprudently stole the sail of a keel owned by one of the Tyne's largest coal magnates (and Tory MP), John Brandling Esq.[20]

One final puzzle remains in discussing the keel's rig: the method by which the mast was raised and lowered. This was a relatively frequent occurrence owing to the constant need to change between sailing and either poling or rowing, together with the necessity for keels to pass under the arches of the Tyne Bridge. No surviving account or illustration explains this process, though the term used for it, 'kepping' the mast, is emphasized by Heslop (below) and others:

A single mast was stepped in a tabernacle forward, where the coal-shuts and heed-sheets joined each other . . . on the port-side of the mast a space, called "a spencer" was kept vacant by means of a shifting board for the purpose of allowing the mast to be unshipped in passing under the Tyne bridge. After the operation of unshipping and "kepping", the mast was laid on top of the cargo and it remained there . . . when[ever] the sail was lowered.[21]

'Kep' he defines elsewhere as 'to catch in falling, or to catch and retain at one and the same time', or 'to intercept, to meet', all definitions that imply a dynamic process involving something in motion.[22] Lacking further description, the best interpretation seems to be that the mast was simply manhandled without mechanical intervention, maybe with one man lifting its base from within the security of the 'spencer' compartment before sliding the heel forward and down the head sheets ramp, whilst another riskily arrested, 'kepped', its downward and backward fall from a stance on top of the coals. To raise and re-step the mast the process was presumably reversed. The open dumb sheave no doubt allowed rapid disengagement of the yard and sail when lowering the mast, for there would have been no need to untie or unreeve the halyard, but care in re-positioning will have been required when stepping the mast again. If comparable to tossing a caber afloat, such lowering and stepping techniques would have been in keeping with the reputation of keel crews for sheer muscular strength and temerity.

Unfortunately, Heslop's comments on the nature of a mast-supporting 'tabernacle' and the role of the 'shifting board' are imprecise.[23] In the SANT model the function of the former is realized by a notch in the diagonal (spencer) beam where it meets the fore beam, making an immovable fixture which would have meant lifting the mast vertically over 3 feet before obtaining clearance to lower it aft (see Fig. 2.7).[24] In fact, the acute angle formed by the junction of these two beams provides support in itself, and a number of cheap, simple restraining systems – including wooden or iron latches – may have been fitted. But, whatever kind of 'tabernacle' was devised, the constraints of space meant that at some point in time the foot of a mast weighing over 200 pounds had to be raised and lowered bodily to-and-from deck level.

Although fitted with side stays (shrouds), the mast's overall diameter and degree of bury, i.e. the proportion below deck-level, suggests it had sufficient inherent strength to have easily carried the sail unstayed.[25] Interestingly, Bell delineates two stays each side but the keelman's sketch shows only one, so staying practices most likely varied. Whatever, stays will not only have helped safeguard the mast against breakage but must have reduced detrimental flexibility and masthead sag to leeward too. Its heavy scantling, of up to 7-9 inches diameter, was perhaps a reflection of the robustness required to survive rough usage rather than the strength needed to carry sail alone.

There are few reliable contemporary accounts of the keel's performance under squaresail, and effectually nothing that describes its management and handling, so retrospective assessment relies much upon inference and hypothesis. But later assumptions that the squaresail was purely for downwind use can be challenged since the surviving evidence indicates that keels could be sailed on a beam reach and, to a certain extent, might work close-hauled too (Fig. 4.5). In 1838 for instance, the well-respected Newcastle sailmaker (and songster) Robert Gilchrist (1797–1844) remarked that, 'Even with the old square sail the keel could be turned to windward hardly giving a shake [of the sail]', and Carmichael's lively depiction of a trio of keels in Shields Harbour, c.1830, shows them with sails well aslant reaching fast upriver, hard on a northerly wind (see Fig. 2.16).[26][27] Some degree of windward ability is also implied by the two 'Bowlynes' (bowlines) fitted to each leech of the squaresail in the keelman's sketch, though regrettably the working lead – to the bow – that their name suggests is not shown (Fig. 4.4). Indeed, the practice of using bowlines may also be inferred from Gilchrist's observation that a squaresail-rigged keel could be 'turned to windward' without the luff (i.e. windward leech) of the sail 'giving a shake' through stalled airflow. Overall, the Tyne keel joined a select list of East Coast watercraft, including the Humber Keel (which also employed bowlines), Norfolk keel, and Fair Isle Yoal, whose crews continued to use the medieval style of squaresail well into the nineteenth century.

Effective windward sailing depends upon hydrodynamic as well as aerodynamic efficiency and, until relatively recently, empirical design theorists would have considered the disposition of the squaresail keel's rig markedly unbalanced in relation to its underwater form.[28] Consequently, for historic or obsolete vernacular vessels, the general archaeological opinion was that, 'Hull-types in which there is archaeological evidence for a forward mast position (typically around one-third

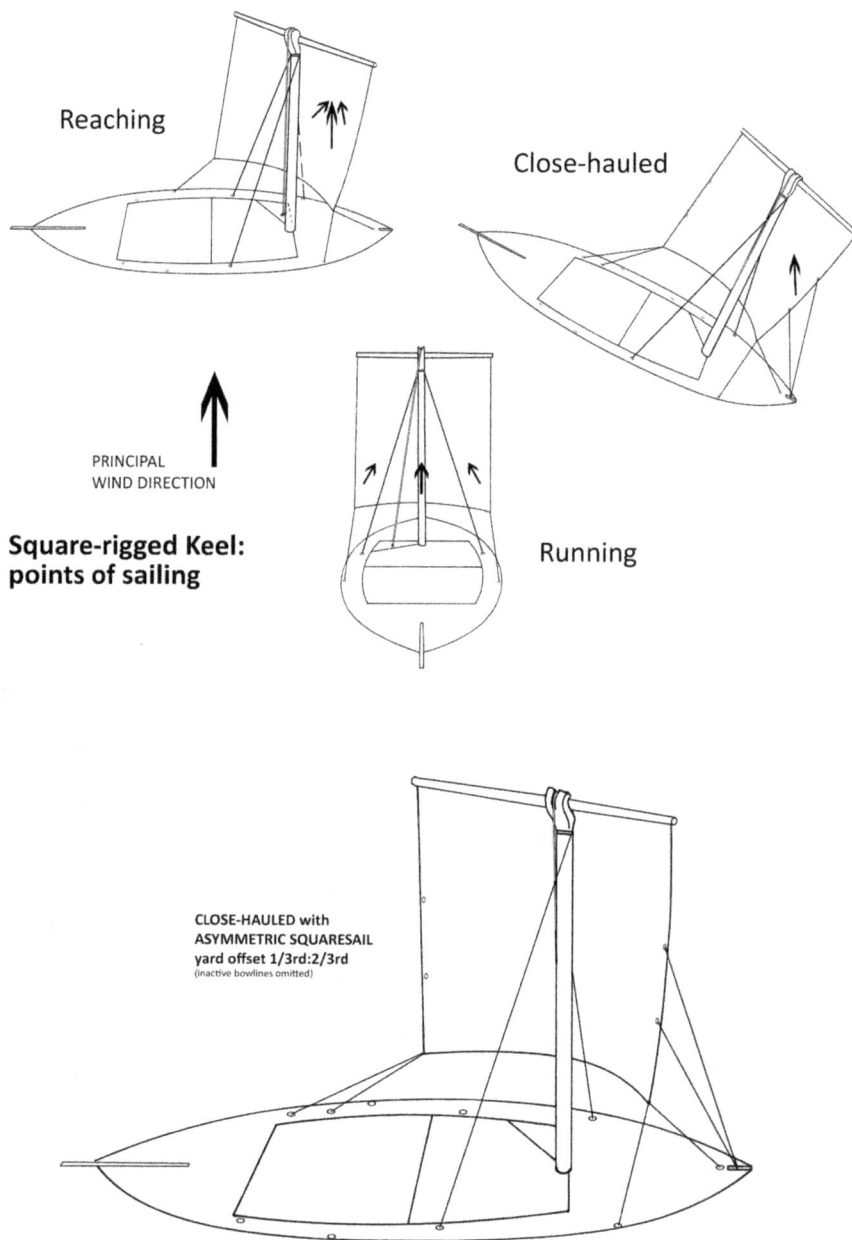

Reaching

Close-hauled

PRINCIPAL
WIND DIRECTION

**Square-rigged Keel:
points of sailing**

Running

CLOSE-HAULED with
ASYMMETRIC SQUARESAIL
yard offset 1/3rd:2/3rd
(inactive bowlines omitted)

FIGURE 4.5 Top, disposition of rig and points of sailing of a square-rigged Tyne keel (reconstructed from contemporary textual and graphic evidence); bottom, sailing to windward with the yard slung off centre to create a more efficient, asymmetric sail shape (based on SANT model, using the positions of assumed holes for rigging in the deck and the rubbing strake).

of the waterline length from the bow) have been interpreted as being poorly balanced (with a tendency to 'fall off' from the wind) if fitted with a single square sail'.[29] In this context the Tyne keel's mast position is even more extreme, at one-quarter of the load waterline length (or 30% of the length overall) from the bow. However, utilizing late twentieth-century techniques of physical analysis developed by Marchaj, Garrett and others, together with associated tank-testing results, naval architect Colin Palmer has demonstrated (2009) that the degree of balance achieved by historic craft of this type was far more favourable than conventional, heuristic, determinations would suggest. He concludes that 'the centre of lateral resistance [CLR] of a hull that does not have a distinct and yacht like keel generally falls between 20% and 35 % of the waterline length aft . . . significantly further forward than the [formerly used] geometric centroid of the underwater area' (Fig. 4.6). Furthermore, and of especial relevance to the Tyne keel, 'The more rounded the hull-sections, the further forward it [the CLR] will tend to be'. Not only that, but towing-tank tests revealed that a sharp forefoot – of the kind found in the keel – caused the CLR to shift rapidly forward when the side force on the hull was reduced, beneficially 'helping turn the vessel into the tack' when beating upwind.[30]

All-in-all, there is reason to believe that, despite its forward mounted squaresail, the Tyne keel may have been adequately balanced under sail, as a comparison

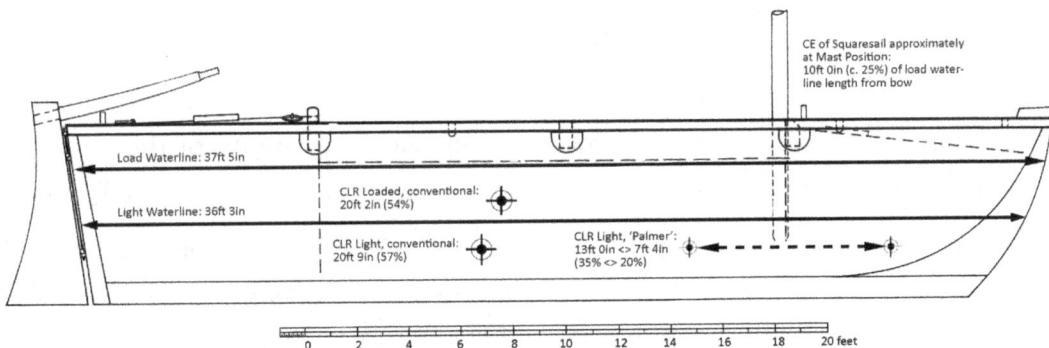

FIGURE 4.6 The differing positions of the centres of lateral resistance of a Tyne keel as predicted by conventional practice and by modern theory.

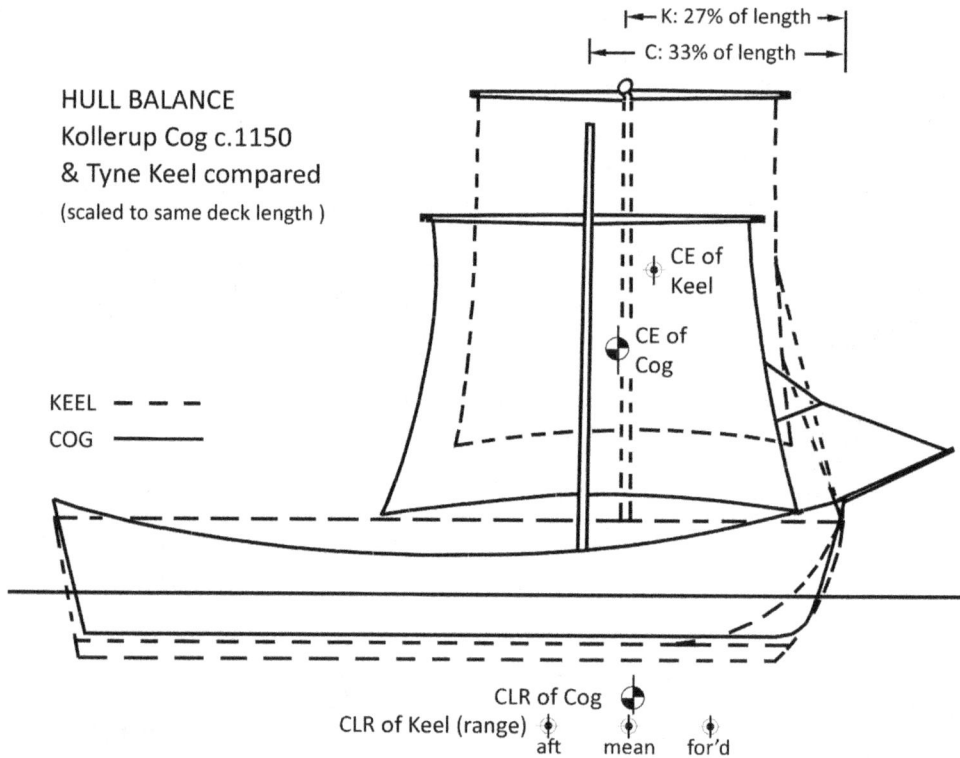

FIGURE 4.7 Comparison of the predicted hull balance of two craft carrying forward-mounted squaresails: a medieval cog, c.1150; and a Tyne keel, c.1820 (cog profile after Palmer).

with Palmer's analysis of, for example, the Kollerup Cog, c.1150, infers (Fig. 4.7).[31] Significantly, Palmer's work also revealed the potential influence of an extended forefoot on windward sailing capabilities. Tank-testing of a 'round-bilged hull of moderate fullness . . . not dissimilar to many traditional sailing vessels' revealed that when 'fitted with a deep forefoot or deep skeg' the ability of the vessel to resist leeway, the reduction of which is crucial for working upwind, was effectively doubled. The Tyne keel's forefoot and (to lesser extent) its sternpost mounted rudder would, intuitively, lead a practical sailor to expect greater windward ability than the same hull without those appendages but, nonetheless, Palmer's tank-test results provide objective confirmation of the potential gains afforded. After extensive analysis of the results from computational studies, tank-testing and replica ship trials, the conclusion was reached that 'under historic, single squaresail rigs '[seagoing] vessels can make modest progress to windward (as measured by their sailing angle to the true wind direction) in moderate winds and calm water', but that 'As wind-speed and associated sea-state increases, progress to windward becomes more problematic' and frequently is impossible.

In hypothesizing the keel's windward capabilities however, two ameliorating factors need to be taken into consideration. Firstly, it was not a seagoing vessel, and although the wind and wave conditions found in Shields Harbour – then unprotected by piers – might approximate to those found coastally, the greater part of a keel's work was carried out in relatively calm water. Secondly, keel passages were almost invariably made with the tidal flow, enabling crews to take full advantage of the commonplace technique known to sailors as 'lee-bowing', i.e. using the flow of the tide to help push the boat up against an adverse wind. Furthermore, according to that reliable professional observer Robert Gilchrist, 'by the old square-sail being slung two-thirds to leeward Keels could [be made to] tack with great facility'.[32] By re-slinging the sail yard off centre, the squaresail could be turned into an aerodynamically more efficient asymmetric sail, approximating to a standing lugsail (Fig. 4.5, bottom).[33] However, this would have meant having to either dip (lower) and re-hoist the sail on the opposite side of the mast during every tack or, alternatively, re-sling the yard. Speculatively, it would have been a technique employed only when long boards (legs of a tack) could be made.

Unfortunately, no description survives of the actual process of swinging the squaresail to tack, but it seems possible that – on occasion at least – the swape may have been used to supplement the rudder and help swing the keel's stern round. In the era before the adoption of the stern rudder, when the swape alone was used for steering, that clearly must have been the case. Correspondingly, more than one source indicates that the rudder was primarily for use when under sail, and that the pintle pin was commonly withdrawn and the rudder 'pulled up' (lifted aboard) when rowing and poling.[34] Theoretically at least, the adoption of a stern rudder provided keel users not only with steering convenience but a marginal gain in hydrodynamic efficiency. This marginal gain results from a stern rudder's wave-making drag being beneficially subsumed into that of the hull, whilst the use of a steering oar (swape) creates an additional wave-train drag. More significantly, if a vessel's sailing rig is set up so that it provides slight weather helm, a stern rudder produces 'an action analogous to a flap on an aeroplane wing, and may increase the efficiency of the hull', added to which it encourages a desirable forward shift of the CLR at a much shallower (less drag inducing) angle than that of a side-mounted rudder or steering oar.[35] An empirical grasp of these potential gains and conveniences seems to have ensured that keels were generally outfitted with stern rudders by the beginning of the nineteenth century.

Too much emphasis should not be placed on the keel's windward capabilities, however, for it is reasonable to assume that the best part of its time under squaresail was spent utilizing following winds: either running, or broad reaching with wind partially astern (Fig.4.5, top). For these points of sailing the relatively small sail area might be perceived as a disadvantage, but a couple of reliable book illustrations together with an early nineteenth-century reference demonstrate that, when sailing before the wind, keels might readily supplement the power of their single, iconic squaresail. Borrowing from seagoing practice, they deployed additional sail area in the form of a studding sail. Though such sails are commonly associated with higher status, oceangoing square-riggers – especially clippers and warships – they were also carried by the mundane collier brigs and coasters employed in the London-bound coal trade, whose captains frequently needed to make smart, competitive passages to be first to market, or gain speedy dispatch of their coals:

The wind at North a pleasant gale
Below the Middens [mouth of the Tyne] we make sail . . .
. . . Square away your yards, my lads, right square,
And all your steering-sail [studding sail] gear prepare;
Look sharp, my lads come bear a-hand,
Set every steering sail that will stand . . .[36]

The transfer of the coastal collier's studding sail technique to the square-rigged keel is thus readily explained, although it does not seem to have been adopted by East Coast rivercraft elsewhere. On the Tyne the practice seems to have occurred quite early, probably in the eighteenth century, for during a legal case concerning the impressment of a keelman in 1801 it was stated that 'the keels are navigated with one and sometimes two masts and large lug sails, and sometimes with studding sails'.[37] Although this statement was obviously designed to bolster the Crown's case that a keelman was a 'seaman', and thus liable to impressment, there seems to be no reason to doubt its factual substance. True, the reference to 'two masts' is unsupported elsewhere, but it is possible that – like some local fishing cobles – a few keels may have sported a small jigger mast aft, and any lawyer's confusion between the common lugsail and plain squaresail is understandable, especially when (as described above) the squaresail was sometimes set asymmetrically.

Two complementary bookplates, dated to c.1847 and 1885 respectively, make the deployment of studding sails on keels abundantly clear (Fig. 4.8).[38][39] The veracity of the earlier of the two is beyond doubt since the original sketch was by the Ovingham-born artist John Jackson jnr. (1801–1848), a former apprentice of the famed Newcastle wood engraver Thomas Bewick (1753–1828), and the bookplate concerned was engraved by Jackson's London-based brother, Mack (1819–1903). W J Palmer's subsequent illustration, published in 1885, appears to pay direct homage to John Jackson's earlier work, but exhibits extra detail and substitutes a backdrop of industrial riverside in place of Newcastle's bustling bridge and its environs.

Technically, the two depictions both suggest the use of a single, low-footed, studding sail set from a short yard hung from a yard arm, its leech providing considerable overlap of the squaresail, with the tack hauled down to the end of a temporarily positioned spar – perhaps the puoy – and a sheet led to the lee bow. Overall, this sail appears to have increased the keel's sail area by around a half and, in both plates, it is clearly set in a light following wind. With its lower edge set forward at deck level the studding sail also advantageously filled the gap below

FIGURE 4.8 Tyne keels running before light winds with their studding sails set: top, by J Jackson, 1847; bottom, by W J Palmer, 1885.

136

the foot of the squaresail, which was unavoidably cut high to clear the deck cargo. Palmer's slightly more detailed depiction suggests a squaresail of higher aspect ratio than that shown by Jackson, one of sufficient height to carry not just one but two rows of reef points. Both artists, however, depict two shrouds per side, and Palmer also seems to delineate the tie halyard of the squaresail leading down to port. Unlike a seagoing studding sail, which was sent aloft by means of a separate halyard, the graphic implication here is that the keel's studding sail was made fast to the yard arm of the squaresail whilst both were on deck, and they were subsequently hoist (and lowered) together. Conversely, a keel in T M Richardson's painting of Forth Banks (note [44]) appears to have pendant blocks at the yard arms, the conventional fittings for hoisting studding sails from deck level. So perhaps both methods were practised.

Since few keel passages were completed under sail alone, assessments of the actual sailing speeds attained are problematic. But a rare account by the mid-eighteenth-century apprentice Ralph Jackson of a positioning trip in an unladen keel from Newcastle Quay to Wincomblee staith does allow of calculation: 'Thursday Fifteenth [March 1753] . . . went to order Thompson to Winkhamlee [Wincomblee] . . . I went to the Cann House [pub] till they drank their Cann then I went down to Winkhamlee in the Keel, was 40 minutes in going down against the tide with a strong westerly wind'.[40] Given an along-river distance of just over three miles (2.6nm) this equates to an average speed over the ground of 4 knots which, with allowance for the adverse tide, might be raised to 5 to 5½ knots through the water, approaching the unladen keel's theoretical maximum speed of 7 knots. The young lad's trip was obviously a noteworthy one, made before a following wind estimated at around Beaufort Force 5 (17-21 knots), and with the set of the river channel allowing the keel to run or broad reach throughout – optimum squaresail conditions.

Fore and Aft Rig

The well attested shift away from the Tyne coal keel's old-established squaresail rig to fore-and-aft rig, which occurred during the second quarter of the nineteenth century, has gone largely unremarked by modern regional historians including Rowe (1969) and Fewster (2011). Its significance was apparently not appreciated or was misunderstood. Nevertheless, a strong argument can be made that this shift was a response to economic drivers elsewhere within the Tyne's coal transport chain, and that the universal adoption of this more efficient rig resulted in – admittedly unquantifiable – productivity gains that helped offset the keel's declining status as a transhipper of coals. In the context of British rivercraft alone, it may also be argued that this change from a near-medieval rig to the historically well-known spritsail rig, was unique both in its belated occurrence (the early Victorian era) and the totality of the change involved, encompassing over 200 vessels (Fig. 4.9).

Luckily, a comprehensive account of the move survives in the succinct but comprehensive text of a letter (note [26]) written by sailmaker Robert Gilchrist to John Bell in the summer of 1838:

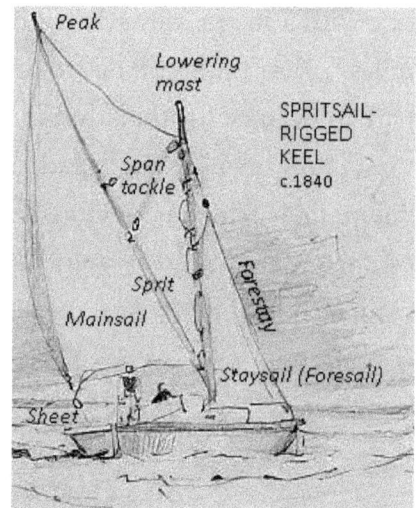

FIGURE 4.9 The main features of a fore-and-aft, spritsail-rigged keel, c.1840 (after J W Carmichael).

Respecting the alterations which have in latter [sic] years been made upon Keel Sails, wherein a Sprit Mainsail and Foresail [staysail] have entirely superseded the large square sheet [squaresail] once so much in vogue, such change appears to have taken place influenced by the following circumstances.

When the shipping [loading] of so much coal [by drops] between Tyne Bridge and the Harbour was resorted to, many Keels were laid aside from the employment in which they had been up to this time engaged; many were purchased by various individuals and fit up with hatches upon Deck for the purpose of rendering them sea-going craft. About the year 1830 T.C. Gibson & Co. began largely in this way trading between Newcastle & Sunderland, Blyth, Hartlepool etc etc It soon became obvious that such vessels as Keels, having to proceed so much along-shore would require headsail to keep them from running too much into the wind . . . hence the adoption of the fore & aft Mainsail and Jib . . .

The appearance and dexterity with which the Keels were thus managed at sea, soon produced a revolution in the ideas of the Keelmen upon the River Tyne. By <u>Holywell Main</u> Keels the <u>New Cut</u> was speedily adopted, <u>Townely Main</u> [sic] followed, succeeded by Wylam, Surtees [?] & Co. bringing up the rear. Great objections were raised by many of the running Fitters and old Keelmen, but the square sails if good, were soon converted into spritsails; and now the <u>old cut</u> is seldom or never seen . . .[41]

To summarize, the marked increase in the use of 'spouts' and 'drops' (direct shore-to-ship loading systems) 'below bridge' during the first quarter of the nineteenth century caused many keels to fall idle, and some of these were bought up to be converted for use on the nearby coast as general carriers.[42] Here, the old squaresail was found to have limited windward ability at sea, and consequently was replaced by fore-and-aft rigs. Appreciating the latter's performance advantages, the owners of coal keels servicing the 'above bridge' collieries – from which keel transport remained vital – commenced to follow suit. Despite the initial opposition of some keel-owning 'Fitters' (brokers) and older keelmen, on the grounds of increased cost and conservatism respectively, the comprehensive change in rig that then took place occupied only a few years, c.1830–c.1837. Although only a single (quite personal) piece of evidence, Robert Gilchrist's richly detailed account may be considered authoritative as to the process and timing of the change.[43] Visual impression of this decade of change is given moreover in the work of contemporary artists, for instance in a waterfront scene (dated 1835) by T M Richardson Snr. which depicts a sprit-rigged keel dried out at Forth Banks – just upriver of Newcastle Bridge – whilst two squaresail-rigged keels linger, symbolically becalmed, in midstream.[44] By the early 1840s, surviving pages of J W Carmichael's on-the-spot sketchbooks depict spritsail-rigged keels only, including a moored *Coal Keel* (Plate 4), five others underway in a busier scene, and finally a pair of fast-sailing *Newcastle Keels* (Plate 5).[45]

Gilchrist's account of the changes in technology and equipment involved are supported and augmented by two retrospective sources which have, until quite recently, lain largely unrecognized: R O Heslop writings of 1902; and the anonymous contributor to *Smith's Dock Journal* (*SDJ*, 1932). Heslop's text, although vague in chronology, reflects the wider picture:

Early in the century a change from square to fore-and-aft was coming into use . . . [the keel's] short mast was replaced by a tall spar carrying a large and lofty sprit-sail with jib. The sprit extended much higher than the mast head. The mast itself was hinged on a pivot and the jib-stay formed part of its lifting and lowering tackle. This was arranged by shackling a chain to the head of the jib stay and the chain, after being roved through a pulley block at the mast-head, was brought down to the heed-sheets where it was passed through a hawse-hole and was wound on the drum of a small winch, fixed in the forecastle below. On approaching the Tyne Bridge the winch pawl was let go and a break [sic] applied; then mast and sail were lowered until they lay aslope at an angle sufficient to clear the crown of the arch. As soon as the passage under the bridge was made the mast was immediately raised again by means of the winch . . . The new rig, well-proportioned to the keel itself, not only changed its appearance entirely but added greatly to its sailing qualities. It could now sail well up into the wind, or on a tack, and under all conditions could be freely handled. In the middle of the century the passage of a large fleet of keels each under its own sail was a familiar and stirring sight on the Tyne.[46]

The basis of the new rig's success lay in the combination of two innovations referred to by Heslop, the spritsail and a pivoted mast which could be raised and lowered by mechanical means rather than crude manhandling. Evidence for the pivoting mechanism is sparse, with only the Mitcalfe model providing any structural detail (Fig. 4.10).

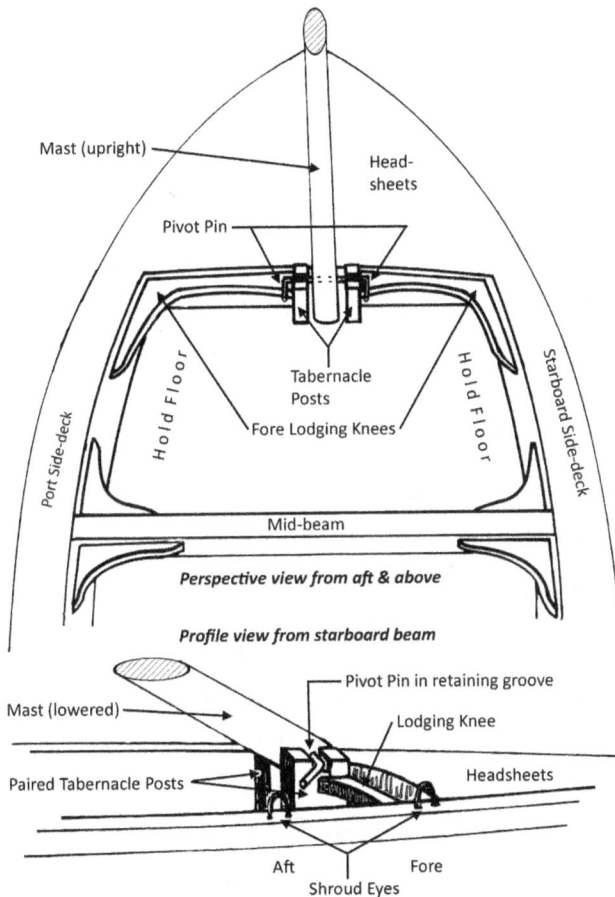

FIGURE 4.10 Schematic diagram of a spritsail-rigged Tyne keel's tabernacle, and associated structural elements, as represented on the Mitcalfe model.

On this model, two stout vertical posts protrude up through the fore end of the hold floor to form a loadbearing 'tabernacle' that engages a pivot pin which passes through the very base of mast. Strong lateral support is provided for these posts by a pair of purpose-fashioned, full-width lodging knees that substitute for the keel's usual fore-beam. Unusually, the pivot pin does not pierce the tabernacle posts themselves but is borne in a deep slot on their respective upper faces, allowing the heel of the mast to swing freely forward as the mast is lowered. The adoption of this freely disengaging pivot pin may have been because it was sometimes necessary for the keelmen to unship the mast foot completely (as in a squaresail keel), allowing them to lay the mast even flatter than its usual 30-degree slope on top of the coals for passing under the Tyne Bridge (Fig. 4.11). Heslop emphasizes that the mast and sail had to be 'lowered until they lay aslope at an angle sufficient to clear the crown of the arch', and a conventional fixed pin may not always have allowed this.

The *SDJ*'s anonymous author concurred as to the use of a tabernacle, although positioning the mast 'just forward of the hold' rather than within it, an alternative also suggested by the Caverhill I model.[47] And he also stated that the mast was secured athwartships by stays (shrouds) made of wire, not rope. This almost certainly records the first regular use of this material in a vernacular watercraft and is consonant with Tyneside's pioneering approach toward the use of wire rope for ship's standing rigging – from 1841 onwards.[48] Contemporary depictions and the Mitcalfe model indicate that two stays were generally fitted on each side, one pair directly in line with the mast's pivot axis and the second pair less than a foot aft of them, both pairs being fastened (via deadeyes and lanyards) to deck-mounted eyes at the edge of the hold. Geometrically, this arrangement must have simplified mast handling, for there would have been little or no need to adjust the stays when raising or lowering the mast – always a chore with stays that led conventionally, more supportively, further apart. The fitting of a forestay of sufficient strength to support the mast longitudinally during the raising and lowering process was, however, a more complex (and costly) business. Chain had to be resorted to for adequate strength allied to flexibility, for the leverage exerted by the mast – plus

RECONSTRUCTED SAILPLAN of
'MITCALFE' MODEL (TWAM B9779)

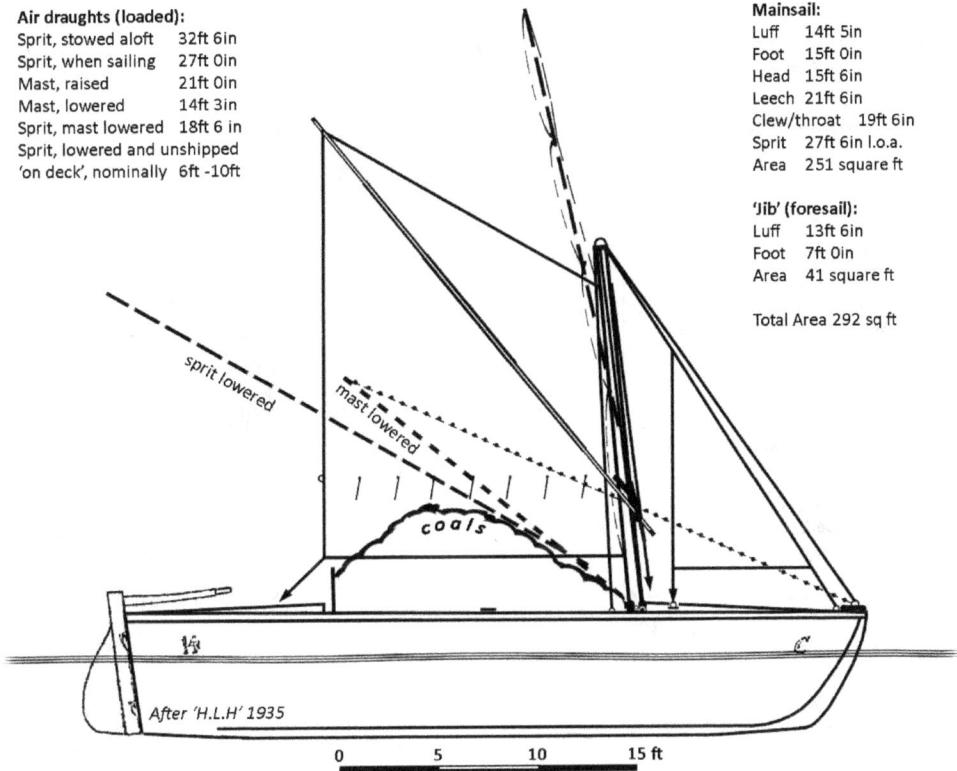

Air draughts (loaded):
Sprit, stowed aloft   32ft 6in
Sprit, when sailing   27ft 0in
Mast, raised   21ft 0in
Mast, lowered   14ft 3in
Sprit, mast lowered   18ft 6 in
Sprit, lowered and unshipped
'on deck', nominally   6ft -10ft

Mainsail:
Luff   14ft 5in
Foot   15ft 0in
Head   15ft 6in
Leech   21ft 6in
Clew/throat 19ft 6in
Sprit   27ft 6in l.o.a.
Area   251 square ft

'Jib' (foresail):
Luff   13ft 6in
Foot   7ft 0in
Area   41 square ft

Total Area 292 sq ft

sprit lowered

mast lowered

coals

After 'H.L.H' 1935

0   5   10   15 ft

FIGURE 4.11 Reconstructed sailplan of a spritsail-rigged Tyne keel based on the Mitcalfe model, with positions and heights of the spars when stowed aloft or lowered for passing under Newcastle Bridge.

the weight of the sprit and sail – produced great loading whilst swinging through its lower angles (Fig. 4.12).

Even the considerable muscle power of a keel's crew needed mechanical assistance when raising and lowering the mast and spritsail gear, with both Heslop and the *SDJ*'s contributor highlighting the use of a winch or windlass mounted under the deck in the forecastle. The latter writer detailed the device used in the 1860s and 1870s 'as of the old barrel type with detachable cranks, a descendant of the old *handspec*, of which it is said by Falconer in his *Marine Dictionary* [1780]

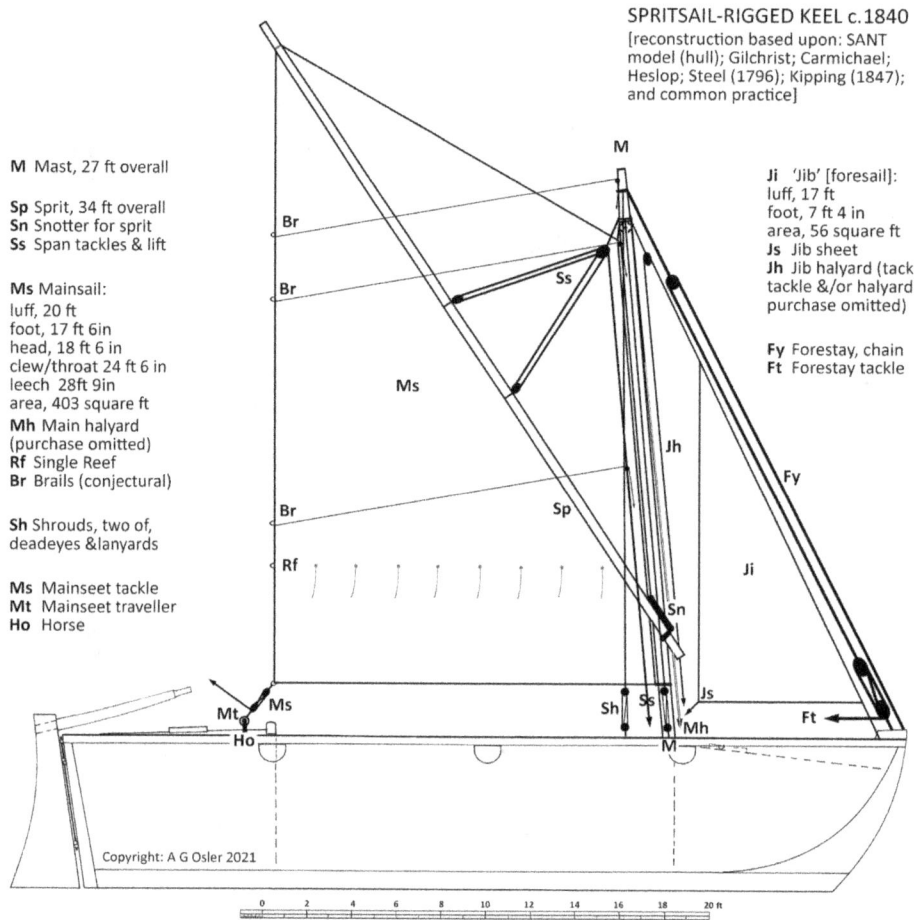

SPRITSAIL-RIGGED KEEL c.1840
[reconstruction based upon: SANT model (hull); Gilchrist; Carmichael; Heslop; Steel (1796); Kipping (1847); and common practice]

M Mast, 27 ft overall

Sp Sprit, 34 ft overall
Sn Snotter for sprit
Ss Span tackles & lift

Ms Mainsail:
luff, 20 ft
foot, 17 ft 6in
head, 18 ft 6 in
clew/throat 24 ft 6 in
leech 28ft 9in
area, 403 square ft
Mh Main halyard
(purchase omitted)
Rf Single Reef
Br Brails (conjectural)

Sh Shrouds, two of,
deadeyes &lanyards

Ms Mainseet tackle
Mt Mainseet traveller
Ho Horse

Ji 'Jib' [foresail]:
luff, 17 ft
foot, 7 ft 4 in
area, 56 square ft
Js Jib sheet
Jh Jib halyard (tack tackle &/or halyard purchase omitted)

Fy Forestay, chain
Ft Forestay tackle

Copyright: A G Osler 2021

FIGURE 4.12 Reconstructed sailplan of a Tyne keel carrying a large spritsail rig and employing the heavy forestay tackle indicated by some contemporary sources for mast raising and lowering (see Plate 4).

that the colliers of Northumberland [coal trade seamen] were the most dexterous managers'.[49][50] The exact positioning of the forestay system's hawse-hole and winch are unknown, for no additional pictorial or textual evidence has been found and the model 'showing this rig and the lowering mast [that] was exhibited by Harry Clasper in the Polytechnic Exhibition at Newcastle in 1848' has been lost – not unsurprising, it was 7 feet long![51][52] The operation of such a rude winch within the confines of the forecastle must have been strenuous and risky, and the effort lost to inherent friction considerable. In fact, mast raising and lowering by a winch may have been uncommon before the late 1840s, for prior to that time the pictorial evidence points towards the use of heavy, above deck, tackles.

A system employing tackles is implied, for example, in Carmichael's sketch, *Coal Keel on the Tyne*, which can be contextually dated to the early 1840s (note [45]). This sketch not only shows a massive tackle attached to the stem-head but, on close inspection, also reveals the chain forestay leading up through a heavy 'pulley block at the mast-head' that was alluded to by Heslop (Plate 4). Helpfully, it also confirms the use of deadeyes and lanyards for tensioning the keel's paired shrouds, but conversely suggests that Heslop, a non-sailor writing retrospectively, misunderstood the set-up of the 'jib' (or, more properly, 'foresail').[53] Together with Carmichael's sketches, the presence of a separate securing eye (to starboard of the stem-head) on the Mitcalfe model apparently indicates that the jib was flown independent of the forestay. The loosely stowed jib dangling from the mast of the moored keel in the sketch cited above, together with the sagging luffs of the craft underway in others, also argue for such an interpretation. A 'jib' that literally ran up-and-down the chain forestay would seem improbable, so a more conventional alternative seems likely.[54]

No quantitative descriptions of a keel's sprit mainsail survive other than Gilchrist's statement that the 'sails of old time [squaresails] were considered large when they took from fifty to fifty-six yards, the [sprit] sails at present have frequently eighty-two yards put into them'.[55] Compared with its squaresail-rigged predecessor the sprit-rigged keel deployed approximately half as much area again in its mainsail; adding in the jib, this probably amounted to around three-quarters more in total. Surprisingly perhaps, this much larger area was still accommodated on a relatively short mast, although when proceeding under sail the top of the 'spreet' (sprit) may have risen to more than 30 feet above deck level.[56] However, rig size clearly varied. For example, a reconstruction of the rig for a keel like that depicted by the Mitcalfe model amounts to little more than that of a squaresail in area (Figs. 4.3 and 4.11). Conversely, a sprit mainsail drawn up according to proportions given in sail-making treatises of the period produces a much larger area, close to the 'eighty-two yards' cited by Gilchrist, and makes a close visual match with contemporary illustrations (Plate 5).

For a cargo-carrying barge or lighter, the principal virtue of spritsail- over squaresail-rig lay in the fact that neither the mainsail nor its spar, the sprit, had to be lowered to the deck when the vessel stopped sailing. The spar and its sail were simply secured aloft with a span tackle and brails respectively: 'When the sprit-sail was not in use a line rove through a pulley at the masthead pulled the sprityard hard up to the mast, and the sail was secured by two brails' (Fig. 4.12). This not only kept the deck clear for cargo handling but, as pointed out by Gilchrist, promised to reduce maintenance costs since 'the sails are by the changes [to sprit rig] never allowed to lie upon deck as heretofore; a considerable saving will ultimately be effected.' As a self-interested sailmaker, maybe Gilchrist's cost-saving prospect was accentuated to help offset the freely admitted fact that 'the cost at first [of sprit rig] is at least double, from so much heavy & expensive gear being to provide . . .'. [57]

Unfortunately, the procedures for sailing a keel under sprit rig are touched upon by one writer only, and that retrospectively.[58] He ascribes a good deal to the effectiveness of the jib, 'a most useful sail because it enabled the keel to change her tack speedily', continuing rather ambiguously, 'Just previous to "ratching" [going about] the jibsail was set up and the keel's helm put over. As soon as the spritsail filled with wind the jibsail was lowered until the next "ratch" '. This implies that the jib was backed (backwinded) to ensure that the keel's head came round through the wind when altering tack – a technique familiar to small boat sailors today – but it also intimates that this was the jib's only function, a statement that is contradicted by several contemporary illustrations showing sprit-rigged keels (and Tyne wherries) reaching and running with jibs fully deployed. Miniature jib-sheet eyes on the Mitcalfe model suggest that the jib could be set at a close-hauled angle, some 22-30° to the keel's centreline.[59] Curiously, these sheet eyes lie almost vertically below the (supposed) clew, raising three possibilities for the sheet lead: modelmaker's error; accepted keel practice; or the use of a rope horse. This last seems possible, for late in the keel era the fitting of an 'iron horse to which the foresail is fastened' seems to have been commonplace.[60] And as was common practice elsewhere, control of the mainsail's sheeting angle seems to have been achieved by the use of a tackle working on a transverse 'horse' via a 'traveller', which the *SDJ*'s author rather confusingly described thus: 'To the lower corner of the spritsail was attached an eye which ran on a rail set up at the after end of the hold, and called the iron horse traveller'. This arrangement is well demonstrated, at larger scale, in surviving Thames Barges and (gaff-rigged) Norfolk wherries today. Unlike these, however, there is no evidence that Tyne keels used vangs to help control the angle and sway of the top of the spar, but the possibility cannot be discounted.[61]

Regarding the sprit rig's actual sailing performance, Gilchrist gave an enthusiastic first-hand endorsement, writing:

Unwieldy as keels appear they can be brought very close to the wind, and sail very swiftly, the activity displayed by their navigators, and skilful management of their lumpen vessels, have frequently called forth the astonishment and admiration of men of the most competent nautical knowledge . . . now with a heavy gale from the westward, they fearlessly turn [tack] up the Long Reach to the amazement of seamen who behold the hardy fellows working their Tide when nobody else dare stir.[62]

By the mid-century the superior sailing qualities of the spritsail rig were taken for granted, as evidenced by a Lemington keelman, William Boyle, at the Admiralty Inquiry in February 1849:

. . . last Friday morning we left Shields at 1 o'clock; when we got up to Newcastle Bridge I looked up at the Gateshead clock and saw it was ten minutes past 3. With a N.W. wind we sailed up Bill Reach and Shields or Tail Reach, and turned [tacked] up the rest of the road. If I had told old [squaresail] keelmen this they would have thought I was mad . . . The old keels used to have square sails; they have now fore and aft sails. This rig is better, but the build of some of the old keels cannot be beaten.[63]

Boyle's account records a – no doubt tide assisted – trip of around 9 river miles (7.8 nm) in some 2¼ hours, indicating an average speed over the ground of some 3½ knots, no mean feat considering that, in contemporary seamen's terms, there was a 'scant' (adverse) wind. And his final caveat about changes in keel 'build' is intriguing. Perhaps this suggests that when keels were built to accommodate the new sailing rig some of the desirable older qualities, perhaps those aiding rowing and poling, had been weakened.

At a greater distance in time, it may have been R O Heslop's own youthful memories of keels being worked like this that caused him to look back and enthuse that, 'In the middle of the century the passage of a large fleet of keels each under its own sail was a familiar and stirring sight on the Tyne'.

The Wind Regime

The employment of sail, both squaresail and spritsail, depended upon the wind regime of the lower Tyne valley, a latent force that was far less predictable than the river's cyclical tidal flow. Although daily local weather observations are sparse and intermittent prior to the early-1860s, historical meteorology indicates that the wind regime will have followed some specific long-term trends during the period 1700–1870.[64] But short term, monthly and annual variations remain harder to characterize and sum-up. All such wind variables must be considered in relation to the geographic configuration of the river's 15½ mile course, three-quarters of which lay broadly upon a west to east axis.[65] The proportion of 'westerlies' to 'easterlies' that was experienced was thus a significant issue, for keels required to make prompt passages both downriver (east-going) when loaded and upriver (west-going) when returning light again (Map 5).

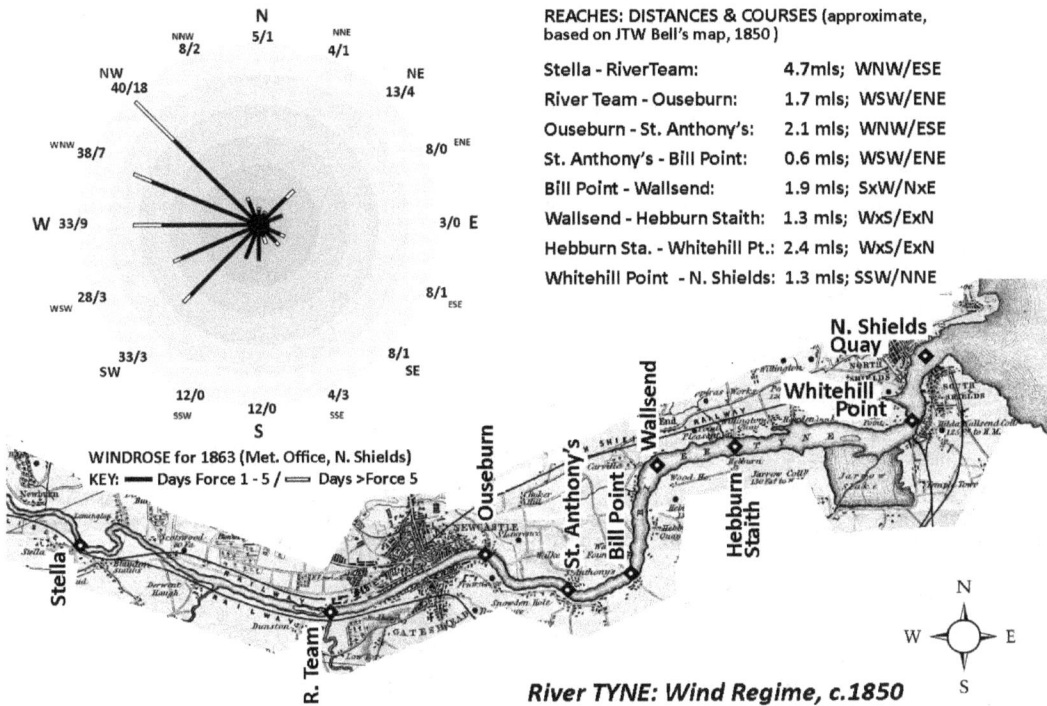

REACHES: DISTANCES & COURSES (approximate, based on JTW Bell's map, 1850)

Stella - RiverTeam:	4.7mls; WNW/ESE
River Team - Ouseburn:	1.7 mls; WSW/ENE
Ouseburn - St. Anthony's:	2.1 mls; WNW/ESE
St. Anthony's - Bill Point:	0.6 mls; WSW/ENE
Bill Point - Wallsend:	1.9 mls; SxW/NxE
Wallsend - Hebburn Staith:	1.3 mls; WxS/ExN
Hebburn Sta. - Whitehill Pt.:	2.4 mls; WxS/ExN
Whitehill Point - N. Shields:	1.3 mls; SSW/NNE

WINDROSE for 1863 (Met. Office, N. Shields)
KEY: ▬ Days Force 1 - 5 / ═ Days >Force 5

River TYNE: Wind Regime, c.1850

MAP 5 The main 'reaches' of the River Tyne navigation with their orientations and lengths, together with the annual wind regime c.1850.

Between the turn of the eighteenth century and the end of the keel era there were certainly enough changes in the national weather pattern to have affected the use of keels under sail, although these effects were probably not recognized by operators at the time. Indeed, one prominent climatologist refers to the period from 1780 to 1850 as being the 'last main stage' of the relatively cold period known as the 'Little Ice Age', c.1550 to c.1850. The last decade of the eighteenth century was a particularly turbulent one, producing three northerly storms of exceptional strength, whilst the 1780s were notable for their want of westerly winds and a succession of bad easterly storms. This last reflects the fact that the balance between westerly and easterly winds changed significantly between 1700 and 1870. In the first phase, from the 1730s until the first decade of the nineteenth century, there was a general decline in the prevailing south westerlies, and these winds eventually reached a nadir of about 60 days per annum (p.a.) around 1807, compared to a peak of some 115 days p.a. in the 1730s. During the second phase, from around 1810 to 1870, the balance shifted cyclically back to the south westerlies again, and they finally regained the same level as their preceding (1730s) peak during the early 1860s when, for example, North Shields weather station recorded 114 days of south westerlies in 1863.[66]

Though this upward trend in south westerlies was well defined it did not proceed altogether unrestrained, for a noticeable decline (of 10 days p.a.) occurred during the 1820s and early 1830s and there was a minor regression in the 1850s as well. Interestingly however, the late 1830s and 1840s saw a rapid increase in frequency (of up to 30 days p.a.), an increase that happened to coincide with the period when sprit rig was introduced.[67] Although there is no suggestion here of cause and effect, this increase in westerlies will undoubtedly have advantaged those keels which had adopted sprit rig over those that retained their original squaresails. With their larger, loftier sprit mainsails the downriver trips of these newly-rigged keels will have been enhanced and, in addition, their ability to work – if only modestly – to windward under mainsail and jib would have provided a significant advantage over any squaresail-rigged counterparts when working back upriver against the prevailing westerlies.

Wind strength was the second critical element in a keel's operation under sail. Unfortunately, consistent local data for wind strength is presently unavailable before 1863, the year in which the Meteorological Office began recording observations at North Shields. But analysis of the surviving (twice daily) wind observations for Shields allows an assessment of the conditions that would have affected the sailing of keels: firstly, through finding the number of days which were likely lost to sail through excessive wind speed or calms; and secondly, through detailing the seasonal patterns of wind strength and direction. From these appraisals an informed calculation can be made of the number of days per month that had winds favourable to up- or down-river passages under sail.[68] Admittedly, a degree of estimation is required when converting such raw data into nineteenth-century sailing practice, but it seems reasonable to suppose that sprit-rigged keels operated satisfactorily in light winds of Beaufort Force 1 through Force 3 and may have achieved their optimum performance in moderate conditions of Force 4 and 5. Above this windspeed the ability to progress will have depended much upon the circumstances pertaining and a crew's skill or determination, whilst steady windspeeds of Force 6 and higher seem likely to have been considered excessive, and thus infrequently used.[69] With respect to wind direction, it is suggested that loaded keels will generally have taken advantage of following or beam winds, but when returning upriver empty are more likely to have engaged in windward sailing, perhaps working some two compass points or so (say, 20-25°) into the wind.

Although affording only a single snapshot in time, an analysis of the North Shields' observations for 1863 is instructive (Fig. 4.13). It suggests that at least half the recorded days in every month, including those of winter, provided opportunity for downriver passages under sail. And throughout the main coal shipment season

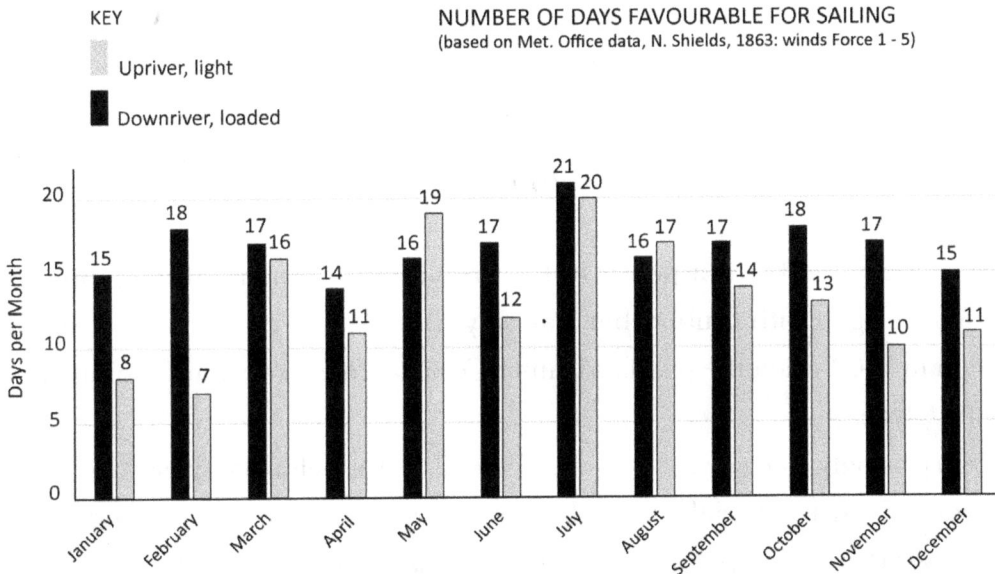

FIGURE 4.13 The frequency (days per month) of wind conditions that were favourable for keels making passages downriver or upriver under sail during the year 1863.

151

of March to October, the difference between the number of downriver and upriver sailing opportunities was relatively slight, indeed March itself and the midsummer months of July and August offered near-equal chances of both.

Considered annually, however, there was an entrenched westerly regime with a striking difference in the proportion of winds of all strengths from westerly (SSW through NNW) as opposed to easterly (NNE through SSE) directions, indeed 70% of all recorded days comprised winds from the South West to North West sector alone (Map 5). But this should not hide the fact that in wintertime, from November to February, the prospects of making a straightforward upriver passage under sail were much reduced owing to consistently adverse or dangerously high winds, and favourable upriver opportunities barely averaged nine days per winter month.

All that said, by the mid-1860s any consideration of the wind regime and its effects on keel movements was of limited everyday significance, for the numbers of keels in use was rapidly declining and steam towage was undoubtedly the prime mover for those that remained.

STEAM

Pioneers

The application of steam power to the propulsion of watercraft was pioneered in the late eighteenth century but was only realized as a practical proposition in Britain in 1802 when the paddle-steamer *Charlotte Dundas* was successfully trialed on the Clyde.

Surprisingly perhaps, it was another 12 years before a river steamer was introduced on industrial Tyneside: the locally-built and locally-engined (14 horsepower), wooden paddle steamer *Tyne Steamboat* of 1814.[70] Intended to run an along-river passenger service, she failed to achieve profitability and, following purchase by industrialist Joseph Price of Gateshead in 1817, was aptly re-named

FIGURE 4.14 The ps *Perseverance* towing a brig upriver against the wind in the approaches to Newcastle; a loaded, squaresail-rigged, keel sails past downriver (far right).

Perseverance and entrepreneurially adapted for the towage of colliers and coasters between Shields Harbour and loading places below Newcastle Bridge (Fig. 4.14).[71] She made the first such trip in July 1818. This work proved to be so advantageous and profitable that, by 1822, no less than 15 such vessels reputedly provided ship towage on the Tyne.

And in that same year, 1822, the first formally recorded towage of a 'string' (group) of keels by steam took place, although it was no more than an unintended by-product of a prolonged and unusually vicious labour conflict: 'The Long Stop' (Keelmen's strike) of October to December 1822. At the height of that protracted and impassioned strike in 1822, the owners of Wylam Colliery took the unprecedented step of placing one of their two locomotive engines, the *Wylam Dilly*, aboard a keel for short-term use as a keel-towing tug, removing its wheels and connecting its drive mechanism to temporary paddle wheels. The expedient worked and this strange vessel, which could tow a string of several keels, apparently continued in operation for some months afterwards.[72] Though technologically retrogressive, it was – as the colliery owners intended – not only a short-term solution but a salutary reminder to the keelmen of the long-term potential for transshipping coal by means of steam-powered river craft, built either specifically for keel towage or (a more difficult proposition) as self-propelled coal carriers.[73] Despite the fact that the keelmen effectively lost their three-month strike it seems that their collective power was still sufficient to deter coal owners and shippers from introducing direct steam towage for keels. Nevertheless, the technological threat to the keelmen's services was publicly underlined by the owners of Wylam Colliery who, a year later in June 1823, let it be known through:

. . . the appearance of a keel with a powerful high pressure engine on board, calculated to tow vessels of great burthen up and down the river . . . and in any future desertion of the keelmen, they can, in a great measure dispense with their services. It is highly creditable to the colliery owners, that having the means thus amply at their command of using machinery to the exclusion of manual labour to their manifest advantage, they are determined not to avail themselves of such a power except in case of actual necessity.[74]

Though admittedly a little slower than the existing steam-boats used for towage, Wylam's proposed new vessel had the advantage of shallower draft, presumably no more than that of a laden keel.

Steam Towage, 1825–1875

In reality, it is likely that in some circumstances keel crews had already been taking discreet advantage of the facility to move their craft against adverse winds or tide by the casual use of steam towage. But what the keelmen presumably did not want was extensive or owner-initiated use of the practice, for that would be an existential threat to their occupation. Newspaper reports of the late 1820s support that impression, with complainants directing their ire not at the keelmen themselves but at the skippers (who were often the owners) of the river's small steam packets for taking on the impromptu towage of a keel to the detriment of their promised schedules. Fare-paying passengers objected, since delays and even lengthy tidal groundings often resulted, as explained in 1828:

We have another word to say of this Mary & Isabella steam-packet. It had hardly left the quay [Newcastle Quay] when the master, Captain Blacklock, bargained with the crew of a loaded keel and absolutely took her in tow in defiance of the united remonstrances of the passengers. Nay, Captain Blacklock even went so far as to treat their complaints with great insolence, declaring that he was not licensed, and cared not a straw for passengers . . . No steam-packet owner has a right to complain that he is kept to his business; let him carry passengers or tow ships or other vessels, but do not let him say "I will take passengers" and then drag keels too.[75]

Neither were keel crews averse to taking surreptitious advantage of the regular, more powerful tugs that now towed sailing colliers to and from the staiths. In that same year (1828) Captain Ralph Storey, whose ship was being towed upriver by a tug, brought a claim for damages against a keel crew who by 'putting their large hook [boathook] into his ship's boat [made fast astern], obliged him to set it adrift to save it from being broken to pieces'. Storey's claim failed, for the magistrates probably took the view that he may not have cast the boat adrift to save it from damage – it was soon recovered – but to deter a keel crew who were seeking a free tow![76] Although infrequent, anecdotes like these reinforce the impression that towage by dedicated tug was too expensive for low-earning keel crews, but it was not uncommon for them to negotiate a cheap casual tow from a small river steamer if it avoided a costly delay or unwonted effort. They certainly had choice, for it has been estimated that nearly 40 steamers plied the Tyne by this time, although the majority were dedicated to handling seagoing sailing ships.

Curiously, there is little record of keel towage during the next two decades, the 1830s and 1840s, a period that – coincidentally or otherwise – was marked by the rise to dominance of keels equipped with faster, more efficient sailing rigs. But from the middle of the century onward references to keel towage become more common, a reflection of the fact that, although the keel fleet had declined in numbers and the proportion of coals loaded by keel was much reduced, the demand for individual promptness of dispatch had almost certainly increased as coal shipments from the port expanded at a record rate.[77] The total tonnage shipped doubled from around 2.4 million tons in 1830 to 5.2 tons by 1865. For steam towage, the pressure of demand resulted in an increased supply of towing units, and by the mid-1860s there were no less than 250 river and seagoing tugs working in and out of the Tyne, the majority of them locally built and engined. Typically, the tugs employed during the third quarter of the century were larger and far more powerful vessels than their early dual-purpose predecessors; for example, the North Shields built *Vanguard* of 1858 had a 40-horsepower engine and, although 86 feet in length, possessed a beam and draught no greater than that of a (loaded) keel.[78]

Within the river it seems that tugs generally towed groups of two to four keels or wherries, though the towage of eight was not uncommon, and strings even longer than that were sometimes reported (Fig. 4.15). A selection of reported accidents serves to illustrate this unregulated situation:

- 1847, tug *Princess* towing a keel and two wherries collided with moored craft in Shields Harbour
- 1860, the passenger carrying *Champion* collided with and sank the *Wanderer*, 'the possession of an industrious seaman [John Hopper] who had purchased her with his savings', which was engaged in towing two keels upriver
- 1862, four keels 'awaiting a steamer towing them away' suffered the loss of a crewman by suicide
- 1866, tug *Effort* (proceeding upriver) received damage from one of three keels 'cast off' from the tail of a 'number of laden keels in line coming down[river] in tow of another steamer'
- 1867, tug *William Cargill* towing two keels downriver (in fog) sunk by ss *Fairy*
- 1867, moored tug *Sunbeam* damaged by the third (and last) keel in a string being towed upriver when a sailing wherry attempted to join the tow
- 1868, the ss *Bolivar* inadvertently caused a fatality (a following boatman) near Dent's Hole through colliding with the last of 'a long string of keels (from 15 to 20)' being towed upriver past her by the tug *Mary*.[79]

On closer examination this last tragic incident is instructive in several respects. *Mary* was obviously the largest (45 gross tons; length 70.4 feet), youngest (1860) and, significantly, the most powerful (30 nominal horsepower) of the four keel-towing tugs cited above. By comparison *Princess, Wanderer,* and *William Cargill* were tugs of an earlier generation, built 1841–1851, and although of similar length and displacement (65–71 feet; 36–41 gross tons) were equipped with engines that had barely half (14 to 16 nominal horsepower) the power of the *Mary*.[80] Clearly the *Mary* had the ability to tow a lengthy string of 15 or more keels, whilst the inference is that her older counterparts could only handle a quarter of that number at best. Though providing increased efficiency (and profitability) this increased keel-towing capacity came at a potential cost to life and property, as made clear by Mr Turnbull, the father-in-law of the boatman tragically drowned in the incident (1868) between the tug *Mary* and the steamship ss *Bolivar*. Turnbull publicly pronounced that 'keels coming in long strings were an impediment to the [river] traffic as well as dangerous'. This pointed comment indicating that the multiple towage of keels was commonplace in the late 1860s.[81][82]

It is also of interest that all four of the tugs exampled above were under Newcastle (not Shields) ownership, a bias which may reflect the fact that keel usage was increasingly concentrated in the navigation above Newcastle Bridge where the collieries had no option but to deliver their coals indirectly to ships by water or rail. Collieries at Benwell, Elswick, Garesfield, Chopwell, Wylam and Stella still transported 'all or part of their coal' by keel as late as 1860, and Walbottle's exclusively so, whilst just ten years earlier, c.1850, the 70-80,000 tons (approximately 3,500 loads) of coal and coke handled through the Marquess of Bute's Derwenthaugh Staith had been dispatched solely by keel.[83] The Admiralty Report of 1849 suggested that on average 600 laden keels passed under Newcastle Bridge each week, say

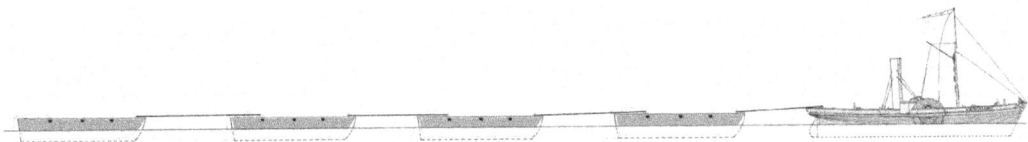

FIGURE 4.15 The 86-feet long Tyne tug *Vanguard*, built in 1858, towing a string of four 'dumb' keels (to scale).

30,000 per year, and even as late as the mid-1850s it was estimated that one-seventh (14%) of the 3.7 million tons of coals shipped from the Tyne was still carried in keels, a figure (522,000 tons) that if correct represented more than 24,500 delivery trips by keels each year.[84][85] It is reasonable to assume that a substantial number of those trips will have involved an element of towage by steam.

The practice of towing long strings of keels may well have resulted from, or been encouraged by, the decision of some upriver collieries to formally contract out the towage of their keels to individual tug owners. In July 1867 for example, the Holywell (Stella) coal agent's office in Newcastle sought competitive tenders from 'steamboat owners' for the towage of keels from 'Lemington to Shields', and a couple of months later Walbottle Colliery did likewise, although specifying that interested 'Steamboat Proprietors' must make a written 'Proposal' that included 'Size of [engine] Cylinder, condition of Boat, Depth of Water she draws. Price per Keel from Lemington to: Newcastle; Jarrow; and Shields'.[86][87] It seems that Walbottle's especial dependency on the use of keels (cited above), or an unsatisfactory experience with a tug owner, may explain their advertisement's contractual caution. Despite the potential drawbacks, it seems that colliery owners generally appreciated the economy of contracting-out keel towage rather than investing in a tug themselves; for instance, in 1851 the owners of Barrington Colliery, Cramlington auctioned off their recently reconditioned, Blyth-based 'Towing Boat' *Mallard*.[88] On the Tyne, the 1860s may have marked the highpoint of keel towage by steam with the River Commissioner's engineer, J F Ure, claiming (1863) that the previous few years had seen the navigation 'so far improved, by about two or three feet [more], that the small passenger steam-boats are never interrupted in their passage at low water . . . the increased depth at the same time benefiting the general trade, and the upper river can be navigated by keels during all tides'. This contrasts with the previous situation when, 'Above Newcastle the navigation was only used by keels, which were interrupted in their passage by not being able to pass over the Scotswood shoal [even] at high water of neap tides'.[89] Both below, and especially above, Newcastle Bridge the Tyne of the 1860s was increasingly being opened to

FIGURE 4.16 As there is no provision for a mast, the deck plan of the Marr model suggests it represents a keel built for the steam era. It is fitted with two pairs of heavy 'billets' (timber heads) forward for securing towing and mooring warps, whilst the central billet aft serves both for mooring and to take the warp of the next keel astern when towing in a string.

steam-towed traffic of all kinds.[90] For instance, in 1865 a witness at a local Inquiry reported that 'a keelman told me the other day that he thought they would soon have to take all their masts and sails out of the keels and tow them up', adding that half the river's keels were already towed by steam rather than navigated by oar and sail, and tugs commonly towed up to eight keels at a time (Fig. 4.16).[91]

By the mid-1870s, the predictions of the keelman quoted above had largely proved correct, although it was true that a crew's use of oars, poles and the tidal flow continued to some degree since they still had to manoeuvre into position to pick up their tow and traverse the final stretch of tideway to a moored ship or a quay after casting off. And this skill was undoubtedly continued amongst the wherrymen who succeeded them. For instance, Ouseburn-born George Cowell remembered how as a boy in the 1920s he was:

> Always fascinated by the manner in which the wherrymen handled their craft . . . for example, when towing 4 or 5 [in a string] to Hood Haggies [ropeworks] at Willington Gut from Newcastle Quay they would cast off, and using the tide and speed would sail into the Gut without any further towing, rowing etc. Excellent River Men. [92]

As to their immediate predecessors, the last generation of keelmen, there is little reason to doubt John McKay's retrospective assessment of the 1880s that: 'Wind and tide are [now] of little moment, and sails are a thing of the past. Steamboats now do the work; keels are towed to and from the ships.'[93] Nevertheless, even when steam towage had gained dominance and the upper navigation was fully opened-up by the removal of Newcastle's stone bridge – replaced by Armstrong's famous swing bridge in 1876 – steam towage's capacity as a transport agency for river-borne coal began to decline since progressively fewer numbers of (mostly smaller) ships required to be loaded from keels. By the end of the following decade, the 1890s, even the towage of the Stella Coal Company's 'genuine old, caulker built, eight chaldron keels' reported by J I Nicholson in 1889 appears to have ceased.[94]

This successful mid-nineteenth century period of steam towage had undoubtedly helped cover an otherwise serious logistical gap in the river's coal transport system but, in the broader context of the keel's history and usage, it proved to be little more than a brief and terminal one.

NOTES

1. Stammers, *Sailing Barges*, 20-21.
2. McKee, *Working Boats*, 31-32, 139-141.
3. Uglow, *Nature's Engraver*, 116-17.
4. Carmichael J W, *The Mayor's Barge on the Tyne*, c.1826-30, TWCMS: B6661.
5. TWMCS: K16524; the nature and content of this undated drawing strongly suggests that it was made by a, perhaps elderly, keelman.
6. Heslop, *Northumberland Words*, 373: 'The upper end of a keel's mast. The pronunciation is like *huun* – a long soft *u*.'
7. Charleton, *Newcastle Town*, 327.
8. Robands: literally, rope-bands. Earing: the rope tie used to fasten the top corner of a squaresail to its 'nock' (yard end).
9. Steel, *Sail-Making*, 32, 99-100, 123, 127-128, 152.
10. In *Sail-Making*, Steel remarks (1796, 15-16) that 'lightermen &c. use the following composition to colour and preserve their sails, viz. horse grease and tar, mixed to a proper consistence, and coloured with red or yellow ochre, with which, when heated, the sails are payed over'. Reporting the 300-400 boats that went out to observe the Royal Squadron pass the Tyne in 1822, a local paper pointedly remarked that 'one of the keels that went out had its sail *clean washed* [their emphasis] – It had also colors [flags] and 14 oars, the oarsmen sitting' (*Tyne Mercury* 13 August 1822).
11. *Newcastle Courant* 3 March 1753; in that same year the Quayside-based hostman's apprentice Ralph Jackson noted: 'I went . . . to get a new [keel] Saile that was in Mr Raphills garrett' (Jackson, Diary E, 28 June 1753).
12. *Newcastle Courant* 1 March 1777; Wall Knolls lay barely a furlong inland from the Newcastle Keelmen's principal riverside community, Sandgate, and after 1716 the Wallknoll Tower housed the Ship Carpenter's Company.
13. *Newcastle Courant* 16 March 1782; 'Port Sails' were spread between ship-and-shore or ship-and-keel as a measure to reduce ballast or cargo spillage and would also have been made of inferior material.
14. *Newcastle Courant* 18 October 1806.
15. *Newcastle Courant* 3 April 1830.
16. *Newcastle Journal* 27 June 1835.

17 *Newcastle Courant* 9 May 1807; auction advertisement listing four new keel sails amongst a large quantity of rope and an assortment of ships' sails.

18 *Newcastle Courant* 8 December 1781; a reward corresponding in value to some £650 today.

19 *Newcastle Courant* 10 October 1807.

20 *Tyne Mercury* 3 September 1822.

21 Heslop, 'Keels and Keelmen', 6-7; the lowered mast of a keel passing under Newcastle Bridge is well represented in J W Carmichael's painting *The Mayor's Barge on the Tyne*, c. 1826-30 (TWCMS: B6661); the mast rests aslant on the coal cargo at an angle of around 15°, with its foot forward on the head sheets.

22 Heslop, *Northumbrian Words*, 419; correspondingly, a 'keppy baa' was a purpose-made ball that was simply thrown up and re-caught in the hand (especially during counting games); it was not bounced.

23 One interpretation of Heslop's term 'shifting board' is that it was a kind of triangular hatch board that covered, and perhaps made safe, the open spencer compartment except when the mast was being raised or lowered. Brockett (1846) defined spencer as a dialect term for an inner apartment or storeroom and, significantly, noted it as 'a very old word indeed'.

24 There is no evidence of the conventional tabernacle gate shown on Viall's plan of 1942.

25 McKee, *Working Boats*, 149-51; McKee's formula of: length/55 = diameter, for an unstayed mast suggests 5½ inches would have sufficed. This is some 30% under the 8-9 inches diameter suggested by the SANT model's, but its maker may well have fashioned a particularly sturdy mast – less likely to get broken.

26 Letter, Robert Gilchrist to John Bell (surveyor), 23 July 1838, in: Bell Collection, Newcastle University Library, Special Collections, R.B. Folio 942.82 – BEL., Box 1. I am grateful to Grace McCombie for first drawing this item to my attention.

27 Lambert, *Pictures of Tyneside*, plate 25.

28 Kinney, *Skene's Elements*, 109-110; basically, the empirical method of forecasting balance relied on determining the relative positions of the centre of effort of the sail area and the centre of the underwater hull area, with balance achieved when the 'lead' of the former over the latter was 7% -16% of the waterline length. But, as calculated from the SANT model, the keel's lead was around 30%!

29 Palmer, 'Reflections on the Balance', 93.

30 Ibid., 91-92.

31 Ibid., 91-92.

32 Gilchrist to John Bell (1838).

33 Osler, *Open Boats of Shetland*, 74; describes a similar practice employed by nineteenth-century Fair Isle fishing yole crews who 'when on the wind' would position the 'rakki' (yard sling) well off centre 'thus peaking the sail and setting the main area both to leeward and aft of the [centrally positioned] mast.'

34 Nicholson, 'Keels and Keelmen'; '. . . the keelman frequently "pulled up" his rudder.'

35 Palmer, 'Reflections on Balance', 94-95.

36 Anon, *A Voyage in the Coal Trade*, 5.

37 English Reports Decisions, 1801, *Ex parte* Robert Softley, 181.

38 Knight, *The Land We Live in*, 'Tyne Bridge', 144 (opp.).

39 Palmer, *The Tyne and its Tributaries*, 'A Keel of the Old Type', 156.

40 Jackson, Diary E, 15 March 1753.

41 Gilchrist to Bell, 1838; the letter's recipient, John Bell, was one of the area's foremost land surveyors and a noted bibliophile, but the reason for his original inquiry remains unknown.

42 Powell, *Staith to Conveyor*, 38-41.

43 Gilchrist, 'Hail, Tyneside Lads', 35-39; at the time of writing this ballad in 1838 Robert Gilchrist (1797–1844) was steward of Newcastle's Incorporated Company of Sailmakers, held parochial responsibilities, and was a renowned local 'Broadside Balladeer'.

44 'Near Newcastle – Tyne –1835', watercolour by T M Richardson Snr, Guy Peppiat Fine Art (London); www.watercolourworld.com (accessed 23/04/2021).

45 Sketches by J W Carmichael, Tyne & Wear Archives and Museums, Laing Art Gallery: 'Coal Keel on the Tyne' (pencil & w/c), TWCMS K12183; '[Two] Newcastle Keels' (pencil on paper), TWCMS : B663; and '[Five] Newcastle Keels', TWCMS : B664.

46 Heslop, 'Keels and Keelmen', 12-14.

47 Anon., *Smith's Dock Journal*, 67.

48 In 1841 R.S. Newall of Dundee established a (later world famous) factory in Gateshead that advertised the manufacture of patented wire rope for 'mining, railway, ship's rigging etc.'; in 1843, for example, the innovative iron-hulled, 139-ton, Tyne-built schooner *Flash* was fitted out with 'Newall & Co.'s Patent Wire Rigging'.

49 Anon., 'The Tyne Keels', 67.

50 HANDSPEC, *anspec*, [handspike], a wooden bar used as lever to heave about [rotate] the windlass . . . particularly in merchant ships (Falconer, 1780).

51 Heslop, 'Keels and Keelmen', 13; as a young man Clasper had worked as a wherryman for a time and, tragically, his brother John had drowned only three months previously, December 1847, whilst poling a wherry at night (Clasper D, *Rowing*, 17).

52 *Newcastle Polytechnic Exhibition Catalogue, 1848,* 57; 'Entry 221, Model of a Keel, by H. Clasper' (Newcastle, 1848); its length as reported in the *Newcastle Courant*, 31 March 1848.

53 Sailmaker Robert Gilchrist was keen to get the contemporary terminology correct: 'the fore & aft Mainsail and Jib (as the latter is [commonly] called, but more properly a Foresail setting entirely in-board)'. Technically, a jib was set from a bowsprit which – for good practical reasons – a keel did not carry.

54 For example, it may have been set 'flying' hanked to its own halyard.

55 Comparison of Gilchrist's squaresail area with that derived from the SANT model (250 square feet) indicate that his calculations (225 and 252 square feet) were almost certainly made according to Steel's navy canvas width of 18 inches.

56 SPREET, the boom, a long pole used to spread or stretch the sail of a wherry (Heslop, *Northumbrian Words*, 680).

57 Gilchrist to Bell, 1838.

58 Anon., *Smith's Dock Journal*, 68.

59 The port and starboard variation (30° and 22° respectively) owing to the jib's tack eye being offset to starboard of the stem-head.

60 *Newcastle Courant* 3 March 1867; report of a fatality aboard a keel caused by a towline hook accidentally fouling the iron foresail horse.

61 For instance, a vang is evident in John Scott's painting (TWCMS G4204) of the 'half-sprit' (or 'standing gaff') rigged Tyne wherry *Jane*, dated 1850.

62 Gilchrist to Bell, 1838.

63 *Admiralty Inquiry 1849*, 78

64 Regrettably, the daily observations of James Losh for 1802-1833 (Newcastle Literary and Philosophical Society Library) were unavailable to the author owing to Covid-related constraints.

65 11½ miles out of a total distance of 15½ miles (North Shields to Stella) are oriented as follows: WNW-ESE; W-E; or WSW-ENE.

66 In 1807 the westerlies had sunk to little more than 15% of the total winds recorded, but by 1863 that proportion had more than doubled, rising to 37%.

67 This long-term summary, c.1700–1850, is drawn principally from: Lamb &Heyerdahl,

Historic Storms, Fig.7; local newspaper reports; together with: https://premium.
weatherweb.net/weather-in-history-1750-to-1799-ad (accessed 07/06/2021) https://
premium.weatherweb.net/weather-in-history-1800-to-1849-ad (accessed 07/06/2021).

68 Met Office, Digital Library and Archive, Daily Weather Reports, North Shields: DWR,
1863, 01-12.

69 The wind strengths reported at North Shields in the 1860s used Beaufort's original
scale which related not to a measured wind speed (as today) but to the speed and
behaviour of a large naval vessel under sail. However, for the purposes required, the
original and new scales may be treated as broadly the same.

70 Built 1814 by John Bowlt (boatbuilder) of Gateshead, 60 tons (shipbuilder's measurement),
14 hp engine by Crowther's Ironworks, Newcastle, driving two paddle wheels.

71 Anon. *Smith's Dock Journal*, 'Tyne Tugs', 64.

72 Appleby Miller, 'The First Tug-boat', 249ff; National Museum of Scotland, https://
www.nms.ac.uk/explore-our-collections/stories/science-and-technology/wylam-dilly/
(accessed 30/09/2021).

73 Fewster, *The Keelmen*, 163, 166.

74 *The Tyne Mercury* 24 June 1823.

75 *The Tyne Mercury* 15 July 1828; in 1849, Samuel Bell, the long-term owner of a passenger
steamboat, stated that he had 'towed ships up and down the river for 30 years', i.e. since
c.1820 (*Admiralty Inquiry* 1849, 13).

76 *The Tyne Mercury* 16 December 1828.

77 Fewster, *The Keelmen*, 177-78; below Newcastle Bridge the decline in deliveries made
by keels to ships as opposed to direct loading by spout was especially significant: at
Heaton Staith, the proportion delivered by keel fell from nearly 9% (291 keels) to barely
3% between 1837 and 1847; and at Gosforth & Coxlodge Staith, from 9% (498 keels) to
just 2% between 1841 and 1849.

78 Anon. *Smith's Dock Journal*, 'Tyne Tugs', 67.

79 *Newcastle Journal* 23 January 1847; *Newcastle Journal* 29 September 1860; *The Tyne
Mercury* 2 August 1862; *The Shields Gazette* 25 January 1866; *The Shields Gazette* 13 April
1867; *The Shields Gazette* 17 May 1867; *The Shields Gazette* 15 October 1868.

80 www.tynetugs.co.uk (accessed 14/07/2021).

81 *The Shields Gazette* 15 October 1868.

82 Photographic images from the turn-of-the-century show that the towing of multiple
rivercraft, principally lighters and wherries, continued well into the post-keel era.

83 Fewster, *The Keelmen*, 183; this tonnage was equivalent to some 3,500 deliveries by keel, averaging 9-10 trips per day throughout the year. The Walbottle fleet was large enough to warrant the colliery contracting out its maintenance annually (*The Tyne Mercury* 27 January 1855).

84 *Admiralty Report* 1849, 13.

85 Fewster, *The Keelmen*, 183 (from *Gateshead Observer* 1 April 1854).

86 *Newcastle Journal* 19 July 1867.

87 *The Shields Gazette* 17 September 1867.

88 *The Tyne Mercury* 9 August 1851; *Mallard* had been built in Shields in 1839 and was of 28 horsepower.

89 *The Shields Gazette* 10 September 1863; quoting the text of a recent lecture given at a British Association meeting (Newcastle) by J F Ure, engineer to the Tyne Improvement Commissioners.

90 This period also saw the development of wooden, purpose-built, self-propelled steam lighters for general cargo carrying. The first such 'steam screw wherry', engined by Smith of St Lawrence, was introduced in 1856 (*Newcastle Journal* 3 April 1856).

91 Newcastle Corporation, 'Report on a proposed New Bridge over the Tyne', 1865.

92 Personal communication, letter to author from George M Cowell, n.d. (c.1977).

93 McKay, 'Keels and Keelmen'.

94 Nicholson, 'Keels and Keelmen'.

PLATE 1 *The Tyne at Low Water*, unfinished watercolour, T M Richardson Snr. (1748–1848), c.1840 (© National Maritime Museum).

Lying aground at the river's edge a keel displays its bowl-shaped form. A man working from a crude floating pontoon tars the vessel's topsides and another four individuals, barely sketched in, gather on deck beside the upstanding 'jells' and 'deals'. A brig – most likely a collier – lies lightly heeled on the exposed foreshore beyond.

PLATE 2 *On the Tyne – Bill Point*, watercolour, Luke Clennell (1781–1840), c.1797-c.1804 (Tyne & Wear Archives & Museums / Bridgeman Images).

About to discharge its coals, a keel lies alongside a Low Countries schooner that has moored in the narrow, deep-water channel below the bluff at Bill point – a familiar riverside landmark and hazard. The artist employs licence in exaggerating the height of the keel's cargo, but nevertheless his atmospheric scene rings true.

A Keelman getting his orders

PLATE 3 *A Keelman Getting his Orders*, watercolour, artist unknown, c.1810 (Tyne & Wear Archives & Museums / Bridgeman Images).

A pugnacious coal fitter, with dog, giving instructions to an impassive keel skipper who is garbed in typical 'war-day duds' (working clothes), including 'his short jacket, waistcoat and knee breeches, dusky with the grime of his work . . . relieved by the bright blue of his stockings'. This humorously observed scene gives life to apprentice coal fitter, Ralph Jackson's, bare diary entry: '15th March 1753, went to order [skipper] Thompson to Winkhamlee [staith]'.

PLATE 4 *Coal Keel on The Tyne*, sketch, J W Carmichael (1799 –1868), c.1840 (Tyne & Wear Archives & Museums / Bridgeman Images).

An unhurried corner of the Keelmen's world. A spritsail-rigged keel has moored-up off a wooden jetty during a calm, its mainsail brailed up to the sprit whilst the foresail hangs loosely stowed. Nearby, an early paddle tug with characteristically tall slender funnel and plain deck, lies astern of an anchored brigantine whose forecourse is spread in bunts to air.

PLATE 5 *Two Newcastle Keels*, sketch, J W Carmichael (1799–1868), c.1840 (Tyne & Wear Archives & Museums / Bridgeman Images).

The artist depicts two fast-moving keels in boisterous conditions. The crew to the left is sailing hard upwind under full sail with the helmsman straddling the tiller and keeping a good lookout ahead. By contrast, the crew on the right have partly brailed in the mainsail and shortened the foresail, measures needed to moderate the keel's speed and maintain control as they broad reach downwind.

PLATE 6 *Newcastle from the Tyne*, watercolour, T M Richardson Snr. (1748–1848), c.1838 (Tyne & Wear Archives & Museums / Bridgeman Images).

Mid-stream, a characteristically black-sailed keel with deeply-laden hull barely visible forges its way downstream. Beyond, a large common lighter –with a keel-like rig mounted far forward – makes its approach to the bridge just upriver. Meanwhile, a hard driven, ketch-rigged passenger boat (left) heads into Newcastle Quay and a couple of cargo-filled rowing wherries busily occupy the artist's foreground.

FIVE

COAL HANDLING
AND RISK

COAL HANDLING

Over the centuries, relatively few changes occurred in the way in which coals were transferred into keels at the riverside and subsequently discharged into seagoing ships afloat. Unremitting hard labour with coal shovels remained the norm, although from the mid-eighteenth century onward the loading process was facilitated and speeded up through the adoption of gravity fed 'spouts', whilst unloading was somewhat eased through the evolution of the keel's heightened load platform (coal shuts).

Loading and Discharging

The customary work of a keel's two crewmen continued to be summed up by the formal, written term used to describe their occupation: 'common Shovel-men'.[1] The total volume of coals handled by these men is best imagined through the number of 21-ton keel loads which crews needed to transport downriver annually

(Fig. 5.1). In the sixteenth century the Tyne's keelmen probably totalled less than 2,000 trips per year and, even after the coal trade's steady expansion in the seventeenth century, the figure still aggregated barely 26,000 journeys annually. At this time, by best guess, they were carried by rather more than 400 crews averaging some 70 passages each. By comparison, the hundred years that followed saw massive growth. Shipments almost quadrupled between 1710 and 1810 and the last decades of the eighteenth century probably saw the use of keels at apogee, with some 400 to 650 keels reputedly deployed and a crew's workload probably reaching 100 or more journeys per year. Technological change during the first half of the nineteenth century subsequently caused a proportionate decline in the volumes of seagoing coal transported by keel, but this reduction was counterbalanced by an exponential growth in gross shipment volumes which, if anything, placed even greater pressure on the remaining crews to compete and perform.

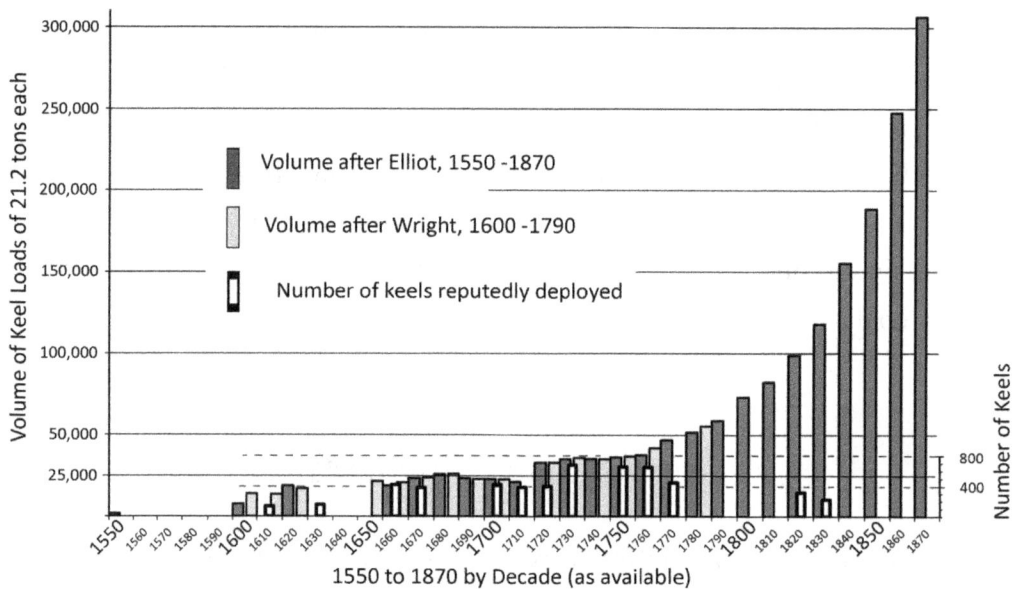

FIGURE 5.1 The growth of coal shipments from the Tyne: 1550–1880, expressed in 'keels' of 21.2 tons (Note: The surviving records are incomplete and, especially prior to 1800, are subject to interpretation).

In practical everyday terms, successive generations of shovel men thus faced a slowly evolving workplace. Prior to the late seventeenth century, the coals 'won' (mined) from a Tyneside 'seasale' colliery were 'led' (transported) overland to a low-lying stretch of tidal riverbank nearby for storage and onward transfer by keels, which were loaded by the simple expedient of plank gangways and barrows from the 'dyke' (jetty).[2] Loading keels in this way implies that the major part of the 21-ton cargo was tipped down into an open hold rather than, as was the case later, piled up on a load platform.

Coal stockpiled at riverbank depots in this way, however, was subject to deterioration through bad weather, loss by flood, and pilferage. Consequently, as the coal trade increased markedly in volume and value during the early eighteenth century, bulk storage undercover in plain, single level, roofed, riverfront buildings known as 'staiths' became the norm and, in turn, these simple covered staiths evolved into much larger two-tier structures. Upon arrival in horse-drawn 'chaldron wagons' the coals could then be shot from an upper level direct down a long, iron-plated 'shoot' or 'spout' by gravity into a waiting keel, or transferred to the building's lower, riverbank floor for temporary or long-term storage. If stored, it was eventually shifted to a wooden spout and tipped down into a keel lying alongside or, alternatively, barrowed out along a plank or gangway direct to the keel's hold.[3] Later still, 'the multiplicity of gangways required for barrow loading gave way to a handful of spouts from the upper floor'.[4] Nevertheless, the practice of loading by barrow and spout persisted at a few staiths well into the nineteenth century. There the keels were filled by keelmen using 'corf barrows [which] measured twenty to the chaldron, and had to be wheeled and tipped from a "shoot" into the keels'. (Fig. 5.2).[5]

Eventually, in the late eighteenth and early nineteenth century, the extensive, complex staith buildings largely became redundant, and were supplanted – especially below Newcastle Bridge – by a variety of newly invented mechanical 'drops' and 'cranes' for the direct loading of ships. The elevated, pier-like wooden trestles known as 'geers', which carried many of these new machines out into the

FIGURE 5.2 Top, keel being loaded by barrow at
a staith across a broad, adjustable, drawbridge-style
gangway (from Taylor, 1850); bottom, barrowloads of
coal being shot into keels down spoon-shaped wooden
shoots (from Barrass, 1766).

deep-water channel, often incorporated an auxiliary, old-style spout intended solely
for the loading of keels (Fig. 5.3).[6] Such an arrangement at the much disputed
'Wallsend Gears' was succinctly described by surveyor John Bell in 1828: 'There
is also, near the outer end of the staith, a spout for loading a keel at the same time
as the ship receives her cargo by means of the cradle [drop], the keel lying inside
in shallower water'.

In places, purpose made keel-loading 'trunk staiths', or spouts, were simply
situated at the end of crude wooden jetties (Fig. 5.4). Altogether, it seems likely that

FIGURE 5.3 A collier brig receives
its cargo via the drop (coal crane)
at the outer end of a lengthy geers;
meanwhile, a keel completes its
lading under the inner spout (coal
ticket, courtesy The Common Room,
NEIMME: 'Riddell's Wallsend Coals',
1859).

the shift towards loading keels from relatively high-level spouts promoted alterations in the keel's internal structure, changing it from a conventional cargo carrier whose coal cargo was tipped from quay level into a hold cavity, to a modified form in which it was piled high upon a raised load platform from above. Quite how quickly a keel could be loaded at a spout is not recorded. But, by way of indication, it was claimed (1824) that a 300-ton ship could be loaded at a drop in around 2½ hours, i.e. at a rate of 120 tons per hour. Consequently, with fast dispatch, a keel taking on its 21 tons at a spout might well have reckoned in tens of minutes, a fraction of a 6-hour tide.[7]

Having made the passage downriver a keel had to find the ship allotted its cargo, and that was not always an easy matter, as sympathetically recounted by Heslop:

Much difficulty was often experienced in the crowded harbour [Shields] to discover the vessel to which the coals were consigned; the classical and other outlandish names of ships adding to the perplexity of the Skipper and his bullies. Local writers have not failed to perpetuate this phase of the Keelman's occupation. A typical instance shows his vocabulary sufficiently copious in his mother tongue but quite unequal to the comprehension of "Amphitrite", the name of the vessel to which his cargo was intended.[8]

FIGURE 5.4 A keel loads from a relatively high-level spout at the end of a short, rather basic, wooden geers (coal ticket, courtesy The Common Room, NEIMME: 'Oakwellgate Colliery', 1846).

171

When taking in a lading from keels, ships tried to move into shallow water where the tide ran slowest, although large, deep draught vessels were sometimes forced to stay out in the deep-water channel facing the full force of the stream. Whatever the case, the keels generally secured alongside with chains and hooks so that they could unmoor quickly if either they or the ship got into difficulties. Most often the receiving vessel accommodated just two keels, one on each side, but vessels of large capacity – like the big mid-eighteenth century 'Collier Cats' from Whitby and Ipswich – or those that required a fast turnround might accommodate four: 'Four keels may discharge at the same time; they then lie on end fore and aft of the ship, two at each side.'(Fig. 5.5) [9]

Discharge was by means of the shovel-men's and Skipper's manual labour alone, but had its niceties, as described by Heslop:

[the keel's] cargo was transferred by "casting", an operation more or less arduous as the ship happened to be light [empty], and therefore higher above the keel, or brought down as the coal was passed inboard and the loaded trim of the ship was approached. The work of casting was facilitated by the method practiced in loading the Keel, which was, to place "shuts", or loose boards, upon the coals at intervals upon the coals as they were received from the spouts. These afforded what was called a "shut run" in casting, or a clean run for the shovel along their surfaces. [10][11]

Although a keel crew's annual bond (contract) with a keel owner invariably obliged them to 'Aid and Assist each other . . . in casting and delivering the same [coals], when two or more Keels are lying alongside of any Ship, Vessel etc.' (note [1]), there might also be a practical competitiveness in their work, as recounted by McKay (Fig. 5.6):

When a ship was empty, she stood a considerable distance out of the water. If keels were on both sides of a vessel, the keelmen worked their hardest to

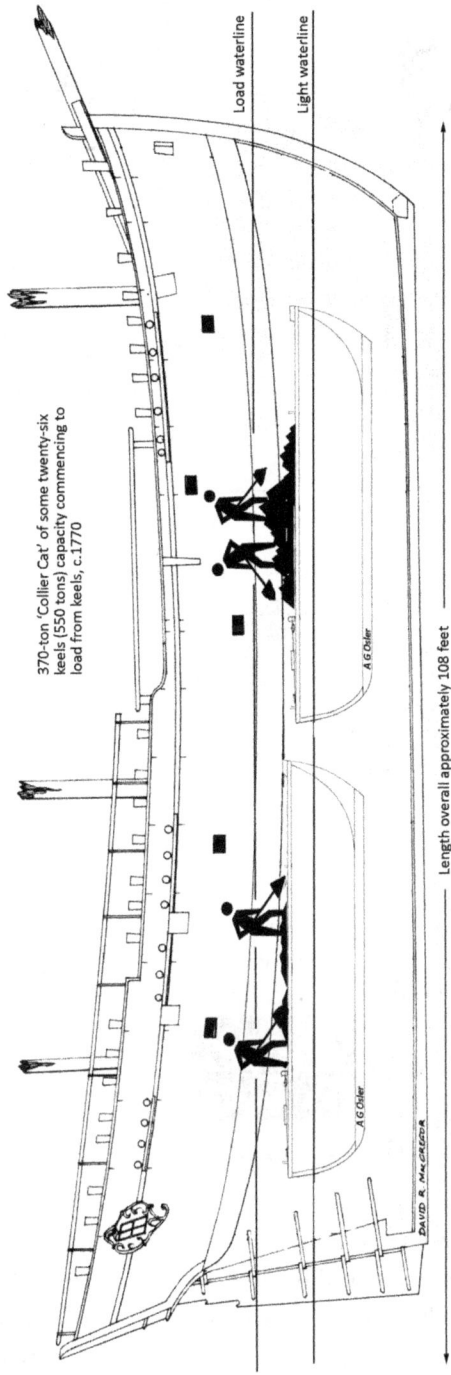

FIGURE 5.5 A typical East Coast 'Collier Cat' of the mid-1700s just beginning to load from four keels, i.e. two keels each side. With the unladen vessel still riding high, the keel crews are having to cast much of their coal to above shoulder height through the narrow – 18 inch by 10 inch – cargo ports cut in the vessel's topsides. The keels themselves are of eighteenth-century form having open, symmetric holds without raised 'shuts', and rounded, rudderless sterns ('Collier Cat', adapted from a drawing by David R MacGregor, 1980, of the *Earl of Pembroke*, built 1764, Whitby; later, HMS *Endeavour*).

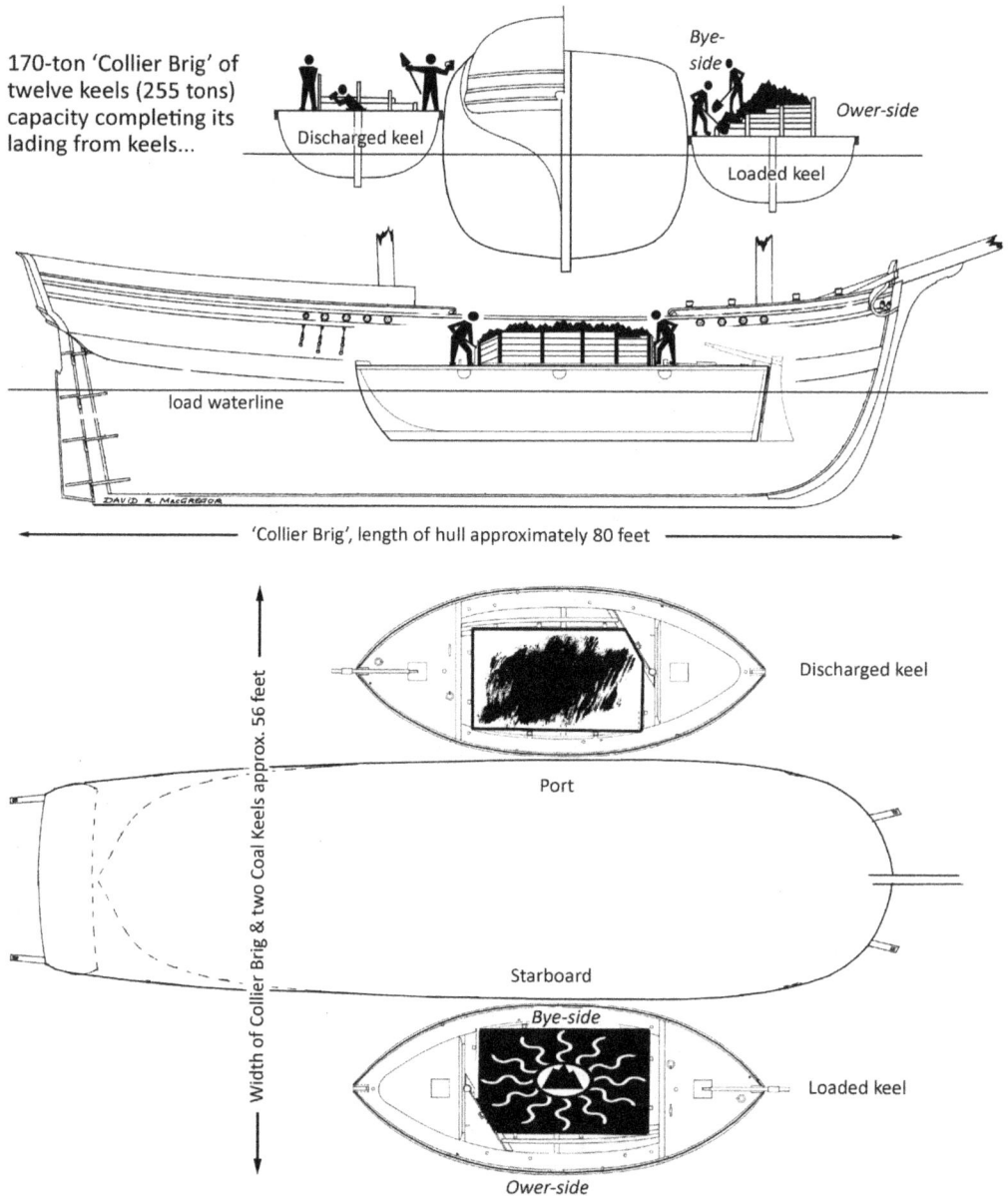

170-ton 'Collier Brig' of twelve keels (255 tons) capacity completing its lading from keels...

Bye-side

Ower-side

Discharged keel

Loaded keel

'Collier Brig', length of hull approximately 80 feet

load waterline

DAVID R. MACGREGOR

Discharged keel

Port

Width of Collier Brig & two Coal Keels approx. 56 feet

Starboard

Bye-side

Loaded keel

Ower-side

FIGURE 5.6 During the early nineteenth century, two-masted, brig- and snow-rigged vessels of 'handy size' (170- to 200-tons) were widely adopted by shipowners engaged in Newcastle's coastal coal trade. Manoeuvrable and of relatively shallow draught, they could be loaded with dispatch at drops, spouts or by keel (170-ton Collier Brig adapted from a drawing by David R MacGregor, 1980, based on plate XXII in David Steele's *Naval Architecture*, 1805).

make the vessel lean or "list" in their direction, as it saved a few inches in the "cast" or the throw of the spade. In wet weather, the "casting" of the coals was most laborious. The men always stripped off to "cast" and wore an old pair of drawers or "hoggers".[12]

In earlier times especially, coals were often cast direct onto a receiving vessel's deck through its open rails or via a removeable 'gate' in solid bulwarks. But most commonly it was shovelled through square, open 'ports' high up on the ship's side, ports which were solidly infilled and caulked before she sailed. Of chief concern to the keelmen, however, was the height to which they had to cast, and – with some justification – they regularly attempted to gain additional payments for heights above what they considered normal (Fig. 5.7).[13] In fact, the final agreement that was reached (in negotiations of 1819) stipulated that 'one shilling per keel for casting be paid by the master of the ship when the port is above five feet from the [keel's] gunwale, and one shilling more per foot for all that is above the stated height'. Additional pro rata payments were therefore to be made for all coals cast above shoulder height.

As direct loading by spout or drop became commonplace, keels were often reduced to the service of topping up a vessel's lading after she had dropped downriver to a deep-water berth. Correspondingly, 'shifting keels' might be called for to put sufficient coals aboard an un-ballasted ship for stability before she moved

FIGURE 5.7 Plying their pointed shovels, keelmen cast coals up through a collier vessel's open ports at night – their work lit by a brazier (detail from *Rivers of England* [plate I], 1827, JMW Turner engraved by Chas Turner,).

upriver to load at one of the many drops or spouts. In 1824, Henry Young (sea pilot) stated that those ships which took a full lading by keel alone were generally 'loaded in one, sometimes two days', but given urgency – and no doubt suitable reward – 'they [the fitters] can load a vessel of 300 tons by the keels in about five hours'. He further claimed that a single keel could, at best, be 'discharged in 40 minutes', although under normal circumstances, 'They sometimes take an hour, sometimes an hour and a half'. These statements suggest that a keel might achieve a discharge rate of some 14 to 21 tons per hour (4¾ to 7 tons per man), with a ship receiving its cargo at some 30 to 40 tons per hour from two keels, or twice that if four were employed. Consequently, if serviced by two keels at a time, the master of a 100-register tons coastal schooner might anticipate loading his full cargo of '8 keels', some 170 tons, in a little over four hours in favourable conditions, whilst a commonplace 'handy-sized' brig or snow employed in the Home Trade would receive its '14 keels', around 300 tons, in eight or ten hours. This last conjectural figure for everyday practice, fits well both with Henry Young's timespan of five hours for an expeditious loading and his associated comment that ships 'sometimes load within a couple of tides'.[14]

One contentious nineteenth-century issue that was never resolved when loading ships by keels was the degree to which it obstructed the waterway, for a common sailing collier with keel's alongside took up some 60 feet of the waterway's width. Indeed, it was claimed that on some occasions up to three adjacent mooring tiers in Shields Harbour might thus be occupied, creating an obstruction some 180 feet (60 yards) wide! Conversely, the keelmen railed against the reduction of navigable water caused by the unchecked extension of staiths out into the deep-water channel, a grievance which reached the courts in 1824 and 1828, but whose eventual equivocal judgement (1828) left the matter – for all practical purposes – still unresolved (Fig. 5.8). Even a subsequent regulation that required staith owners to leave a 28-foot-wide gap in their structures for the passage of keels and similar craft was, quite literally, obstructed and 'rendered of no avail by the Balance Weights [coal drop counterweights], Stay Timbers and Mooring Posts being placed in the way'.[15]

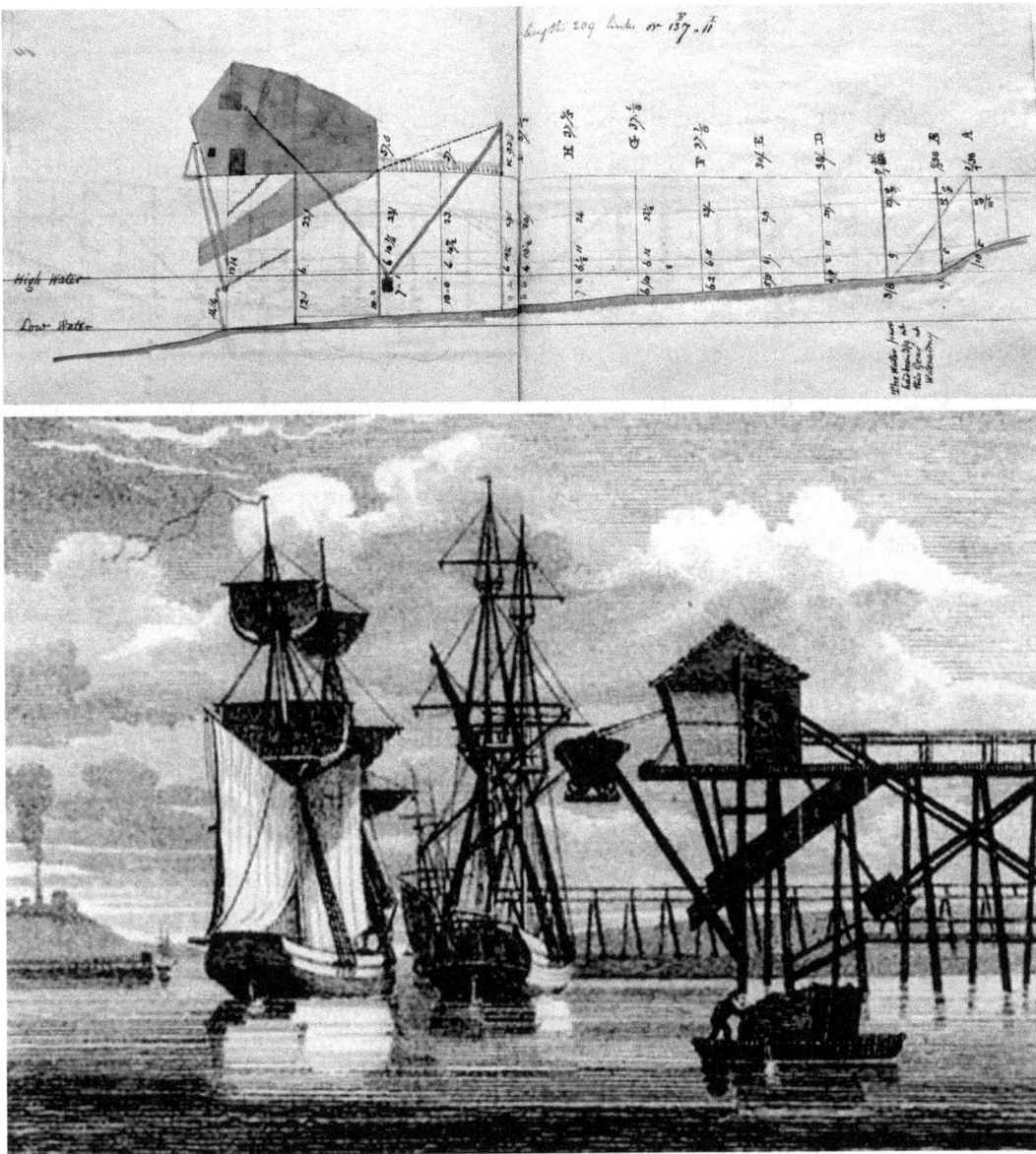

FIGURE 5.8 Top, survey of a 138-foot long staith indicating 12-foot gaps between the supporting piles and showing the location of the swinging balance weights (Wallsend Gears by J Bell); bottom, detail from a coal ticket depicting a coal drop of this kind (coal ticket, courtesy The Common Room, NEIMME: 'Heworth', n.d.; note- image reversed for visual comparison).

RISK

That the keelmen's working life was a potentially hazardous one is certain, but exactly what level of risk the keelmen ran compared to other skilled manual workers in the Coal Trade is unclear. By comparison, memories of the losses incurred amongst pitmen and seamen – through mine accidents and wreck – have become part of North-East posterity, with the causes of their occupational deaths and the resultant economic impact investigated closely by contemporaries and historians alike.[16] Underlying this disparity in perception is the fact that, by the mid-nineteenth century at least, an elementary degree of state scrutiny, regulation, and recording had been instituted for miners and seafarers, but common watermen apparently received none.

Hazards and Accidents

Although this lack of labour regulation has resulted in an absence of dedicated records and statistics for watermen, it is possible to build up a qualitative impression of the nature, number, and whereabouts of workplace casualties suffered by members of the Tyneside keelmen's community through an examination of the – admittedly imperfect – medium of local newspaper reports over a 160-year period: 1710–1870.[17] Indeed, these casualty reports occurred so frequently as to occasion the employment of stock journalistic phrases, routinely for example, 'a keelman fell out of his keel' or, in Coroner's parlance, made a 'misstep'. And though the victim was often named, they were just as readily anonymized as a 'skipper', 'keelman' or, more poignantly, 'keel boy'. For the most part these reports dealt with fatalities where, as might be anticipated, drowning was the cause of decease, although death caused by equipment failure, poor judgement, or just plain bad luck comprised around a tenth of the tragic total.[18] Severe injury alone was rarely reported but may well have lain at much the same level as these latter events, and likely resulted from similar causes. A conditional search of local newspapers discloses some 103 deaths between 1728 and 1870 and, in consequence of under-reporting, source gaps and incomplete detection, it is reasonable to estimate 1 to 1.5 fatalities for keelmen annually. That annual rate is supported by the four highest decadal totals: 1750s, 17; 1760s, 15; 1820s, 16; and 1860s (a reduced workforce), 11, and is reinforced by the fact that it is not uncommon for single years to show three news-reported drownings. Consequently, an estimate of one to three drownings per annum may be set against an average workforce size of 700 to 900 keelmen.[19] Individual incidents varied widely but may be epitomized by the very first and last newspaper accounts discovered. Firstly, the vague obscurity of the 'several keels sunk and some of their men lost' in April 1728, and lastly, the detail afforded the unfortunate William Smith who, in mid-December 1870, 'was anchoring his keel at Lemington [when] he slipped his foot and fell into the water. A boy on board rendered him every assistance by flinging ropes, but Smith was carried away by the strong tide and drowned . . . leaving a wife and a large family'.[20][21]

Random as such events may appear when considered in isolation, patterns of loss do emerge when they are collated and examined. To begin with, there is a clear bias in respect of location, with two-fifths of all the drownings that were reported by place, 69 in total, occurring between Newcastle Bridge and St Anthony's (less than 3 miles downstream). Above Newcastle Bridge, the 6-mile passage up to Stella accounted for a little more than a quarter, with the greatest frequency of incidents in the relatively short section between the bridge and Dunston. The two long, mid-river reaches between Bill Point and Jarrow (5 miles in total) saw the lowest proportion of all, barely one-eighth, whilst the comparatively short final stretch from Jarrow to Shields Harbour returned almost one-fifth. If those accidents with unreported locations, 22 in total, are then allocated pro rata to the above geographic figures, it appears that around 7-in-10 drownings occurred downstream of the bridge and 3-in-10 upstream of it. The explanation for these uneven geographic distributions is not hard to extrapolate.

The river from Newcastle Bridge to St Anthony's was not only physically constrained but carried a high level of river traffic. This busy waterway had to accommodate not only seagoing ships arriving, departing, or mooring at Newcastle Quay, but coasters and lighters which needed to moor mid-stream, together with numerous passenger- and light goods-carrying craft which (under oars, sail, or steam) hurried about their owners' cross-river and along-river business (Plate 6). Finally, there was a constant, determined stream of coal keels negotiating the bridge in both directions. The Sandgate area, next to Newcastle's flourishing Quayside, also housed the keelmen's largest riverside community, one that was replete with the 'Canhouses' (beer houses) that helped tie these men to their respective keel owners. And along the stretch of river in front of the Sandgate lay the 'Fest', the mooring place occupied by keels whose crews were either awaiting orders or engaged in domestic and recreational matters ashore, and others might lie nearby downriver at, for example, St Anne's (Fig. 5.9). As John McKay later recollected, 'It was a common occurrence, especially on a Saturday [when 'owner's wages' were paid], to see as many as twenty keels moored alongside the *Robin Hood*, a famous rendezvous for keelmen, situated in the Close, Newcastle'.

Of nearly 30 drownings reported for this stretch of the river, nearly a half involved keelmen falling from moored keels when they were boarding or disembarking, including the unfortunate Charles Boag who, on the 9th of November 1821, 'having got up out of the huddick of his keel about five o'clock . . . was distinctly heard to fall into the water . . . and call out several times for help', but was swept away by the strong ebb tide.[22] His body was found three hours later at St Peters quay, and it seems likely that he had got up in the early-morning winter dark to micturate. Drink was probably implicated in a number of these quayside drownings but, although its effects can sometimes be inferred, it is cited as a cause only once, in the case of Joseph Hardy of Whickham who 'on Friday afternoon [6 July 1832] was going on board of his keel at the High Crane [Newcastle Quay], when in a state of intoxication, he fell into the Tyne, and though not more than ten or twelve minutes in the water, his death was the consequence'.[23] In the nineteenth

FIGURE 5.9 A couple of characteristically black-hulled keels (centre left) with gear protruding over their bows lie moored by the shore at St Anne's – the home of many watermen – just downriver from Newcastle Quayside (from a late eighteenth-century painting, courtesy Michael Greatbatch).

century, resuscitation was often attempted in such cases but on Tyneside it was rarely successful, a failing which caused local humanitarian concern.

Next only to accidental falls as the cause of drowning from keels in this locality were the effects of collision, either with other vessels or fixed structures, especially the bridges (Fig. 5.10).[24] One-third of all fatalities here were attributable to collision. Typical were the fates of two mid-eighteenth-century skippers, one lost through his keel 'running rapidly against a [moored] ship . . . and in rebounding he fell overboard', and the other, George Dixon of Newcastle, was lost at three o'clock on a foggy September morning 'owing to the accidental meeting of another keel at the entrance of one of the arches of the bridge . . . The weather was so hazy, that he was not seen to fall'. Or was he on deck alone at the time?[25]

Even though the new bridge of 1781 had wider arches than the old medieval one, keels still occasionally failed to negotiate them, as in April 1792, when 'a keel by the inattention of the crew, run against one of the piers' throwing one man clean overboard and causing another serious injury; the newspaper's appended diatribe, which shamed the crew's 'indolence' and unprofessionalism appears justified, if rather emphatic.[26] Over 50 years later similar accidents still occurred, for example a boy was lost from a keel proceeding upriver when its mast hit a bridge arch 'in consequence of not having been lowered at the proper time.'[27] Saddest of all such collisions perhaps is the earliest known bridge casualty when, in November 1764, skipper Thomas Leg was 'setting' his keel through the old bridge (Fig. 5.10) at midday and 'his Set [puoy] slipped, and he fell overboard and was drowned'.[28]

FIGURE 5.10 The old medieval bridge, depicted as it was around 1700. This bridge was always a potential hazard owing to the closely spaced masonry piers that were mounted on broad, immersed, 'starlings' that terminated in sharp cutwaters.

Above the bridging point, in the 6 miles up to Stella and Lemington where keels were largely engaged in loading and passage-making, the pattern of loss was very different. Despite the well-established keelmen's communities, only one drowning from a moored keel is recorded there, together with another where the individual concerned was 'much intoxicated' and, although quickly retrieved, could not be revived by a surgeon.[29] However, most of the accidents in this locality occurred when keels were underway, including two men who were knocked overboard by their sails and, in the mid-eighteenth century, 'Thomas Pescod, of Swalwell, who 'was pushing [poling] a keel from the staith at Lemington'.[30] More unusually, two men (one with seven children) were tragically lost in the sudden sinking of a keel 'laden with ironstone' near Dunston and another, near Swalwell, was drowned after falling overboard during a quarrel, sadly 'leaving a wife and three children'.[31][32]

Below Newcastle, in the long open reaches from Bill Point to Jarrow, the situation was rather similar, with drownings largely from keels on passage. One remarkably unfortunate incident arose from a unique equipment failure when 42-year-old George Henderson 'was steering, and while in the act of pressing his foot on the spoke of the rudder [i.e. the tiller], the spoke suddenly snapped, and he was precipitated into the river'.[33] Owing to the tiller's low sweep across the after deck, keelmen frequently steered with their feet whilst standing.[34] The only recorded fall from a moored keel in this locality resulted in a macabre outcome when George Gray's body was found at low water 'with the keel resting upon it'. And, though the sinking of a fully laden keel with the loss of all its crew in the 'Long Reach' in January 1754 was a relatively rare occurrence, it was followed less than a year later by another such loss on a stormy night in Shields Harbour when 'four men and a boy . . . were all drowned before any Assistance could be had'.[35][36] A century later, in February 1863, Shields harbour also saw the wreck of the river's only iron-built keel with the loss of its father and son crew. These sinkings act as a potent reminder that the lower stretches of the river could produce conditions almost as harsh as the open sea.[37] Lastly, the fate of Peter Sinclair who 'in stepping from a keel on board the ship *Amphitrite* . . . fell into the River and was drowned', emphasizes the fact that danger lay even at the very end of a keelman's journey.[38]

Viewed on a river-wide basis, it seems that nearly half of all drownings happened whilst keels were on passage and, more unexpectedly perhaps, a quarter of them took place whilst moored up. Drownings through keels sinking accounted for almost one-fifth of the total and collisions for just one-eighth, but collisions were the only (recorded) cause of loss of life for third parties, i.e. non-keelmen. Surprisingly perhaps, adverse weather conditions were linked to relatively few drownings and were generally associated with use in wintertime or passages under sail. Examples of the former include: the 'three days violent wind' experienced in January 1756 when several keels 'drove on shore, having some of their men blown overboard and perished'; and the massive flood of January 1816 when a keel was swept down onto the new bridge to be 'laid across [an outer arch] with her head and stern resting on two of the jetties', when a man and boy drowned as onlookers attempted to heave it clear.[39] [40]

Significantly, the half-dozen reported accidents under sail all occurred following the introduction of spritsail rig, and three of them were evidently caused by a sudden gybe of that rig's heavy gear. Tragically however, one of them occurred through poor judgement or inexperience when, in September 1869:

Just before dark last evening a melancholy case of drowning occurred just above the High Level Bridge. Two young men got into a keel for the purpose of taking it down the river. Owing to the strong west wind blowing during the afternoon the water was very rough, and a strong current was running at the time. Soon after leaving the shore the young men attempted to set sail but only partially succeeded in doing so on account of the wind. No sooner did the wind fill the sail than the keel scudded along at a tremendous rate. The two men frightened [that they would hit the bridges] . . . quickly let loose the sail. One of them caught hold of the bottom of the sail and attempted to fasten it to the mast; but unfortunately just then a heavy gust of wind jerked the poor fellow out of the keel right into the current . . . His companion attempted to bring the keel to, and save his companion, but to no avail.[41]

It sounds suspiciously as though this incident occurred during an equinoctial gale, and an analysis of the relevant statistics reveals that the months of September and December had the highest drowning totals of the year: 14 drownings over the 150 years from 1720 to 1870, as against an average of 7.5. But these September and December maxima were not caused by weather alone, rather they reflected a combination of weather conditions and the intensity of coal shipping activity. As shipment levels built up slowly in the generally more clement weather from late March through to early summer, casualty levels remained well below the 7½ mean, but as activity increased in mid-summer the rate began to rise. Then, during the second shipment rush of late autumn and early winter drownings reached double the mean, with the commonplace risks presumably exacerbated by a growing combination of cold, wet, and windy weather allied to shorter daylight hours. By comparison, mid-winter's environmental risks seem to have been offset by the 30 per cent reduction in coal shipping activity during January and February, producing a level of losses only slightly above average.

Winter was also the time of greatest worry about an exceptional danger – that of keels being driven out to sea. This happened not infrequently in the eighteenth- and early-nineteenth century when ships loaded largely by keel in and around Shields Harbour, but with the advent of steamboats and the increased use of spouts and drops upriver such incidents declined. Notable eighteenth-century occurrences, however, included a 'great fresh' [flood] after a thaw in January 1741 that drove many keels to sea, and a singular loss and recovery in late January 1767 when a loaded keel broke its moorings at Lemington staith under pressure of ice and was carried 15 miles downriver and then out to sea, where it was eventually recovered by fishermen 6 miles out, still with its '20-ton load' of coals intact![42] [43] Coincidentally, just two months later, in March, a ship collided with a keel in Shields harbour leaving the latter's crew powerless through the loss of their oar and swape, whereupon they quickly cast anchor only to have the anchor cable cut by another keel. Out of control, the keel drove helplessly out to sea where its crew were lucky enough to be saved by a fishing coble, the fishermen effecting the keel's salvage too.[44] A few keelmen drifted even further than that and survived. In February 1793, a keel that was neglectfully 'without an anchor' was followed coastwise by a 'five-man [Tyne] foyboat' to Sunderland and towed in there, whilst as late as January 1816 several keels that had been driven out to sea by floodwater eventually drifted down the coast as far as Whitby, where the three men still aboard one of them were taken off.[45 46]

Reports of fatalities other than through drowning were relatively few, with deaths caused by the direct, or indirect, failure of equipment prominent among them.[47] In 1858 for instance, David Watson was fatally injured when the mast of his spritsail-rigged keel fell on him whilst it was being lowered to pass under Newcastle Bridge and, even more unluckily, James Muckle of Jarrow suffered a similar fate when the rigging of a schooner being towed upriver became entangled with his keel's mast, tearing it 'from its socket' and causing it to fall on him.[48] Indeed, the danger from falling spars was a well-recognized one; for example, in 1771 a 'young man' had been killed 'on the spot' by the fall of a squaresail yard during a collision whilst under sail.[49]

Collision was an ever-present risk and the collisions that were reported in print probably represented a mere fraction of all those that took place, chancing to reach the newspaper columns only if a fatality, damage to property, or a court case resulted – when the irresponsibility and pugnacity of keelmen often became apparent.[50] In May 1805, for example, as the Mayor of Newcastle's annual Ascension Day procession proceeded upriver from the bridge, a fatal accident occurred when one of the boats in company: 'The *Dispatch*, one of the covered boats [a 'comfortable', i.e. passenger ferry] that plies between Newcastle and Shields . . . was run down by a coal keel, the crew of which was intoxicated', causing the son of the boat's owner to be knocked overboard and drowned. The subsequent coroner's inquest pronounced a verdict of 'wilful murder' against the two Swalwell keelmen concerned.[51] But that perhaps was not the end of the affair, for during the following year's procession (August 1806) the 'Mayor's barge was run into danger by the misconduct of some keelmen, who drove their keel against it'. An attempted retaliation against Novocastrian authority seems likely, and three of the individuals in the keel concerned were quickly 'taken up' for trial at the next assizes.[52]

Most of the non-fatal collisions and accidents occasioned by keels were far more mundane, although no doubt distressful for the parties who suffered. A small representative sample gives a vivid impression of these commonplace events:

- 1768, Robt. Clark's 'fish wherry' run down but all occupants saved
- 1785, Samuel Lawton's 'Long Boat' run down en route to Shields with '8 casks of Dublin Mess Beef' – the beef was lost but Sam was saved
- 1822, a court awarded £7-15s-3d damages (plus costs) to John Oliver whose keel had been 'wilfully and maliciously' fouled by another
- and, in 1826, the master of the *Thomas and Isabel* (of Newcastle) was twice thrown in the river by recalcitrant keelmen when he tried to board and identify a keel that had run into his vessel![53]

To balance such unhappy matters, the local press also gave accounts of praiseworthy rescues and the recovery of keel property. Again, a small selection illustrates some very human stories:

- 1780, a violent October gale drove six keels with only two men aboard from the upriver staiths down to Newcastle, where 'a keelman leapt from the temporary bridge into one of the keels' and succeeded in mooring them securely
- 1784, during the 'Great Frost' many keels became 'stuck fast amongst the large bodies of ice, carried by the tide' leaving one dangerously close to being wrecked on the bridge, where its crew were 'drawn up by ropes onto the Bridge' to safety
- 1793, in late March, when the Tyne was undoubtedly icy cold, 'a keelman's wife, with a young child in her arms, in stepping from her husband's keel

into another' fell overboard into the fast-running tide 'but was happily picked up, together with the child, by the crew of a keel lying below'; it was a most remarkable escape

- 1832, three young children stood on the edge of Newcastle Quay in summertime watching a keel tack upriver, but unfortunately it missed stays and failed to go about, striking the quay wall 'with such violence' that the children were thrown into the water, only to be bravely rescued by two lads from the nearby 'Bottle Works'; even innocent land-dwellers were occasionally vulnerable to keel traffic!

- and finally, a keelman falling overboard could be lucky too; whilst poling his keel near his home at Penny Pie Stairs (South Shields) in June 1865, William Doughat fell overboard and was already sinking fast 'when a man from another keel caught hold of a few hairs of his head and succeeded in keeping him above water till he was rescued' – after a short 'sit down' in his keel he 'resumed his work'.[54]

Bizarrely, in March 1771 a keel was drifting past Bill Quay when a fox pursued by John Wardale of Bumper Hall's hunt suddenly 'leaped off the Quay and the hounds after him; and a boy likewise leaped into the river in the hopes of bringing him [the fox] out.' The hounds were quickly taken aboard the keel and the impetuous boy was saved after much difficulty but, alas, 'Renard was drowned.'[55]

NOTES

1 Bell, *Keelmen*; annual keelmen's bond (contract) between, 'Nathaniel Clayton, of Newcastle upon Tyne, Hoastman, and the Several Persons whose Names or Marks are afterwards subscribed', dated 11 January 1822.

2 The output from 'seasale' collieries was destined for shipment by sea, as distinct from that of 'landsale' collieries which was sold locally. According to Heslop (1892), the term 'dike' properly referred to the 'jetty or pier by the river side' where coals were stored, and keelmen continued to refer colloquially to their loading at the 'dyke' until the end of the keel era.

3 Barrass, 'Coal Staith', 39-41; Barrass's description and illustration features a Wearside staith, but the principle arrangements held good on the Tyne too.

4 Powell, *Staith to Conveyor*, 10-11.

5 McKay, 'Keels and Keelmen'; loading in this way entitled the keel crews to an extra beer allowance.

6 Powell, *Staith to Conveyor*, 28-29.

7 *Durham Chronicle* 14 August 1824; witness Henry Young (sea pilot) in the case of, *The King v. Russell & Others*.

8 Heslop, 'Keels and Keelmen' 49-50.

9 *Newcastle Courant* 28 August 1828; witness Henry Young (sea pilot) in the case of, *The King v. Russell & Others*.

10 Ibid., 50-51; in a later era, coal trimmers working in the holds of large ships put down steel sheets on which to slide the coals along.

11 Heslop, Northumbrian Words, 637-38.

12 McKay, 'Keels and Keelmen'.

13 Fewster, *The Keelmen*, 145-46.

14 Much of the section on discharge rates is drawn from anecdotal information in witness statements made during two court cases in 1824 and 1828: *Rex v. Russell and Others* (as reported in *The Durham Chronicle* 14 August 1824, and *Newcastle Courant* 28 August 1828).

15 Bell, *Keelmen*; manuscript note by John Bell detailing abuses of the regulation that was ordered after the 1824 trial, *Rex v. Russell and Others*, at York.

16 Even Joseph Fewster's authoritative social and labour history of the Tyneside keelmen (2011) contains no specific mention of accidents and casualties.

[17] Newspaper texts reporting keel accidents included, in order of yield: *Newcastle Courant* (1728–1831); *Newcastle Chronicle* (1765–1831); *Newcastle Journal* (1832–1863); *Tyne Mercury* (1816–1862); *Durham Chronicle* (1824–1858); *Shields Gazette* (1863–1870); *Durham County Advertiser* (1814).

[18] In a sample of just over 100 accidental workplace deaths (1728–1870) barely a dozen resulted from causes other than drowning.

[19] Fewster, *The Keelmen*, 129, 150, 181.

[20] *Newcastle Courant* 27 April 1728.

[21] *Shields Gazette* 17 December 1870.

[22] *Newcastle Courant* 10 November 1821. Wm. Daniell's (1769–1837) 'View of Newcastle upon Tyne', c.1802, finely depicts the keel moorings, river traffic, and bridge (TWAM, Laing Art Gallery).

[23] *Newcastle Journal* 7 July 1832.

[24] The arches of the old (pre-1771) bridge were some 27 feet wide at water level with piers supported on dangerous, partly awash, wooden 'starlings' of around 30 feet in width. In 1845, Newcastle's then river engineer commented, retrospectively, that 'he had not heard of keels being "wrecked" on it; but sometimes . . . they ran foul of the piers.' The maximum span of the arches of the new bridge (1781) was 57½ feet, with an air draught (i.e. arch height) of some 18 feet, considerably less than the height of a keel's masthead.

[25] *Newcastle Courant* 15 September 1770.

[26] *Newcastle Courant* 14 May 1792.

[27] *Newcastle Journal* 6 January 1849.

[28] *Newcastle Courant* 10 November 1764.

[29] *Newcastle Courant* 14 May 1796.

[30] *Newcastle Courant* 5 September 1772.

[31] *Durham Chronicle* 18 February 1826.

[32] *Newcastle Courant* 14 May 1757.

[33] *Newcastle Journal* 24 December 1842.

[34] Osler, 'Steering Norfolk Keels', in *The Wherry*, Journal of the Norfolk Wherry Trust, 2021.

[35] *Durham Advertiser* 22 October 1814.

[36] *Newcastle Courant* 29 November 1755; mid-eighteenth-century keels still had comparatively open holds that would have been more susceptible to flooding than later (effectively decked) types.

37 *Newcastle Journal* 22 September 1863.

38 *Newcastle Courant* 10 February 1798.

39 *Newcastle Courant* 24 January 1756.

40 *Tyne Mercury* 2 January 1816.

41 *Shields Gazette* 20 September 1869.

42 *Newcastle Courant* 3 January 1741.

43 *Newcastle Chronicle* 31 January 1767.

44 *Newcastle Courant* 28 March 1767.

45 *Newcastle Courant* 16 February 1793.

46 *Tyne Mercury* 2 January 1816.

47 Only one 'Act of God' has been noted. Whilst working a keel upriver past Whitehill Point with their father on the evening of a thundery day in May 1808, the two sons of James Forster of Blaydon were struck and killed by lightning (*Tyne Mercury* 10 May 1808).

48 *Shields Gazette* 17 May 1866.

49 *Newcastle Chronicle* 2 November 1771.

50 Over 30 collision reports were analysed as to cause and outcome.

51 *Newcastle Courant* 25 May 1805; *Newcastle Courant* 8 August 1805.

52 *Newcastle Courant* 16 August 1806.

53 *Newcastle Chronicle* 27 February 1768; *Newcastle Courant* 2 October 1785; *Tyne Mercury* 1 October 1822; *Tyne Mercury* 17 October 1826.

54 *Newcastle Courant* 21 October 1780; *Newcastle Courant* 3 January 1784; *Newcastle Courant* 2 March 1793; *Newcastle Chronicle* 14 July 1832; *Shields Gazette* 17 June 1865.

55 *Newcastle Courant* 16 March 1771.

SIX

A HISTORICAL
PERSPECTIVE

AS WITH MANY OF BRITAIN'S WATERCRAFT from the age of sail and oar, the keel's early history has been the subject of speculation by antiquarians and modern boat enthusiasts alike, and neither party has altogether avoided the romantic trap of assuming that the type must have a 'Viking' ancestry. This is an unwise assumption, for as Goodburn has perceptively pointed out, 'The waters around England were traversed by the craft of many non-Viking peoples such as the Frisians, Anglo-Saxons, Franks and many Celtic groups'.[1] He also emphasized that 'we know clinker-built craft were being built in England at least as early as the late 6th century AD', that is, well before the Vikings appeared. So, even if it could be established – from documentary or archaeological evidence – that the Tyne's earliest keels were clinker-built in the fashion of Viking vessels, many other factors would need to be taken into account before ascribing them a so-called Viking ancestry. Indeed, in the absence of significant archaeological boat finds, much of what may be said about the keel's origins is necessarily speculative, but at least let it be informed speculation based on informed lines of inquiry.

Three questions must lead any discussion of the keel's pre-nineteenth-century development: what, if any, changes occurred in its mode of construction; how did its rowing technology and sailing rig evolve over time; and finally, did the mid-nineteenth-century keel retain any elements of the medieval keel's fabric? None of these questions are easy to answer because textual and iconographic references to the coal keel are rare before the late eighteenth century, and even nineteenth- and early twentieth-century sources must be treated with caution. Nevertheless, it is possible to achieve a degree of synthesis through a careful combination of circumstantial evidence, inference, and comparison with British watercraft practices elsewhere. That said, the results rarely provide more than tentative working hypotheses – not verifiable conclusions.

EARLY KEELS AND THEIR ANTECEDENTS

The Construction Conundrum

When, in 1935, R S Mitcalfe wrote that keels 'were carvel or caulker built . . . [but] latterly wherries, which were not keels properly so called, were clinker built' he not only made a division resulting from differences in appearance but, quite unknowingly, raised questions which still exercise maritime archaeologists and boat historians today.[2] Briefly, Mitcalfe simply reiterated a distinction that would have been taken for granted by any nineteenth-century Tyne waterman, seaman or even lexicologist:

> CARVEL-BUILT. A vessel or boat, the planks of which are all flush and smooth, the edges laid close to each other, and caulked to make them watertight: in contradistinction to clinker-built, where they overlap each other. CLINCHER OR CLINKER BUILT. Made of clincher-work, by the planks lapping one over the other. The contrary of *carvel-work*.[3]

> CLINKER-BUILT, having the edge of each plank or layer overlapping, not butting, the next to it.[4]

That this binary distinction implied an origin in separate boat and ship building cultures was not apparent to historians in 1935, and it took several decades of incremental study by maritime scholars to formulate a coherent theory which explained the ramifications of the everyday distinction between 'carvel' and 'clinker'. Then, in the mid-1960s, Professor Olof Hasslöf introduced the terms 'shell-built' and 'skeleton-built' to describe two different sequences, or traditions, of European shipbuilding (Fig. 6.1).[5] The first – shell-built – employed overlapping planks whose edges were through-fastened to each other to produce the vessel's primary hull form, whilst the vessel's stiffening frames were inserted later. The second – skeleton-built – relied upon establishing the vessel's hull form by means of pre-fashioned transverse frames, clad in turn by flush laid planks that were fastened to the frames but not to each another.

More recently, as succinctly explained by the late Sean McGrail, these two terms and subsequent nomenclatures (e.g. Greenhill's, 'edge-joined' and 'non-edge joined') have been supplanted by the two building-sequence concepts, 'plank-first' and 'frame-first', as follows (Fig. 6.2):

'plank-first' and 'frame-first' – terms that may have originated in North America. Those terms also specify the nature of the two types of hull: either an edge-joined, planked structure subsequently further supported by framing, or as a (partial) framework to which planking was subsequently fastened. Furthermore, they indicate how the builder obtained the hull shape he wanted:

'Plank-first': by eye, based on personal experience and inherited wisdom, and possibly using some 'rules of thumb'.

'Frame-first': hull shape was encapsulated in a framework 'designed' by 'rule of thumb' or by building a small-scale model. Where frame-first techniques were used to extend an existing 'plank-first' lower hull, such design work would be minimal.[6]

FIGURE 6.1 Top, interior of a 'shell-built' Shetland leisure boat with the frames being inserted after the clinker planking is complete (Burra Isle, 1974); bottom, construction of a large 'skeleton-built' motor fishing vessel showing the framing system under erection (St. Ayles, Fife, 1973).

PLANK- FIRST with overlapping
'clinker' planks riveted together .... and the frames fitted afterwards

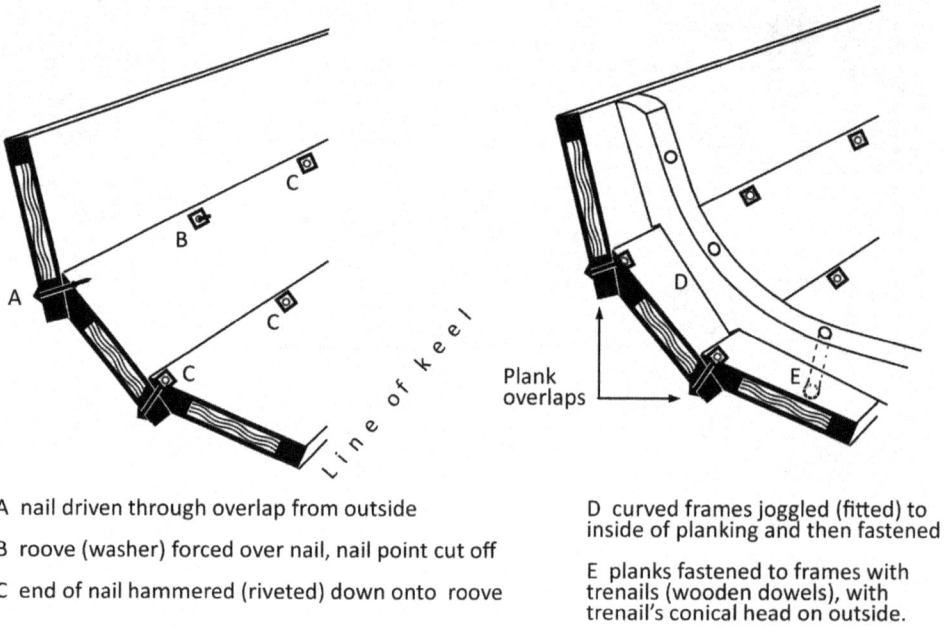

A nail driven through overlap from outside

B roove (washer) forced over nail, nail point cut off

C end of nail hammered (riveted) down onto roove

D curved frames joggled (fitted) to inside of planking and then fastened

E planks fastened to frames with trenails (wooden dowels), with trenail's conical head on outside.

Plank overlaps

Line of keel

FRAME-FIRST with frames
erected, fixed and aligned... before cladding with flush laid planking

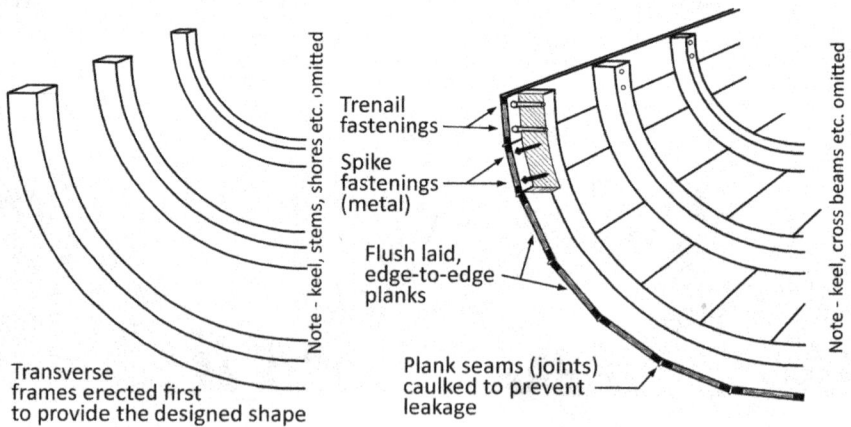

Note - keel, stems, shores etc. omitted

Transverse frames erected first to provide the designed shape

Trenail fastenings

Spike fastenings (metal)

Flush laid, edge-to-edge planks

Plank seams (joints) caulked to prevent leakage

Note - keel, cross beams etc. omitted

FIGURE 6.2 The elements of Plank-first and Frame-first construction schematically compared.

Such theoretical arguments have considerable significance with regard to the development of the Tyne keel. All printed commentaries and dependable illustrations (including models) indicate that keels were carvel planked and, consequently, were built frame-first. But it is a well-established fact that frame-first construction of Mediterranean pattern, with flush laid carvel style planking, was not adopted by British shipbuilders until the mid-fifteenth century.[7] Yet Tyne keels had existed for at least two hundred years prior to that.

Previous writers on the subject have thus stated, or implied, that they were originally clinker-built but that, at some unspecified point in time, there was a shift to carvel-planked construction. So far however, no documentary or pictorial evidence has emerged to verify the change. If such a shift could be proven and described it would constitute a singular example of a long-established, plank-first built type of vessel that was purposely transposed into a frame-first built vessel which – owing to strict statutory regulation – exhibited the same characteristics, and probably form, as its progenitor. But whatever the case, where exactly might the ancestry of the earliest recorded, thirteenth century, Tyne keels have lain?

The Precursor Problem

In the present state of historical knowledge, and that is an ever-shifting baseline, the Tyne's medieval keels will have originated in one or more of the three recognised streams of early European boat and ship building practices (Table 6.1).[89]

The oldest, termed 'Romano-Celtic', dates in Britain from around the beginning of the second century AD to the end of the fourth century, and is known chiefly through archaeological finds of river- and estuarine-based vessels. Then, after the withdrawal of Rome from Britain, the succeeding centuries saw the introduction and apparent primacy of ships and boats constructed on 'Nordic' principles. These Nordic craft comprised Anglo Saxon vessels, including the famous Sutton Hoo ship, Scandinavian (so-called 'Viking') ships and boats, and the watercraft of Britain's immediate post-Conquest, Norman era (>1066 AD). Reinforced by impressive archaeological finds, a rich narrative literature and a striking – if sometimes puzzling – iconography, this Nordic boat culture spanned over a thousand years and has become the best-known of all streams in European watercraft development. Rather less well known in the British maritime context is the milieu of the North European Cog. Chronologically, this was concurrent with the later stages of the Nordic era, whilst geographically it arose in the adjoining coastal regions to the south, focused on the seaboards of the western Baltic, Frisia and the Low Countries. Exhibiting an intriguing and perhaps historically derivative shipbuilding technology, the construction and deployment of cogs accompanied the aggressive rise of commercial seaports and increasing urbanization in the regions cited.

TABLE 6.1 A chronology of select finds and associated events from three European boat/shipbuilding traditions, together with the advent of Mediterranean carvel-style building (second to fourteenth century AD, dates in parentheses approximate).

C'y AD	Romano-Celtic	Anglo Saxon/Nordic (ceol/'keel' tradition)	North European Cog	Mediterranean 'Carvel'
2nd	Blackfriars I (mid-century)			
3rd	St Peter Port I (late-century)			
4th	County Hall Ship (290-300) Barland's Farm boat (300)	Nydam 2 (320-330)		
5th	No evidence of continuance, but some techniques possibly retained in coastal Europe			
6th				
7th		Sutton Hoo 2 (630)		Port Berteau II, 'proto-skeleton' build (600)

C'y AD	Romano-Celtic	Anglo Saxon/Nordic (ceol/'keel' tradition)	North European Cog	Mediterranean 'Carvel'
8th			Some Romano-Celtic techniques possibly retained in European coastal vessels	
9th			Appearance of 'cog' as a ship type in Denmark, Frisia, North Germany and the Low Countries.	
10th	*Graveney boat* (mid-century)			
11th		*Skuldelev 3*, 'Viking' coaster (1040)		
12th		Edward I's *Newcastle Galley & barge*	*Kollerup cog* (1150) four cogs impounded in Tyne	
13th		Median rudders on town seals *Kalmar I* (early 14th?)	median rudders, 1242 *Kolding cog* (1250)	Full 'skeleton' build practiced, fusion with northern square-rig & median rudder; Medit'n 'carracks' trade to Britain.
14th		*Gedesby* (1320)	*N243 cog* (1300) *Bremen cog* (1378-80)	'Carvels' in North Europe; several two-masted 'carracks' taken by British Crown; first British-build, c.1463.

Seamen and boatbuilders on the Tyne were definitely exposed to two of these three maritime technologies, namely, those associated with vessels of Nordic type and those practiced by builders of the North European Cog. But the degree of involvement that local people may have had with the earlier Romano-Celtic watercraft is more open to speculation for, although the existence in fourth-century,

Roman-occupied South Shields of a group of 'Tigris lightermen' – *Numerus barcariorum Tigriensium* – has been widely quoted, that unit's presence and exact function there remains unproven.[10][11] Nevertheless, in view of Rome's well attested use of waterways for commercial and military purposes in mainland Europe, it seems unlikely that the Tyne's potential for reliable, efficient water transport would be neglected.[12][13] Topographically there is nothing to suggest that – for watercraft of limited load and draught – the Tyne navigation was any more difficult during the Roman occupation period than it was over a thousand years later at the time of Ralph Gardiner's *Grievances* (1655). Correspondingly, there is solid evidence that all the propulsive and steering techniques practiced by, say, an eighteenth-century Tyne keelman, were known to fourth-century Romano-Celtic watermen too: rowing; poling; squaresail; steering by sweep oar; and the use of tide or stream.[14][15] The siting of some local Roman facilities may also be indicative, for instance the riverside fort of Segedunum lies immediately at the end of Long Reach, a location that would have provided a natural (near line-of-sight) transhipment point for lighters moving to and from the river-mouth fort and settlement at Arbeia. In fact, seagoing vessels of moderate draught could well have reached this sheltered mid-river locality, the 'North Roade', as well. Upriver, beyond that the natural channel from Segedunum to Pons Aelius (Newcastle) and the higher stretches of the river to the head of navigation around Newburn, may well have been navigable by Roman watercraft whose operational characteristics resembled those deployed elsewhere in Europe.

In a British archaeological context such conjectures (and that is all they are) immediately reference a quartet of Roman era watercraft finds from further south: the County Hall Ship, River Thames, c. AD 290–300; Blackfriars I, River Thames, mid-second century AD; St Peter Port I, Guernsey, late-third century AD; and Barland's Farm boat, Severn estuary, c. AD 300. The first three represent relatively large seagoing vessels but, like the Tyne keel, the open-hulled Barland's Farm boat was clearly built for estuarine and river transport. At 37½ feet it approached the length of a nineteenth-century keel, but with barely two-thirds of a keel's beam and a draught of merely 1 foot 9 inches, its estimated load capacity was just 6½ tons as against 21 tons.[16] With the exception of the County Hall Ship – locally built, but purely Roman in typology – these Thameside vessels are adjudged as of Romano-Celtic construction i.e. characterised by: relatively massive, closely spaced, frame timbers; sawn planks, flush laid edge-to-edge but not joined together; vegetable fibre caulking; and with planks fastened to frames by means of large 'hooked' (self-clenched) nails.[17][18] More widely, the archaeological evidence suggests that the Romano-Celtic boats of Europe's inland waterways were typically slab sided and flat bottomed, although the Barland's Farm boat possessed curved sides, providing rounded sections.

That any such ancient influences should survive on medieval Tyneside seems unlikely, but recent research has revealed the marginal possibility of an indirect path. Attention has recently been drawn not only to significant parallels between some Romano-Celtic construction techniques and those used in the building of North European cogs from the tenth to fifteenth centuries, but to the complementary fact that cogs originated in areas of north-west Europe where the Romans utilized river and estuary transport widely.[19][20] That the Tyne's mariners and artisans were familiar with the seagoing European medieval cog can be surmised from surviving records. No less than 11 storm-driven cogs were impounded at Newcastle as early as 1294 and, more congenially, many of the cog-owning ports along northern Europe's western seaboard (North Sea and Baltic) subsequently became significant trading partners of the town.[21] Undoubtedly the opportunity for maritime technological interchange – from cog to keel – existed during that period, but no firm evidence has emerged from artefacts, local vernacular techniques, terminology or documents to suggest that any transference occurred.

Sufficient twelfth-century documentary evidence does exist, however, to indicate that Nordic methods of ship and boat building were known and practiced at Newcastle in post-conquest times, and this contention is further supported by a limited array of thirteenth- and fourteenth-century archaeological finds.[22][23] But there is little insight into ongoing local medieval watercraft practices, other than a fragmentary and ambiguous terminology. As a consequence, it is impossible to know whether the roots of Newcastle's twelfth-century ship and boat building lay among the preceding Anglian or Scandinavian maritime cultures – or perhaps both. Such a distinction may have little bearing on the origin of the Tyne's earliest coal keels anyway, for the products of the two maritime cultures had much in common. Their established features included: plank-first construction on a backbone of keel and stems; strakes of riven (split, not sawn) boards; overlapping planking, edge-fastened with iron rivets; planks trenailed (dowelled) to shaped frames; double-ended hulls (i.e. pointed at both bow and stern); and, commonly, there was provision for rowing.

Terminologically, it has been postulated (by McGrail) that from the sixth century onward 'OE *ceol* was the characteristic word for a native craft in Britain' and that such Nordic types were 'subsequently known in English manuscripts as the *ceol* or "keel" . . .'.[24][25] Consequently, when the building accounts for Edward the First's 'Great Galley' at Newcastle in 1294 record the payment of one shilling to '*Edmundi Kelman* for one boat to take the said timber to the site of the Galley', and similarly, when in 1367 'xxxiii kelis et una batella [33 keels and one boat]' were used to transport coals from Winlaton to Newcastle on the order of King Edward III, it is reasonable to suppose that both Edmundi Kelman's 'Batellata' (per the original Latin account) of 1294 and the five-man, coal-carrying 'kelis' of 1367 were vessels of Nordic type.[26][27] Significantly, the latter document's anglicised rendering, 'kelis', emphasises the fact that it was spoken of as a distinct local boat type separate from other rivercraft. And that distinction was later reinforced by the term's use in royal legislation during the late fourteenth and early fifteenth centuries.[28] However, no clues have yet emerged as to the form and construction of the 20-chaldron (approximately 20-ton) coal keels thus specified.[29] Early sixteenth-century documentary evidence, however, suggests that Nordic, plank-first construction remained the norm for local rivercraft. In February 1510, for instance, the borough of Newcastle began construction of a multi-oared 'rowbarge' in order to impress the visiting Lord Chancellor that summer, and the relevant Newcastle Chamberlain's accounts clearly indicate an ongoing pattern of Nordic building with, for example, expenditure on 'reuyn burrd' (riven planking), 'seym and royff' (iron clench nails and washers) and the thrifty collection, by a 'boye', of the 'yirn' nail points cut off whilst clenching.[30]

Towards a New Technology: cost and control

Meanwhile to the south, in the Mediterranean frame-first construction with flush-laid planking had long prevailed, although by the thirteenth century many Mediterranean ships had borrowed advantageous northern features too, especially the squaresail-rig and median rudder. Known as 'carracks' and 'carvels' these early-fourteenth century hybrids regularly appeared in European waters, but it seems that no 'carvel' was actually built in Britain before the middle of the next century: Lord Howard's *Edward*, at Dunwich in 1465–1466 was the first.[31] The location may have significance for Dunwich ranked high amongst those English ports whose ships traded with Newcastle, whilst the shipowners of another prominent East Anglian trading partner, King's Lynn, possessed carvel-built vessels by the early sixteenth century. And as maritime trends are readily transmissible along sea routes, it is reasonable to infer that by the mid-sixteenth century Newcastle's mariners and artisans will have had knowledge of carvel construction, though not yet perhaps the capacity to undertake it.[32] Matters seem more certain a generation later with, for instance, a payment dated 1613 recording: 'Robart Harrigad for a carvell [repair?] 1s.'.[33] More speculatively, the formation of the Newcastle Shipwright's Company (c.1622) was in part engendered by these artisans' perceived need to protect their knowledge of – and control over – this new kind of shipbuilding work. Furthermore, as previously described (Chapter Two), this new and exclusive 'Company' claimed a monopoly over keel building and repair. This interpretation would fit well alongside recent thinking on the subject of the changeover from plank-first (clinker) to frame-first (carvel) construction in northern Europe, which emphasises the need to consider not only the technological aspects of this radical shift, but the social and economic background of the practitioners as well. In other words, even if it was a technologically and economically advantageous changeover, was it also acceptable to the individuals concerned, perhaps better reflecting their status?

By the mid-seventeenth century Newcastle's shipwrights appear to have been fully conversant with this new technique of frame-first construction. For instance, the town's leading shipbuilder, Thomas Wrangham (c.1647–1689), left to posterity his London-made 'adjustable draughting curve', an instrument useful only in the context of frame-first ship design.[34] Concurrently, a large number of Dutch-built, carvel-planked 'Vliebotes' and 'Fluyts' were incorporated into the coal-carrying fleet that worked out of the Tyne, prizes of war acquired cheaply by British owners during 20 intermittent years of conflict with the Dutch (1652–1674). Hence it is reasonable to assume that the skills necessary for building carvel-planked, rather than clinker-planked, keels were now in place in Newcastle.

The pertinent question is, was there a cogent reason to do so? And if so, who might have initiated it? Logically, the successful adoption of a new construction practice for keels will have relied upon the support of that small, exclusive, and monopolistic group of individuals that comprised Newcastle's 'Hostmen'. Also known as 'fitters' (transaction agents), their sale of a cargo of coals to a prospective buyer included the cost of transport to the latter's nominated ship in 'admeasured' keels which the Hostman either owned or procured. Financially, these fitters had the most to gain from any changes in keel construction that would lower a new keel's capital cost, running costs, or rate of depreciation. Secondarily, those shipwrights that practiced keel building might benefit too, either by way of immediate construction profits or by retaining a revenue-generating share in a keel's ownership.[35] This proposed Tyneside scenario would certainly fit a well advocated theory in which 'the adoption of an innovation is heavily influenced by the relationship between the innovators and the potential 'acceptors', and is not promoted by intrinsic technical advance alone.[36]

A New Technology: concept and realization

Despite the absence of documentary or visual evidence from the seventeenth and early eighteenth centuries, an informed guess may be made as to the key issues in the assumed changeover from clinker to carvel. In particular, it seems likely that the regulatory constraints placed on cargo weight (21 tons) will have oriented builders towards the production of standardized vessels of near identical displacement and dimension.

Though repetition of that kind can be achieved by plank-first, free-form methods, it requires the combination of an experienced 'master' boatbuilder and a small team of variously specialised journeymen – such as 'berders' (plank fitters) – to carry out the work of planking up and framing successfully. Furthermore, the master's expertise in design (i.e. hull form) is a singular skill that may entail obscure or non-codifiable concepts. And these concepts are frequently made accessible to chosen individuals only, for example, a son, or a worker with evident ability. Even then, a master's inheritor has to undergo a lengthy period of subservient practical training – Hasslöf's 'visual motor tradition'.

In comparison, once a frame-first, flush-planked design has been proven in practice, it can be recorded for future use in a variety of transmissible modes, including scaled draughts, tabulated dimensions, and full-size templates. The facility for codifying a frame-first vessel's design means that a succeeding new-build does not always require the presence of the initiating 'master', but may be carried out instead by any competent individual or successor (including former apprentices) possessing appropriate technical knowledge. Furthermore, although the amount of labour required might appear little different to that of plank-first construction, it is generally achievable using a workforce of inferior skills and experience.[37] It may be no coincidence that as frame-first construction (and repair-work) expanded on the Tyne in the seventeenth century, there were significant increases in the number of initially low-skilled, low-cost shipwright apprentices. For example, between 1630 and 1680 the annual intake of apprentices more than doubled, from under 10 entrants per year to about 20, with marked peaks in the 1650s (52 in 1656) and towards the end of the period.[38]

Partly through its capacity for ready repetition, frame-first methods tend to offer cost and production advantages when the series production of vessels is envisaged. And in the case of the keel, this propensity may have given an advantage to those Tyneside artisans who first adopted the new technique whilst disadvantaging the river's established plank-first builders. Speculatively (and that word is emphasized) this separation was expressed at a later date in an occupational division between boatbuilders who specialised in plank-first construction, and shipbuilders whose labour forces of shipwrights were engaged primarily, though not exclusively, in frame-first, flush-planked work. But whatever these shifting relationships were, it is necessary to consider the mechanisms by which the supposed shift from clinker to carvel might take place. Informed conjecture may also be made as to the potential shortcomings of plank-first, clinker-built keels, and a number of negative issues are suggested. First, the potential cost and replication concerns outlined above. Next, the susceptibility of the edges of clinker planks and their iron fastenings to impact damage and straining respectively, especially when loaded roughly with a dense mineral cargo – coal. And, linked to that, there is susceptibility to leakage through the plank 'lands' (overlaps) resulting in an ingress of 'bilgewater' that affects measured displacement and requires regular bailing out. Lastly, the fact that any increase in strength and durability sought through the adoption of thicker planks or heavier framing would negate one of a clinker-planked vessel's major assets: lightness of build. In all these instances, a frame-first, flush-planked keel would seem to offer advantages.

How might such a craft be produced in practice, especially considering that it had to retain the characteristics of its plank-first predecessor for regulatory reasons? Reference to the archaeological and ethnographic record suggests various solutions. The simplest perhaps would be by 'doubling' (cladding) an existing – maybe leaky – keel with a layer of flush-laid planking fitted on top of the original overlapping clinker planks.[39] True, this would increase the keel's flotation but, given a dense timber like oak, the resultant downward shift in the unladen waterline would be partly offset by the additional weight. Similarly, a damaged or worn-out keel might have been partially re-built by progressively stripping away the old clinker planking and replacing it with flush-laid planking fastened to the original frame timbers; with the joggled (notched) outer faces of the originals being smoothed off to receive the new carvel-style planks (Fig 6.2). Instances of this technique are affirmed by early sixteenth-century documentary records and archaeological finds elsewhere in Britain.[40] Nevertheless, the two processes outlined above represent discrete expedients, not a systematic shift in the keel's construction. For that, other approaches may be proposed.

For most of the twentieth century maritime historians considered the changeover from clinker to carvel in northern Europe (including Britain) a rather puzzling, conceptually based, total revolution in shipbuilding practice. More recently though, the expanding corpus of knowledge gained from wreck finds and a greater understanding of documentary sources suggests a more gradualist explanation. This interpretation indicates that the shift took place with much greater variability – in time, geography and technique – than previously imagined, and that the historian's search for linearity and typological evolution is not necessarily a guide to what actually occurred.[41] [42] For instance, it has now been recognized that plank-first builders do not always work entirely freeform, by eye, but may use a variety of subtle memory aids or templates (both physical and mental), especially when building large craft. As with the frame-first builder, their work may in effect employ pre-planned designs and controls (Fig. 6.3, left).[43] In like degree, it has become apparent that frame-first builders do not always set up a skeleton comprising a complete set of frames, but frequently just outline the hull-shape by erecting a few pre-planned frames and physical controls, e.g. transverse 'moulds' and longitudinal ribands, before commencing planking (Fig. 6.3, right). Indeed, Dutch carvel builders successfully employed a system in which the ship's bottom strakes – held by temporary fastenings – were laid in their entirety and dictated the vessel's form before any frames were erected.[44]

FIGURE 6.3 Left, templates used by a plank-first, Shetland boatbuilding family for stock open boats: 1, fore- and after-stems; 2, a specific plank edge; 3, part of the keel; and 4, stem 'rebates' (Burra, c.1890–1980). Right, a full-size 'mould', i.e. temporary transverse template, scaled up from a small half-block model and used in the frame-first building of a 40-foot, herring fishing boat (Lerwick, 1910).

Consequently, if keel builders successfully negotiated the clinker-to-carvel transition, it may be that they achieved it through hybrid forms rather than through a single binary shift that suddenly abandoned pure 'by eye' clinker building in favour of a fully framed-out skeleton. Hypothetically, for instance, a practical Tyneside shipwright may simply have 'lifted', i.e. measured up, a number of cross-sections from a clinker-built keel and used them to make enough control frames to produce a basic frame-first skeleton, cladding this with flush-laid planking and inserting additional strengthening frames later (as in plank-first construction). Alternatively, a more theoretically inclined shipbuilder may have used his knowledge of keels to

208

draught at a suitable scale – or alternatively 'loft' full size – a preferred midship-section, using this to develop the shapes of the remaining frames through a contemporary process such as 'whole moulding'.[45]

In overview, the lack of any overt comment or record in local sources may well indicate that the (assumed) shift from clinker- to carvel-built keels was a gradual, rather than an abrupt, process. In both a practical and economic context, it seems likely that many years or even decades would have been needed to replace the entire fleet.[46] As to the precise mechanisms of change, the possibilities are many, but without new discoveries in the written and graphic record, or the archaeological recovery of keels preserved in or beside the river Tyne, they must remain unclear.

VESTIGES, DEVELOPMENT – AND A FUTURE?

Potential Relict Features

From the eighteenth century through to the twenty-first century, writers on keels have emphasized the type's supposed antiquity, though rarely providing facts to support that. In the light of current maritime historical knowledge, however, it is possible to highlight a few details of the nineteenth-century keel that may represent Medieval, or distant Early Modern, survivals. Three such features are of especial interest: beam-end caps; an extended forefoot; and plank ends terminating on the sheerline. The circumstantial evidence that the first of these three, beam-end caps, is a potential relict medieval feature is especially strong.

1. *Beam-end Caps* – prominent on the SANT model and also appearing as distinct details on a dependable watercolour of 1835, are three pairs of semi-circular blocks located immediately below the rubbing strakes, with each pair aligned on a beam's ends.[47][48] Appearing too small and widely spaced to have served

as fenders, and without obvious function otherwise, it is suggested that they originally served as protective caps or fairings for exposed beam ends. If so, they have a clear parallel with several examples in the archaeological and iconographic record where a medieval vessel's transverse beams protruded through the hull planking and were locked in position by rebated ends, or perhaps, were cut and capped off (Fig. 6.4).[49] The archaeological evidence includes beam ends from the eleventh-century Hedeby 3 (south east Jutland) and thirteenth-century Gedesby (Falster, Denmark) wrecks, together with the thirteenth/fourteenth-century Kalmar 1 (south east Sweden) and early fifteenth-century Aber Wrac'h (Brittany) finds, all of which were vessels of 'Nordic' construction type (Fig. 6.5).[50 51 52] Similarly, the iconographic record includes depictions from a wide range of sources and dates, for example: the seals of Dunwich and Winchelsea, c.1199 and c.1310 respectively (Fig. 6.4, B); medieval manuscript illustrations, e.g., in a Bodleian Apocalypse, 1250–1260; and a unique pew end carving from King's Lynn, c.1415–1420.[53 54 55]

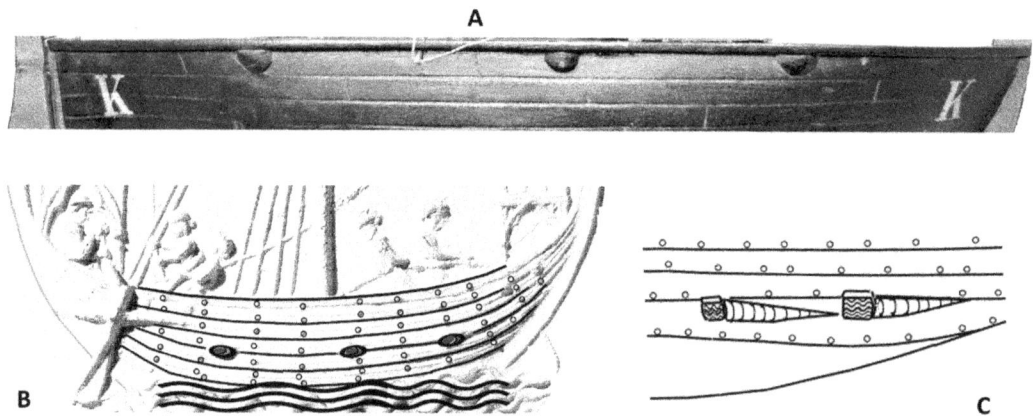

FIGURE 6.4 (A) The three prominent semi-circular blocks below the gunwale of the SANT model are coincident with the ends of the fore-, mid- and after-beams respectively. The keel's plan-form makes their primary use as fenders unlikely since only a single block would bear against a ship's side, or quay wall, at any one time; (B) three beam-end caps or fairings as depicted on a medieval ship (after the second seal of the Corporation of Winchelsea, 1274 AD); (C) two beam ends with forward-facing hemi-conical fairings on the Doel I cog, c. 1325 AD (after Vermeersch & Haneca, 2015).

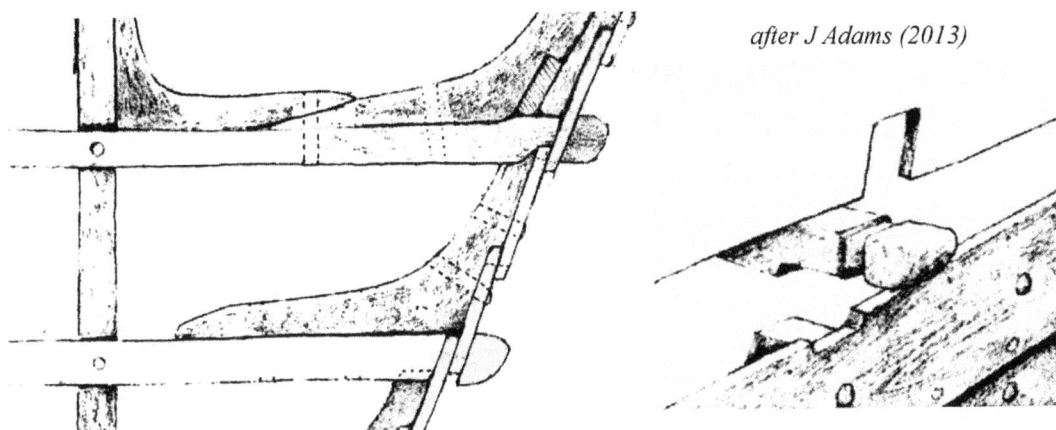

after J Adams (2013)

FIGURE 6.5 The skilfully rebated beam ends and complementary notched clinker planking of the century Kalmar I ship, Sweden, c. thirteenth to fourteenth century (courtesy, Prof. Jon Adams, 2013).

With respect to the nineteenth-century Tyne keel, if the semi-circular blocks described above are relict beam-end caps of medieval origin, then their presence was apparently a limited or merely cosmetic survival. And since most representations omit them, it suggests that the majority of nineteenth-century keels used conventional beam shelves for lodgement.

2. *Extended Forefoot*– this feature is present, to a greater or lesser degree, on three of the four surviving models and is especially pronounced on the SANT model (Fig. 6.6). Linkage to medieval practice is by inference only, but nevertheless merits discussion.

Many depictions of Scandinavian vessels of Merovingian and Viking age (c.450–1066 AD) portray extended, angular stems, a stem form that has been interpreted as a modification associated with the adoption of sail, i.e. as a measure to reduce leeway by increasing lateral plane.[56] These early, mid-fifth to mid-eighth century, angular Scandinavian stems are obviously much too removed in time and place to be considered progenitors of the extended forefoot of the nineteenth-century Tyne keel. Nevertheless, comparable forms are occasionally represented later, and the archaeological record for the period provides intriguing evidence too.

In particular, the latter embraces stem remains from Danish and Baltic underwater discoveries which include the unusually intact Kollerup Cog, c.1150 (Northern Jutland) and the Gedesby wreck, c.1320 (island of Falster), together with a number of other isolated finds (lower Baltic and Sweden).[57] [58] [59] The Kollerup and Gedesby remains were of a coastal cargo carrier and an inter-island sailing lighter respectively, and their stems may well have aided weatherliness. But several of the remaining isolated stem finds suggest they had a specialized regional function as a reinforcement for taking the ground in shallow water or as attachment points for haulage over sand bars.[60]

In Britain, the tenth-century Graveney Boat find in the Thames estuary has also been held to exhibit stem and stern posts which are 'a larger projection beyond the planking than is needed for strength but which is helpful in reducing leeway when sailing'.[61] If this interpretation is correct it provides intriguing parallels with the Tyne keel, for the Graveney boat was an open-hulled, Anglo-Saxon vessel which also functioned as a mundane estuary or coastal lighter, and has been estimated to carry some 7 tons of cargo with a crew of four.[62] Once again, no direct connection with the extended forefoot of the Tyne keel is suggested, but the provision – for whatever reason – of an extended stem is

FIGURE 6.6 The pronounced, extended forefoot of the SANT model.

clearly a feature of considerable antiquity in northern waters. Noteworthy too is the fact that a variety of vernacular sailing craft on both sides of the North Sea exhibited analogous stem features in Early Modern times, the 'Loefjbiter' (forefoot) of the Dutch, cargo-carrying, inland waters Boeier, and the deep 'fore gripe' of the seagoing Northumbrian Coble among them.[63][64] Both boeiers and cobles survived under sail into the early twentieth century.[65]

To conclude, there is no direct historical evidence which connects the extended forefoot of the nineteenth-century Tyne Keel to a particular medieval predecessor, but the archaeological and ethnographic contexts suggest that the feature related to earlier practice.

3. *Plank Ends Terminating on the Sheer* – in modern European wooden boatbuilding practice the upper strakes of a vessel's planking (both clinker and carvel) generally follow the line of the sheer, with the plank ends of each strake terminating fore and aft on the stems or transom, although various devices (e.g. 'stealers') may have to be adopted to achieve this. In the past however, and in some non-westernized cultures too, it was considered acceptable to terminate some of the lower strakes on a separately aligned strake or structure above them. Three examples suffice:

- First, the apparently near-vertical ends of planking, not mated to the stems, that are regularly depicted in medieval illustrations and which some authorities have assigned to a controversial, archaeologically undiscovered, ship type: the 'Hulc'.[66]
- Second, a variety of patterns found in Early Modern European carvel-planked practice where the plank ends of the lower strakes – especially those of bluff-bowed hulls – terminated successively on the bottom edge of a (sheerline aligned) strake or wale in the vessel's topsides (Fig. 6.7).[67][68]
- Third, as described by Greenhill, there are Indian sub-continent watercraft that display strake configurations analogous to these two European forms, and for much the same practical reasons.[69][70]

213

Indeed, the manner in which a Tyne keel's top plank may run out at the ends onto the vessel's flat sheerline suggests a similar concern with the technical problem of planking a beamy or full-ended hull (see Fig. 2.17). In practical terms this solution would enable builders to employ straighter, less costly planks for the topmost strakes, reducing the wastage associated with fashioning curved planks. Although the earlier proposition that this feature has a medieval lineage is tenable, it might equally well signify a somewhat later survival. It could be a vestige of the strake patterns found in the many carvel-planked 'fluyts' and 'cats' employed in Newcastle's coal trade during the seventeenth and eighteenth centuries (Fig. 6.7, right).

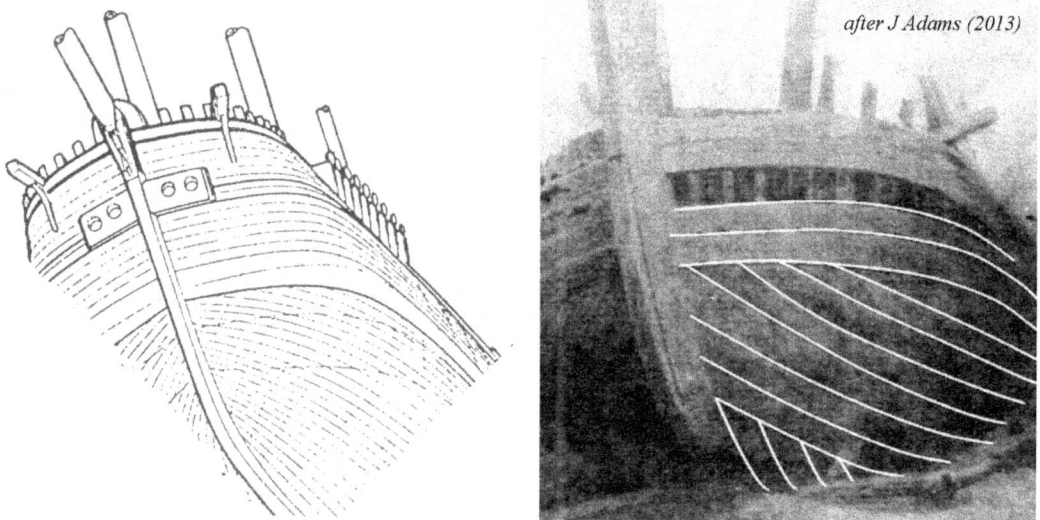

after J Adams (2013)

FIGURE 6.7 Left, the lower strakes of an eighteenth-century 'Cat' terminated at the bilge line on the thickened planking of its wale (after, af Chapman, 1768); right, typically disjunct lines of planking on the bluff-bows of a sunken fluyt, c.1650 (courtesy, Prof. Jon Adams, 2013).

Development: a provisional interpretation

Although the keel first came to prominence as a dedicated coal carrier in the late-fourteenth century, it was chronicled as a local river lighter at least one hundred years earlier than that (Table 6.2). But prior to this its functions and origins are unknown, and without new archaeological evidence this historical lacuna is likely to remain. It may be surmised, however, that as a watercraft type it lay within the Nordic tradition, constructed plank-first with overlapping (clinker) planks, and was probably of double-ended, open-hulled form, reliant on rowing, poling and the tidal flow for propulsion. Though popularly perceived as of Viking lineage, the region's pre-Conquest settlement patterns and cultural history suggest that the keel's technology more likely lay in a well-established Anglo-Saxon (perhaps even Celtic) technology, much as Fenwick explained for the tenth-century Graveney Boat:

> ... there is the clearest evidence for a clinker boat-building tradition [in Britain] established centuries before the Viking invasion ... this, originally south Scandinavian tradition, may be expected to have been influenced by local conditions and indigenous boat-building. In particular the Celtic tradition may have contributed a legacy of heavier framing[71]

Indeed, the fact that a master boatbuilder (William of Wayneflete) was drafted in from Lincolnshire to supervise building King Edward's 'Newcastle Galley' in 1294 might imply that the Tyne's indigenous constructional skills were considered inferior, or of different character, to those of the incoming Norse-oriented Normans.

By the early fifteenth century, official records show that the keel's lading had been formally set at around 20 tons, indicating that it was already close to the displacement and size of keels deployed some five hundred years later. Fourteenth- and fifteenth-century keels probably used multi-oar propulsion, maybe employing two pairs of oarsmen disposed fore and aft of a central open hold, though even that tentative interpretation relies on no more than a single, unadorned, payment account (note [27]). Whether short end decks or walkways were present is unknown but, without the latter, active poling could not have been carried out, only less efficient punting using statically positioned crew inside the vessel.[72] Equipping keels with sail may not have been considered necessary because most were deployed for short trips only, typically working between the staiths a few miles above Newcastle bridge and ships that were obliged to moor either at the customs port of Newcastle itself or, after 1384, at Gateshead opposite.

TABLE 6.2 A simplified chronology of the development of the Tyne Keel together with select Coal Trade and Regulatory factors that may have affected it.

C'yAD	Aspects of the Coal Trade	Relevant Regulations & Acts	Development of the Tyne Keel
13th m	'Sea coal' used by London ironsmiths		
l	Mining at Tynemouth, Wylam & then Elswick		Employment of a 'Kelman' recorded
14th e	1325, first overseas exports; staiths in Newcastle for Elswick's coals; pits sunk on Newcastle's 'town lands'	1356, output limit of a pit set at: 'one keel (20 chaldrons) per day'	
m	Bishop of Durham's pits active at Whickham		
l	1366, significant coal shipments recorded to Windsor Castle	1368, Edward III allows the keel's load to be deemed a taxable measure	1366, transhipment of coals via (c.20-ton) 'Kelis' recorded
l	1384, first shipments allowed direct from the Durham (south) side of the River Tyne	1384, Richard II appoints commissioners for the measurement of keels	Keels probably of clinker-planked, un-decked construction with an open hold for the coals; propulsion by conventional rowing (perhaps employing two pairs of single-manned oars) and also by poling; comparatively, a limited use of sail seems likely, but is uncertain
15th e	1402, significant coal loading from banks of river Derwent; 1404, Henry IV, statute re: Newcastle's 'hoostes'	1421, Henry V, Act limiting keels to 20 chaldrons, and each to be marked with nails	
m/l	Chaldron = c.1 ton, but subsequently increases		

C'yAD	Aspects of the Coal Trade	Relevant Regulations & Acts	Development of the Tyne Keel
16th	'Keel' measure still officially 20 chaldrons		1510, *Newcastle Rowbarge*, clinker-built
e		1530, Act conferring the conservatorship of the Tyne to Newcastle	Keel's status not recorded, but probably similar to that surmised for the late 14th and 15th centuries
m/l	Stella pit significant - pits on south side have 'exceptional advantages for loading into keels'		
l	1583, Queen Elizabeth I grants Newcastle's merchants a monopolistic 'Grand [coal] Lease'		
17th e	During reign of James I, 'sea cole' becomes an accepted domestic (not just a tradesman's) fuel. Incorporation of Hostmen	1600, Queen Elizabeth I grants the town of Newcastle an advantageous 'Great Charter'	1602, 28 Newcastle Hostmen with 85 keels 1600-1622, Shipwrights Co'y established. Overloading of keels a contentious problem
e	Significant Staiths at Newburn & Lemington 1622, restriction of coal Vend (output)		
m	1655, publication of Gardiner's *'Grievances'* 1650s, approx. 21,000 keel loads shipped p.a.	1640s, Charles I tries, unsuccessfully, to monopolise the coal revenues	1660, Tempest & Carr sell '10 keels or lighters', nature unknown
m	1642-51, Civil War; 1652-1674, three Anglo-Dutch naval wars, 'fluyts' taken as prizes		Hypothetically, the building of keels experiences a changeover from the long-established plank-first (clinker planking) methods to newly acquired frame-first (flush laid 'carvel') building techniques . . .
m/l	1683, 'Grand Lease' acquired by the Liddell family (Grand Allies); new, deeper pits open just east of Newcastle	1678, Charles II, Act for the admeasurement of keels; 1679, an amendment for measurement by bulkheads	
l	Chaldron size fixed at 53 hundredweights Keel load set at a 10 chaldrons max., in practice regularized at 8 chaldrons (21.2 tons)	1694, William & Mary, Act for admeasurement of keels; 1695, commission to 'measure & mark' keels	

TABLE 6.2 *continued*

C'yAD	Aspects of the Coal Trade	Relevant Regulations & Acts	Development of the Tyne Keel
18th e	Main coal production still upriver of the bridge First 'fire [steam pumping] engine' used in a pit	1711, 'The Regulation' (Cotesworth family), 'scriven' (mark) their own keels	First sales of keels advertised by newspaper 1725, 55 'keel rooms' on banks of River Derwent
e/m	1730s, approx. 36,000 keel loads shipped p.a. Substantial usage of large collier 'cats' (like Cook's *Endeavour*) in the coastal coal trade	1738, George II, Act re: admeasuring & marking of keels	Keels double-ended & part-decked at least, but retain open unprotected hold for coals, propulsion by: a triple-manned oar plus steering sweep; poles; and a squaresail set on a mast amidships
l	1790s, approx. 56,000 keel loads shipped p.a.	1775, George III, Act re: measurement of wagons, keels etc (1791, supplementary)	As for early 18th century, but now with full after- and fore-decks, the latter
19th e	1800, Benwell, Chapman's direct ship-loading 'drop' unsuccessful 1812, Thompson's innovative 'drop' at Urpeth succeeds and becomes widely adopted Coastal and export shipments largely by 100 to 300-ton sailing vessels 1820s, approx. 99,000 keel loads shipped p.a. 1820-30, low-powered river steamers common	1815, George III, Act to prevent fraud in 'overloading keels etc'	an inclined plane to aid rowing; sweep steering retained; mast moved to fore-beam. Transition from sweep steering to a median rudder mounted on a straight sternpost; elevation of hold floor so as to carry coals on, rather than within, the vessel; use of cargo containment structures and introduction of the asymmetric hold; ancillary sails added to the squaresail; towage by steamers commences

C'yAD	Aspects of the Coal Trade	Relevant Regulations & Acts	Development of the Tyne Keel
e/m	Steady increase in proportion of coals loaded by direct mechanical means		1830s, introduction by the upriver keel owners of lowering masts with spritsail sloop rig
m	Introduction of steam colliers and improved coal-loading equipment 1850s, approx. 190,000 keel loads shipped p.a. 1863, long-established use of the 'keel' as a measure of shipment is replaced by the ton		Sprit-rig becomes universal and squaresail-rigged keels decline; iconic three-man oar falls into disuse as paired-oars with outriggers adopted; steam towage by dedicated 'tugs' more widely practiced, some keels largely dumb lighters
l	1870s, equivalent of 306,000 keel loads of coals shipped p.a., but only a very small proportion of these are transhipped by keel		Few active coal keels remain, many are re-purposed (e.g. as ferry landing stages or general-purpose lighters), the remainder are disposed of

Notes to column one: e, early-century; m, mid-century; l, late-century.

Subsequently, between the late fifteenth and late seventeenth century, there were few significant changes in either the keel's area of operation, its everyday usage, or the commercial framework of the Tyne's seaborne coal trade, although volumes did increase from less than 2,000 keel loads per annum to over 20,000. As a result of this stasis, it seems probable that the keel remained little altered. But, as conjectured previously, towards the end of this period a significant change may have occurred in its appearance and nature owing to the introduction of frame-first, instead of plank-first, building methods. Objectively considered, however, no textual, iconographic, or archaeological evidence has yet emerged which serves as a convincing guide to the keel's form and development between the early fifteenth century and the mid-seventeenth century, at which time pictorial clues start to appear. For example, close scrutiny of the 'Maps and Plans' which accompanied various editions of Ralph Gardiner's *England's Grievance Discovered* (1655), provides an enigmatic picture.[73]Although London-based Wenceslaus Hollar's illustrations of the countless ships on this work's principal map of the Tyne are meticulous, his rivercraft appear as tiny, stylized four-oared boats akin to the rowing craft portrayed in his panoramic *Long View of London from Bankside*, 1647. However, Gardiner's 'Shipwright's Map' (maker unknown) includes two pointedly ovoid craft with long paired sweeps worked well forward, and these appear more credible as Tyne keels, especially since other elements of the map evidence local knowledge. Nevertheless, these vessels also resemble rivercraft depicted on the Thames both in Hollar's *View* and Ogilby & Morgan's new map of London, 1676 (Fig. 6.8).

Most notable of these early visual representations, however, are the panoramic views of Newcastle published in 1723 and 1745 by the famed Buck brothers, their

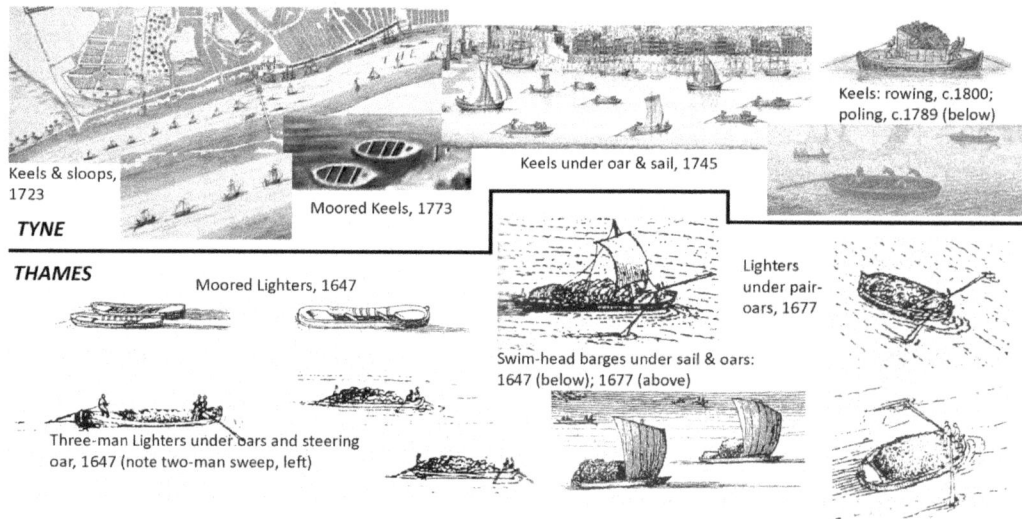

FIGURE 6.8 Some pre-nineteenth century cargo carrying craft of the rivers Tyne and Thames compared (Thames craft from: Hollar's *Long View of London*, 1647; and Ogilby & Morgan's *Map of London*, 1676/7. As reproduced by Marsden, 1996).

FIGURE 6.9 Detail from the Buck brothers *Prospect of Newcastle from the South East*, 1745, showing keels working their way downriver under oar, steering swape and squaresail (courtesy, Society of Antiquaries of Newcastle upon Tyne and NC).

Prospect of the latter year depicting no less than 19 keels on the river: three under sail and the rest under oars.[74][75] Although these keels are rather simplistically portrayed, they nevertheless present consistent, recognisable characteristics: double-ended hulls with raked stem and stern posts; a plain open cargo hold amidships; coals heaped little higher than the sheerline; a single mast stepped amidships (not forward); a squaresail with its yard supported by lifts; oar propulsion by triple-manned sweep (deployed port or starboard); a long stern oar for steering under both oar and sail; and the skipper apparently standing within an un-decked after compartment (Fig. 6.9). The Bucks' work also apparently shaped the records of the Swedish traveller R R Angerstein, although the keels sketched in his *Journal* (1753–55) add a characteristically Scandinavian sheerline.

Bucks' several representations of the keel's iconic, triple-manned sweep effectively allot it a pre-eighteenth century origin, although the reasons for this unusual technical development are a matter of speculation. Practically, the sweep's usage parallels that on contemporary Thames lighters, and transfer through the coal trade milieu cannot be ruled out (Fig. 6.8). On the other hand, it may well have been a response to two very local factors. Firstly, with a four-man crew comprising

221

a skipper, two men, and a boy, a keel was overmanned compared with most river lighters, where just two grown men would have sufficed. However, the keel's two adult crew were not employed primarily as sailors, but as labourers (shovelmen) who expedited loading and discharge. Secondly, the keel's coal-laden hold restricted the room available for rowers amidships, and so the bow compartment (or deck) became the most effective rowing station. Since the double-manning of large sweeps was not uncommon, especially in the navy, the emulation of this by using the keel's spare manpower might well explain the development of the keel's unusual rowing configuration.

By the last quarter of the eighteenth century, it appears that the largely open-hulled keels portrayed by the Bucks had been supplanted by craft fitted with a definite afterdeck and foredeck linked by bow-to-stern walkways (see Fig. 2.8).[76][77] The Rev. John Brand's detailed and definitive bookplate of 1789, which also depicts the keel's uniquely ramped fore-decking, confirms these changes.[78] Similarly, it suggests that the long stern oar was still the recognized method of steering, although worked from a low, narrow platform immediately in front of the afterdeck, not from the afterdeck itself. The following decades saw significant changes which included the fitting of stern rudders, the transfer of the mast position from amidships to the fore beam and, apparently, a marked uplift of the hold floor (Table 6.2). Unfortunately, the evidence for these changes is too fragmentary for a verifiable sequence and chronology to be established, and some changes were perhaps interrelated. It goes without saying that these changes would have enhanced passage times and speed of coal handling, positive attributes during a period of expansion and competition. The fitting of stern rudders does not seem to have commenced until the turn of the nineteenth century when there was clearly a transitional phase of usage.[79] And it may well be that the adoption of the rudder and its straight sternpost were related to an increased emphasis on the use of sail and, perhaps, to the positioning of the mast further forward. Indeed, the rather awkward location of the mast in the spencer, and the reliance on brute strength to step and lower it, has something of a makeshift feel.

More widely, questions remain over the origins and development of the keel's distinctive rig. The surviving early nineteenth-century evidence indicates that masts with unusual open dumb sheaves at the masthead (see Figs. 4.3 and 4.4) were universally fitted to keels, and perhaps largely to keels alone.[80] Nevertheless, the squaresail itself bore close resemblance to historic forms used on single-masted craft. But, as previously noted, some eighteenth-century illustrations portray common stump-headed masts with lifts to support the sailyard (e.g. Bucks' *Prospect*, 1745; and Hutton's map, 1770). Thus the question remains, was the nineteenth-century keel's squaresail rig the product of long held conservatism or a relatively recent development? The former seems most likely but as yet there is no definitive proof.

Meanwhile, an outstanding question also remains over the keel's curious masthead, for which only two similar configurations have been observed. The first dates from Imperial Roman times and the other from the Early Modern era. A significant number of Roman mosaics and wall paintings from around the Mediterranean include depictions of ships or boats with a distinctive 'hooked' masthead which supports either a Mediterranean square-sail or a lateen sail (Fig. 6.10, right).[81] The majority of these representations date from the fifth to the eighth centuries, but the earliest appear during the High Roman Empire and the last of them, which show post-Roman Mediterranean vessels, date from the eleventh to fifteenth centuries. Visually, the type of masthead shown resembles that of the keel and, when used with a squaresail, appears to have performed much the same function although fitted – so far as is known – with enclosed sheaves (pulleys) rather than an open dumb sheave.[82] And as with the keel, masts of this kind had no forestay for support, only paired side-stays (shrouds).

Hypothetically, Roman ships or boats fitted with such masts may have been used on the Tyne, but even if that were the case the adoption and transmission of a specific feature like this through the succeeding centuries of Nordic dominated boat technology seems unlikely. Conversely, in Mediterranean maritime cultures the hooked masthead was retained by some watercraft users and survived well into medieval times. Consequently, it seems that although the Roman iconographic resemblances are conspicuous the functional parallels are less so, and transmission through the Tyne's successor boat cultures of the Anglo-Saxon and Nordic periods would appear improbable.

The second analogous candidate is post-Medieval and European. A common seventeenth-century Dutch shipboard practice involved running the heavy 'ties' (ropes) used to hoist a ship's lower yard over, rather than through, the lower mast cap, the figuratively named *ezel's-hoofd* (ass-head): 'which in longitudinal section was

FIGURE 6.10 Representations of hook-shaped mastheads.

Left: rig and masthead of Tyne keel from a sketch by surveyor John Bell, c.1828 (TWCMS: 2018.614). Top right: Mediterranean masthead, late-12th/early 13th century (after a mosaic, St. Castrense, Duomo of Monreale, Palermo).

Right centre: masthead, yard, and furled sail of a Roman open boat from the 'High Roman' period (after an intaglio, Museum of Berlin, ref: fr.884.2013; also figured in Basch, 1987, 474, No. 1092)

Right lower: rig and mainmast of a two-masted Roman ship, c.200 AD (after a stone relief carving from Utica, British Museum; also figured in Casson, 114).

shaped like a question mark laid on its side. Scores were cut in the after part of the cap which acted like a dumb sheave'.[83] The physical and functional parallels with the keel's masthead seem obvious, but the scaling down of this equipment (from ship to boat size) is harder to account for. Undoubtedly some, perhaps many, of the numerous captured Dutch fluyts which worked in the seventeenth century coal trade will have been equipped with the *ezel's-hoofd*, and the Tyne's earlier seaborne connections with the Low Countries are well recorded. Consequently, transfer through imitation of Dutch techniques cannot be ruled out and, in that context, it is noticeable that some local maritime dialect terms are derived from Dutch.[84]

Three familiar features of keels are more clearly of local origin however: a raised load platform, known as the 'shuts'; the associated coal containment structures; and an asymmetric hold plan. These all appear to have been home-grown innovations of the early nineteenth century, probably developed as competitive measures to aid loading – especially by shoot – and to facilitate discharge alongside ships. Again, as with the rudder, their introduction seems to have occurred within a relatively short space of time, the old-style keels with open holds of the Reverend John Brand's late eighteenth-century era being replaced in the first quarter of the nineteenth century by upgraded keels with much-improved provisions for load carrying and handling. And, as previously described (Chapters 3 and 4), the second quarter of the nineteenth century saw even more radical changes to the keel's sailing rig and rowing configuration, modifications which were introduced in an attempt to extend the keel's viability in an age of unprecedented technical and economic change (Table 6.2).

In the past, the Tyne coal keel has largely been portrayed as an icon of antiquity. But in reality, during the last 50 or so years of its existence keel builders and owners collectively made the effort to modernize it by changing what, in many respects, was a medieval watercraft into one that might meet the much greater water transport demands of the industrial Victorian age. That their endeavours eventually failed may, in essence, be attributed to three factors: the persistence of a fifteenth-century regulatory regime that restricted the keel's capacity to 21 tons; the widespread adoption of steam propulsion afloat; and an overwhelming increase in demand for seaborne coal.

A Keel For The Twenty-First Century?

Two potential futures suggest themselves for the Tyne coal keel: archaeological and experimental, with the one ideally preceding the other. One can only but float some brief thoughts on these matters.

To date, the recovery of even fragmentary historic boat or ship remains has been low in the North East of England. But, despite the adverse effect on the preservation environment caused by extensive dredging works, river improvements and shoreside industrialization along the Tyne, the sheer volume of watercraft historically deployed suggests that – as on the Thames – the potential for archaeological discoveries exists.[85] A formal assessment of riparian areas where past usage and hydrology seem favourable for keel preservation would certainly be a useful archaeological project. The recent discovery (2013) of the keel- and ship-serving Willington Waggonway of 1785 highlights the fact that preservation may occur even in the most industrialized of riverside areas.[86]

Correspondingly, the idea of constructing and trialling informed reconstructions or – where the evidence allows – working replicas of historic boats and ships is an old one, dating back in Europe to the late nineteenth century at least. Modern examples of such reconstructions, like the trireme *Olympias* and the large Viking longship *Sea Stallion of Glendalough*, are often spectacular and are extraordinarily well researched, constructed, and evaluated.[87] As yet, such reconstructions – rather than restorations – have been rare in the North East, but again the potential is there. That the iconic Tyne Coal Keel has not been taken up for such a purpose is understandable, for accessible knowledge regarding its form, structure, and operation has been hard to come by, whilst the investment in cash and manpower needed for such a build would be considerable, and the vessel's operation afloat would pose health and safety challenges. Nevertheless, the potential publicity generated by recreating a living, working image of 'The Keel Row' would be significant, and the yield for the historian substantial. Furthermore, the author is in no doubt that Tyneside has the naval architectural expertise, wooden boatbuilding skills, enthusiasm, and community spirit required to carry out such a reconstruction.

Perhaps the keel might have a future after all . . .

NOTES

1 Goodburn, 'An Archaeology of Early English Boatbuilding', 3/1/4.

2 Mitcalfe, 'The History of', 4.

3 Smyth, *Sailor's Word-Book*, 168, 191.

4 Heslop, *Northumberland Words* v.I, 164; interestingly, Heslop recorded no local dialect word for carvel planking.

5 Hasslöf, 'Wrecks, archives and living traditions', 162-78.

6 McGrail, 'Hornell, Hasslöf', 385.

7 Friel I, *The Good Ship*, 158-59, 166-67.

8 McGrail, *Boats of the World*, 196-247.

9 Adams, *A Maritime Archaeology*, 53-72.

10 Martin, 'Water Transport', 27 (note [108]).

11 Shotter, 'Numeri Barcariorum', 206-09.

12 Roberts, 'Between the brine and', 21-22.

13 Gerrard & Ridgeway, 'A Romano-British Graffito of a Ship', 246; this suggests that Medway-produced pottery (BB2) found at Hadrian's Wall arrived in the Tyne by sea where, in this author's opinion, a degree of onward carriage by lighter (kinder than cart) is plausible.

14 McGrail, *Boats of the World*, 205-07; archaeological finds include evidence for rowing (Mainz), poling (walkway, Pommeroeul boat 4; metal terminals for poles, Rhine), and mast steps for sail (Thames).

15 Casson, *Ships and Seafaring*, 130-33.

16 McGrail, *Boats of the World*, 197-201.

17 Marsden, *First to twelfth centuries AD*.

18 Marsden, *Twelfth to seventeenth centuries AD*, 219.

19 Adams, *A Maritime Archaeology*, 56-57, 59-60.

20 McGrail, *Boats of the World*, 232-39.

21 O'Brien, 'North Sea Trade', 39-42.

22 O'Brien et al, *The Origins of*, 78-85, 104-06.

23 Walton, 'Caulking, Textiles and Cordage', 167-76.

24 Thier, *Old English Sea Terms*, 43-45.

25 McGrail, *Boats of the World*, 223.

26 Whitwell & Johnson, 'The Newcastle Galley', 166.

[27] Taylor, *Archaeology of the Coal Trade*, 12, 61-63; also: Galloway, 'Earliest records', 31.

[28] Galloway, *Annals of Coal Mining*, 47-48, 50, 68-69; to summarize: c.1368, Edward III tacitly acknowledged the use of Newcastle's local measure, the keel, in place of the national standard measure; 1384, to prevent evasions caused by the employment of oversize keels, Richard II appointed commissioners for the supervision and measurement of keels; 1421, following further such evasions, an Act of Parliament was passed enabling King Henry V's Commissioners to measure and 'sign' (mark with nails) keels at 20 chaldrons capacity.

[29] Galloway, *Annals of Coal Mining*, 68-69; between the early fourteenth and mid-eighteenth centuries the size of the Newcastle chaldron was slyly increased two-and-a-half fold, but as the capacity of the 'admeasured' keels remained constant, their loads finally comprised 8, rather than 20, chaldrons.

[30] Fraser, *Accounts of the Chamberlains*, 133-43, 146-54, 164.

[31] Friel I, *The Good Ship*, 170-80.

[32] Whiting's proposition (1936) that the Newcastle Galley of 1294 may have been carvel built is clearly untenable. But his suggestion that, as the galley's accounts make no mention of 'rof' (rooves), the planking's 'seam nails' were through-driven and simply hooked over on the inside does merit consideration. Friel (1986) however, concluded that the same omission in the Lyme Galley's accounts resulted from the fact that the comparatively expensive 'seam nails' included the cost of the rooves too.

[33] Brand, *History and Antiquities*, 343.

[34] Osler & Barrow, *Tall Ships Two Rivers*, 25.

[35] It seems unlikely that, as annually hired labourers of (reputedly) conservative bent, the keelmen would have played a significant role, although maybe eventually welcoming any improvements in performance or ease of maintenance that resulted from change.

[36] Adams, *A Maritime Archaeology*, 194.

[37] Friel I, *The Good Ship*, 66-67; however, Friel questions whether when building large ships, any anticipated labour cost savings were realised in practice.

[38] Clarke, *Building Ships*, 6, 14-16.

[39] Hasslöf, 'Main Principles', 58.

[40] Adams, *A Maritime Archaeology*, 56-57.

[41] Ibid., 53-72.

[42] McGrail, *Boats of the World*, 385-86.

[43] Osler & Barrow, *Tall Ships Two Rivers*, 5, features photographs of the 50-foot Tyne Wherry *Elswick No.2* (the last of her kind, 1932) under construction using typical plank-first, clinker-planking techniques, but employing a midships check mould – probably derived from her predecessor, *Elswick No.1* – to control the lower hull form. Empirically, the author's fieldwork in Shetland and on the North East coast has revealed evidence of the use of mental plans, memorised measurements, and physical templates amongst plank-first boatbuilders, a subject analysed in depth in the historical context by Dhoop & Ollaberia, 2015.

[44] McGrail, *Boats of the World*, 385-86.

[45] Barker, 'Whole Moulding', 33-36, 51; although not formally described in England until the early eighteenth century, this design technique (which uses simple quadrantal arcs) is believed to have originated much earlier, perhaps in the fifteenth century. Initially at least, it was considered best suited to the production of boats rather than ships.

[46] Wright, Thesis, 52-53; citing Moller (1933), Wright states that mid-seventeenth century keels had a longevity of 'fifty or sixty years', their working lives prolonged by being laid up ashore – like most seagoing colliers – in winter. At a nominal 5% p.a. wastage rate, it would have taken 15-20 years to replace even half the fleet of 320 keels quantified by Gardiner in 1655.

[47] TWAM H5541, general arrangement plan (see chapter 2).

[48] T M Richardson, *Near Newcastle upon Tyne*, 1835, Guy Peppiatt Fine Art.

[49] Rieth, 'From Wreck to Shipyard', Fig. 5; this records an analogous through-beam structure much earlier, in a river Charente (France) lighter of the seventh century, Port Berteau II.

[50] McGrail, *Boats of the World*, 230-32.

[51] Adams, *A Maritime Archaeology*, 60-61.

[52] Hutchinson, *Medieval Ships*, 31-34.

[53] Ibid., 48, 154.

[54] Bodleian Library, MS. Auct.D.4.17, Folio 002v. (St John being exiled to Patmos); also reproduced in Friel, *The Good Ship*, 92-93.

[55] Hutchinson, *Medieval Ships*, 58.

[56] Heide & Planke, 'Viking Ships with Angular Stems', 8-18, 21.

[57] McGrail, *Boats of the World*, 231-237.

[58] Andersen, *Kollerupkoggen*, 28-29, 36.

[59] Zwick, 'Conceptual Evolution', 50-52.

[60] Bill, 'Shallow-water craft', 90-98.

[61] Gifford & Gifford, *Anglo-Saxon Sailing Ships*, 4.

[62] Fenwick, *The Graveney Boat,* 295-306.

[63] Kampen, *De Zeilsport*, 47.

[64] Salmon, *The Coble*, 8-9.

[65] The Mariner's Museum, *A Dictionary of Watercraft*, 81, 142-43.

[66] Greenhill, *Archaeology of Boats and Ships*, 250-53.

[67] Chapman, *Architectura navalis mercatoria*, Pl. XVII.

[68] Adams, *A Maritime Archaeology*, 107, Fig. 5.14.

[69] Greenhill, *Archaeology of the Boat*, 87.

[70] Greenhill, *The Archaeology of Boats and Ships*, 254.

[71] Fenwick, *The Graveney Boat,* 249.

[72] This punting technique is clearly illustrated in a twelfth century drawing of St Guthlac travelling by boat to 'Croyland' in the Fens (BL, Harley Roll MS Y6, roundel 4: reproduced in Flatman, *Ships & Shipping*, 55, Fig. 22).

[73] Spence C J, 'Notes on the Plates and Maps of the Tyne'; earlier depictions, including the multi-oared boats naively depicted – with great similarity – on both Speed's plan of Newcastle (1610) and the Duke of Northumberland's 'Mappe of Tinemouthshire' (c.1600) are best interpreted as official row-barges, rather than workaday keels. These were most likely inserted with symbolic reference to the recent grant of Newcastle's 'Great Charter' by Queen Elizabeth I (1600) or the incorporation of its Company of Hostmen.

[74] Buck & Buck, 'Prospect of Newcastle'; whilst it is generally acknowledged that the panorama's depiction of Newcastle's built environment is extremely accurate (e.g. Pears, 2016) that of the keels and their crews depicted seems less so, and particular concern must be raised over the role of the Bucks' London-based engravers. The limning of these provincial vessels appears repetitive and simplistic, perhaps knowingly so. It bears no comparison with the almost photographic quality of the sundry depictions of Thames rivercraft seen in their five-sheet panorama of London published just four years later, 1749, or even the shipping shown in their comparable views of, for example, Bristol, Liverpool, and Yarmouth.

[75] Corbridge's map of Newcastle, 1723, offers nothing by way of comparison. It includes just two miniscule keels, one under sail and the other apparently being rowed and poled whilst approaching the bridge. Oddly however, half-a-dozen square- or gaff-rigged sloops with bowsprits are prominently depicted.

76   Alnwick Castle Collections, 03396/10: John Bell, 'View on the Tyne from the Cinder Kiln to Dent's Hole', 1773; this clearly shows afterdecks (with huddock hatches) and walkways on two moored keels, but the nature of their foredecks is unclear.

77   Walpoole, *New British Traveller*, Plate: 'View of Newcastle in Northumberland'.

78   Brand, *History and Antiquities*, Vol. 1, facing 48, Plate: 'View of the Ruins of the Bridge . . .'

79   For example, Taylor's plate of 1858 titled "The Old Coal Staith – Keels Loading" apparently depicts a scene from the early 1800s, portraying: an empty keel propelled by three-man sweep and guided by steering oar alone; a fully laden keel under sail which is managed by rudder; and a third, being loaded alongside, with rudder raised and stowed on the afterdeck.

80   There seems to be no analogous masthead in either the British or Scandinavian medieval record. Personal communications: Ian Friel (Littlehampton, February 25, 2022); Morten Gotche (Roskilde Museum, September 7, 2021). However, the dialect term 'heughn' for the keel's masthead is an Old English/Old Norse cognate (Thier, *Old English Sea Terms*, 74–75).

81   Beltrame & Medas, 'The Hook-Shaped Masthead', 34-40.

82   Ibid., 40-42.

83   Harland, *Seamanship*, 26-27, Figure 3.

84   Griffiths, *Fishing and Folk*, 214-15, 83; Brand (1789) even attributed the term 'huddock' to the Dutch.

85   Goodburn, Thesis, 4/1 to 4/14.

86   Bell ed., *Setting the Standard*.

87   Nielsen, 'Sea Stallion from Glendalough', 59-82.

CONCLUDING
A 'LANG TIDE'

FROM THE OUTSET OF THEIR recorded history in the fourteenth century, the Tyne's indigenous watercraft known as 'keels' serviced what came to be regarded as Britain's largest waterborne domestic trade: the Coal Trade. Collectively, keel owners maintained fleet levels of several hundred units, numbers that were largely unknown in standardized river craft elsewhere. From the early fifteenth century onward keel users were obliged to operate under inflexible national regulation; added to this, Tyneside's social and commercial structures remained remarkably conservative over the succeeding five centuries. These two factors, one national and the other local, resulted in keel owners and operators perpetuating technologies and practices abandoned in the drive for greater efficiency in cargo-carrying craft on British rivers elsewhere.

In essence, the keel retained a late medieval character well into the industrial nineteenth century, and the material that has been presented in this book may serve to remind scholarly historians of the need to appraise practical – as well as social and economic – constraints (e.g. how often did a west wind blow?), and the benefits that governed and rewarded river transport systems in the age of sail and oar. Correspondingly, the descriptive information provided here provides a baseline against which archaeologists may assess future riparian discoveries of cargo-carrying watercraft, not only on the Tyne but on the Thames, Severn, Humber, and other (un-canalised) rivers in the centuries specified.

The real surprise is that the Tyne keel's importance as a national transport mechanism and as a carrier of maritime cultural practices has lain unrecognized for so long, obscured by the unflattering reports of early commentators, a nostalgic secondary literature, the north–south divide, its abrupt demise, and a continued emphasis by historians on the struggles of its labour force, the Keelmen, rather than on the artefact itself. One always hesitates in applying a superlative in a historical context but, in respect of the Tyne coal keel, the author feels justified in using the word 'unique'. A number of its surviving features and associated practices – from the oddly formed masthead to the distinctive mode of rowing, the 'Keel Row' – warrant the term alone. And, in an economic context, no other single defined class of British rivercraft achieved such a key position in a vital transport chain or, debatably, enjoyed dominance over such a long period in the trade it served.

SOURCES

PRINTED AND TEXTUAL

Adams J, *A Maritime Archaeology of Ships: Innovation and Social Change in Medieval and Early Modern Europe* (Oxford, 2013).

Admiralty Inquiry Under the Preliminary Inquiries Act, 11 & 12 Vict., cap. 129. River Tyne Conservancy Bill (1849).

Admiralty Reports under the Preliminary Inquiries Act, Report of the Admiralty, under the Act 11 & 12 Vict.c.129, 27 – River Tyne Conservancy (1849).

A.H., note in, *The Mariner's Mirror*, Vol 1, No.1, 1911, 93.

Andersen K, *Kollerupkoggen* (Museet for Thy og Vester Hansherred, 1983).

Angerstein R R, *R R Angerstein's Illustrated Travel Diary, 1753–1755* (Science Museum, 2001).

Anon., *Description of A Voyage in the Coal Trade* (Newcastle, c.1840).

Anon., 'The Tyne Keels', in *Smith's Dock Journal*, April 1932.

Archer M, *A Sketch of the history of the coal trade of Northumberland and Durham* (London, 1897).

Barker R, 'Whole-Moulding: a Preliminary Study of Early English and Other Sources', in Nowacki H & Valleriani, (eds), *Shipbuilding Practice and Ship Design Methods From the Renaissance to the 18th Century, A Workshop Report* (Berlin, 2003, Max Planck Institute for the History of Science,).

Barrass E, 'Description of a Coal Staith', in *The London Magazine or Gentleman's Monthly Intelligencer*, vol. XXXV, 1766.

Basch L, *Le Musée Imaginaire de la Marine Antique* (Athens, 1987).

Bell D (ed), *Setting the Standard: research reports on the Willington Waggonway of 1785* (Newcastle, 2018).

Bell J, 'Keelmen', manuscript and ephemera, c.1828, TWCMS 2018.614.

Bell J, 'Collections Relative to the River Tyne its Trade and the Conservancy, Vols. 1 & 2' (NCL, L942.8, T987B).

Beltrame C & Medas S, 'The Hook-Shaped Masthead in Late Antiquity and the Early Middle Ages', *International Journal of Nautical Archaeology*, 50:1, 2021, 34-44.

Bill J, 'Shallow-water craft from medieval Denmark: the identification of a specialized regional ship type', in *Archaeonautica*, v.14, 1998, 87-102.

Bourne, Rev. H, *The History of Newcastle Upon Tyne* (Newcastle, 1736).

Brand J, *The History and Antiquities of the Town of Newcastle Upon Tyne*, 2 vols (London, 1789).

Casson L, *Ships and Seafaring in ancient times* (Austin, Texas, 1994).

Calver E K, *The Conservation and Improvement of Tidal Rivers, Considered Principally With Reference To Their Tidal And Fluvial Power* (London, 1853).

Chapman F H af, *Architectura navalis mercatoria* (Stockholm, 1768).

Charleton R J, *Newcastle Town*, 4th ed. (London, 1885; reprint, 1978).

Clarke J F, *Building Ships on the North East Coast, Part 1, c.1640-1914* (Newcastle, 1997).

Clasper D, *Rowing: A way of life – The Claspers of Tyneside* (Gateshead, 2003).

Clavering E & Rounding A, 'A Map and its Meaning', in *Archaeologia Aeliana*, Fifth Series, v. XL, 2011, 243-58.

Christensen A E, 'Boatbuilding Tools and the Process of Learning', in Hassløf O (ed), *Ships and Shipyards, Sailors and Fishermen* (Copenhagen, 1972), 235-59.

Colman Green G, *The Norfolk Wherry: Its Construction, Evolution and History* (Norwich, 1953).

Dawkes G, Goodburn D & Rogers P R, 'Lightening the Load: Five 19th-century Lighters at Earith on the River Thames UK', *International Journal of Nautical Archaeology*, 38:1, 2009, 71-89.

Dhoop T & Olaberria J, 'Practical Knowledge in the Viking Age: the use of mental templates in clinker shipbuilding', *International Journal of Nautical Archaeology*, 44:1, 2015, 95-110.

Dodd R, *Report on the First Part of the Line of Inland Navigation from the East to the West Sea* (Newcastle, 1795).

Dunn M, *A treatise on the winning and working of collieries* etc., 2nd edition (Newcastle, 1852).

Elliot N R, 'Tyneside, a Study in the Development of an Industrial Seaport, Part I and Part II', *Tijdschrift voor Economische en Sociale Geografie*, No. 53 (1962).

Elliot N R, 'A Geographical Analysis of the Tyne Coal Trade', *Tijdschrift voor Economische en Sociale Geografie*, No. 59 (1968).

Falconer W, *An Universal Dictionary of the Marine* (London, 1780).

Fenwick V (ed), *The Graveney Boat: a Tenth-Century Find from Kent*, British Archaeological Report, 53 (Oxford, 1978).

Fewster J M, 'The Keelmen of Tyneside in the Eighteenth Century', *Durham University Journal*, new series, XIX (1957-58), 24-33, 66-75, 111-23.

Fewster J M, 'The Last Struggles of the Tyneside Keelmen', *Durham University Journal*, new series, XXIV (1962-63), 5-15.

Fewster J M, *The Keelmen of Tyneside: Labour Organisation and Conflict in the North-East Coal Industry, 1600-1830* (Woodbridge, 2011).

Flatman J., *Ships & Shipping in Medieval Manuscripts* (London, 2009).

Fraser C (ed), *The Accounts of the Chamberlains of Newcastle upon Tyne 1508–1513* (Newcastle, 1987).

Friel I, 'The Building of the Lyme Galley, 1294-1296', in *Proceedings of the Dorset Natural History and Archaeological Society*, v.108, 1986, 41-44.

Friel I, *The Good Ship: Ships and Shipbuilding Technology in England 1200 – 1520* (London, 1995).

Fuller M, *How a Norfolk Wherry was built, circa 1825* (privately published, 2007).

Galloway R L, *Annals of Coal Mining and the Coal Trade* (London, 1898).

Galloway R L, 'An Account of some of the Earliest Records connected with the Working of Coal on the Banks of the River Tyne', *Archaeologia Aeliana*, Series Two, v.8, 1880, 167-210.

Gardiner R, *England's Grievance Discovered in Relation to the Coal Trade*, 1655 (reprinted by Akenhead, Newcastle, 1796).

Gerrard J & Ridgeway V, 'A Romano-British Graffito from Gillingham, Kent, UK', in *International Journal of Nautical Archaeology*, 48:1, 2019, 245-46.

Gifford E & Gifford J, *Anglo-Saxon Sailing Ships* (Woodbridge, 1997).

Gilchrist P, '"Hail Tyneside Lads in Collier Fleets": Song Culture, Sailing and Sailors in North-East England', in *Port Towns and Urban Cultures: International Histories of the Waterfront c.1700-2000* (Basingstoke, 2016).

Greenhill B (ed), *Archaeology of the Boat* (London, 1976).

Greenhill B, *The Archaeology of Boats and Ships, an Introduction* (London, 1995).

Griffiths B, compiler, *Fishing and Folk: Life and Dialect on the North Sea Coast* (Newcastle, 2008).

Hails W A, *An Enquiry Concerning the Invention of the Life Boat* (Gateshead, 1806).

Harland J, *Seamanship in the Age of Sail* (London, 1987).

Harris H, *Under Oars: Reminiscences of a Thames Lighterman, 1894-1909* (Stepney, London, 1978).

Hasslöf O, 'Wrecks, archives and living traditions', in *The Mariner's Mirror*, Vol 49, 1963, 162-78.

Hasslöf O, 'Main Principles in the Technology of Ship-Building', in Hasslöf O, Henningsen H & Christensen A E (eds), *Ships and Shipyards, Sailors and Fishermen* (Copenhagen, 1972).

Heide E & Planke T, 'Viking Ships with Angular Stems: Did the Old Norse term *beit* refer to early sailing ships?', in *The Mariner's Mirror*, Vol 105, No.1, 2019, 8-24.

Heslop R O, *Northumberland Words, A Glossary of Words Used in Northumberland and on Tyneside*, vols. I & II (London, 1892).

Heslop R O, 'Pitmen and Keelmen', Annual Address to the Northumbrian Small Pipes Society, Newcastle Weekly Chronicle, c.1894, NCL News cuttings, v.2, 104-05.

Heslop R O, 'Notes on Keels', manuscript c.1902, TWAM F7675.

Heslop R O, 'Keels and Keelmen', manuscript c.1902, NEIMME, D/71.

Holland J, *The History and Description of Fossil Fuel, The Collieries, and Coal Trade of Great Britain* (London, 1835; 2nd edition, London, 1841).

Hutchinson G, *Medieval Ships and Shipping* (Leicester, 1994).

Hutchinson W, *The History and Antiquities of the County Palatine of Durham*, in three volumes (Durham, 1785–94).

Kampen H C A van, *De Zeilsport* (Amsterdam, 1924).

Kinney F S, *Skene's Elements of Yacht Design* (London, 1962).

Knight C, *The Land We Live in: A Pictorial and Literary Sketch-book of the British Empire, Vol. III* (London, 1847–50).

Lamb H. & Fryendahl K., *Historic Storms of the North Sea, British Isles and North West Europe* (Cambridge, 1991).

Lambert M & Collard W, *Pictures of Tyneside: Circa 1830* (Newcastle, new edition 1969).

Leifchild J R, *Our Coal and Our Coal Pits* (2nd edition, London, 1856).

Losh J., 'Meteorological Observations made by James Losh, at Jesmond Grove in the years 1802-1833' (manuscript, 1802–33, Literary and Philosophical Society of Newcastle upon Tyne).

Lethbridge T, *Boats and boatmen* (London, 1952).

Lyons M, 'Keepin' ahad o' wor tung: Richard Oliver Heslop', in *The Northumbrian*, Issue No. 184, October/November 2021.

Malster R, *Wherries and Waterways* (revised edition, Lavenham, 1986).

Manders F W D, *A History of Gateshead* (Gateshead, 1973).

Mackenzie E, *Descriptive and Historical Account of the Town and County of Newcastle Upon Tyne*, vols. I & II (1st edition, Newcastle upon Tyne, 1827)

Mannering J (ed), *The Chatham Directory of Inshore Craft* (London, 1997).

Marsden P, *Ships of the Port of London: First to twelfth centuries AD* (London, 1994).

Marsden P, *Ships of the Port of London: Twelfth to seventeenth centuries AD* (London, 1996).

Martin C, 'Water Transport and the Roman Occupation of North Britain', in Smout (ed), *Scotland and the Sea* (Edinburgh, 1992).

Maxwell J I, *The Spirit of Marine Law, or, Compendium of the Statutes* (London, 1808).

McGrail S, *Boats of the World from the Stone Age to Medieval Times* (Oxford, 2001).

McGrail S, 'Hornell, Hasslöf and Boatbuilding Sequences', in *International Journal of Nautical Archaeology*, 44:2, 2015, 382-87.

McKay J, 'Keels and Keelmen', *Newcastle Weekly Chronicle Supplement*, 9 November 1889.

McKee E, *The Gokstad Faering, Part II, The Sea Trials* (London, 1974).

McKee E, *Working Boats of Britain: Their Shape and Purpose* (London, 1983)

Mitcalfe W S, 'The History of the Keelmen and Their Strike in 1822', in *Archaeologia Aeliana*, Fourth Series, v.14, 1935, 1-16.

Newcastle Corporation, *Papers Relating to the River Tyne, ordered to be printed by the River Committee, March, 1836* (Newcastle, 1836).

Nicholson J I, 'Keels and Keelmen', *Newcastle Weekly Chronicle Supplement*, 9 November 1889.

Nielsen S, 'The Sea Stallion from Glendalough, Reconstructing a Viking Age Longship', in Staubermann K (ed), *Reconstructions* (National Museums Scotland, 2011).

O'Brien C, Brown L, Dixon S, & Nicholson R, *The Origins of the Newcastle Quayside*, Society of Antiquaries of Newcastle upon Tyne, Monograph Series 3 (Newcastle, 1988).

O'Brien C, 'Newcastle upon Tyne and its North Sea Trade', in *Proceedings of the Third International Conference on Waterfront Archaeology, 1988, Council for British Archaeology Report 74* (London, 1991).

Osler A G, *Open Boats of Shetland: South Mainland and Fair Isle* (London, 1983; reprinted Lerwick, 2016).

Osler A, 'Tyneside's Riverworkers: Occupational Dress', *Costume* (Journal of the Costume Society of Great Britain), 18, 1984, 74-82.

Osler A, *Mr Greathead's Lifeboats* (Newcastle, 1990).

Osler A, 'Goods to Newcastle: An Unexplored Coastal Shipping Network, 1800–1840', in *Archaeologia Aeliana*, Fifth Series, Vol. 46, 2017, 157-79.

Osler A & Barrow A, *Tall Ships Two Rivers: Six Centuries of Sail on the rivers Tyne and Wear* (Newcastle, 1993).

Palmer C, 'Reflections on the Balance of Traditional Sailing Vessels', in *The International Journal of Nautical Archaeology*, 38.1, 2009, 90-96.

Palmer C, 'Windward Sailing Capabilities of Ancient Vessels', in *The International Journal of Nautical Archaeology*, 38.2, 2009, 314-30.

Palmer W J, *The Tyne and its Tributaries* (London, 1882).

Pears R, 'An Observation Tower on Newcastle Quayside', in *Archaeologia Aeliana*, Fifth Series, v.45, 2016, 145-148.

Pennant T, *A Tour In Scotland 1769* (London, 1771).

Pennant T, *A Tour In Scotland and Voyage to the Hebrides, Part 2* (London, 1776).

Phillips-Birt D, *Sailing Yacht Design* (London, 1966).

Pomey P, 'Principals and Methods of Construction in Ancient Naval Architecture', in Hocker F M & Ward C A (eds), *The Philosophy of Shipbuilding: conceptual approaches to the study of wooden ships* (Texas A & M University, 2004).

Powell T, *Staith to Conveyor: An Illustrated History of Coal Shipping Machinery* (Houghton-le-Spring, 2000).

Rennison R W, 'The Great Inundation of 1771 and the Rebuilding of the North-East's Bridges', in *Archaeologia Aeliana*, Fifth Series, v. XXIX, 2009, 269-91.

Richardson W, *History of the Parish of Wallsend* (Wallsend, 1923).

Rieth E, 'From Wreck to Shipyard: The Example of the Port Berteau II Wreck, France (VIIth century AD)', in Nowacki H & Valleriani (eds), *Shipbuilding Practice and Ship Design Methods From the Renaissance to the 18th Century, A Workshop Report* (Berlin, 2003, Max Planck Institute for the History of Science).

Roberts B K, 'Between the brine and the high ground: The Roots of Northumbria', in Colls R (ed), *Northumbria: History and Identity* (Stroud, 2007).

Rowe D J, 'The Decline of the Tyneside Keelmen in the Nineteenth Century', in *Northern History*, IV (1969), 111-31.

Rowe D J, *The Records of the Company of Shipwrights of Newcastle upon Tyne 1622-1967, Vols I, II* (Newcastle, Surtees Society, 1971).

Salmon J, *The Coble* (South Shields, 1885).

Schofield F, *Humber Keels and Keelmen* (Lavenham, 1988).

Shotter D C A, 'Numeri Barcariorum: A Note on RIB 601', in *Britannia*, v.4, 1973, 206-09.

Shrimpton C, *A History of Alnwick Parks and Pleasure Grounds* (Derby, 2006).

Skelton L J, *Tyne after Tyne: An Environmental History of a River's Battle for Protection, 1529-2015* (Newcastle, 2017).

Smiles S, *Lives of the Engineers. The Locomotive. George and Robert Stephenson* (London, 1879).

Smyth W H, *The Sailor's Word-Book*, reprint 1991 (London, 1867).

Spence C J, 'Notes on the Plates and Maps of the Tyne in Gardner's [sic] *England's Grievance Discovered* of 1655', in *Archaeologia Aeliana*, Second Series, v.13, 1889, 285-305.

Stammers M, *Sailing Barges of the British Isles* (Stroud, 2008).

Steel D, *The Art of Sail-Making* (London, 1796).

Steel D, *The Art of Making Masts, Yards, Gaffs, Booms, Blocks and Oars* (London, 1797).

Steel D, *The Elements and Practice of Naval Architecture, Or, A Treatise on Ship-building* (London, 1812).

Steinhaus C F, *Die Schiffbaukunst in ihrem Unfang* (Hamburg, 1858).

Stukeley W, *Itinerarium Curiosum; Or, An Account of the Antiquities, and Remarkable Curiosities in Nature Or Art, Observed in Travels Through Great Britain: Centuria I.* (London, 1776).

Tate G, 'On the Stature, Bulk and Colour of Eyes and Hair of Native Northumbrians', in *Proceedings of the Berwickshire Naturalists Club*, 1870, v.VI (1869–1872), 133-40.

Taylor T J, *An Inquiry into the operation of the running streams and tidal waters, with a view to determining their principles of action: and an application of those principles to the improvement of the River Tyne* (London and Newcastle, 1851).

Taylor T J, *The Archaeology of the Coal Trade* (Newcastle, 1858; reprinted, 1971).

Taylor P & Williams A, 'The Newburn wherries: remnants of the River Tyne's industrial past', *Archaeologia Aeliana*, Fifth Series, v. 39, 2010, 401-25.

The Mariner's Museum (ed), *A Dictionary of the World's Watercraft: from Aak to Zumbra* (London, 2000).

Thier K, *Old English Sea Terms* (Ely, 2014).

Tidal Harbours Commission, Second Report of the Commissioners, with Minutes of Evidence, Appendices, Supplements and Index (Command Paper, HMSO, 1846).

Uglow J, *Nature's Engraver: A Life of Thomas Bewick*, (London, 2006; pbk edition, 2007).

Vermeersch J & Haneca K, 'Construction Features of Doel I, a 14th-Century Cog found in Flanders', in *International Journal of Nautical Archaeology*, 44:1, 2015, 111-31.

Viall H R, 'Tyne Keels', *The Mariner's Mirror*, Vol. 28, No.2, 1942, 160-62.

Walpoole G A, *The New British Traveller; Or, A Complete Modern Universal Display of Great-Britain and Ireland* (London, 1784).

Walton P, 'Caulking, Textiles and Cordage', in O'Brien C *et al*, 'Excavations at Newcastle Quayside: The Crown Court Site', *Archaeologia Aeliana*, Fifth Series, v.17, 1989, 167-76.

Warrington Smyth H, *Mast and Sail in Europe and Asia* (2nd edition, Edinburgh, 1929), 144-45

Whitehead I, *The Sporting Tyne: A History of Professional Rowing* (Gateshead, 2002).

Whiting W R G, 'The Newcastle Galley', in *Archaeologia Aeliana*, XIII, Fourth Series, 1936, 95-116.

Whitwell R J & Johnson C, 'The "Newcastle Galley", A.D. 1294', in *Archaeologia Aeliana*, Fourth Series, v.2, 1926, 142-93.

Willan T S, *River Navigation in England 1600-1750* (Oxford, 1936).

Wright P D, *Life on the Tyne, Water Trades of the Lower River Tyne in the Seventeenth and Eighteenth Centuries, a Reappraisal* (Farnham, 2014).

Zwick D, 'Conceptual Evolution in Ancient Shipbuilding: An Attempt to Reinvigorate a Shunned Theoretical Framework', in Adams J & Rönnby J (eds), *Interpreting Shipwrecks: Maritime Archaeological Possibilities* (Oxford, 2013).

MAPS AND CHARTS

John Speed (described by William Matthew): Map of Newcastle-upon-Tyne and Gateshead, 1610.

Grenville Collins: Map of the Tyne dedicated to the Master and Brethren of Trinity House, Newcastle, c.1693 (TWAM D/NCP/5.1.).

'Jas Larken Sculphsit': A Chart of the River Tyne and the Soundings from Tinmouth Bar into the Sea, 1700-1750 (TWAM D/NCP/5.2.).

Unknown: Map of the Tyne (probably amended from Greenville Collins, 1693), 1765 (Bell Collection, Vol. 1, NCL L942.8 T98).

James Corbridge: Map of Newcastle upon Tyne, 1723 (TWAM D/NCP/2/6).

Charles Hutton: A Plan of Newcastle upon Tyne and Gateshead, 1772.

John Fryer: Map of the River Tyne, 1782 (Port of Tyne collection); detail reproduced in Powell T, *Staith to Conveyor*.

John Wood: Plan of Newcastle-upon-Tyne and Gateshead, 1827.

Lambert (publ. D Akenhead, Newcastle): Plan of the Rivers Tyne & Wear with the Collieries etc., 1807.

John Rennie (in John Taylor, *An inquiry into the operation of tidal streams and running waters etc.*, 1851) : Channel of the Tyne between Bill Point & Jarrow Slake, 1813.

William Collard (publ. in M A Richardson, *Handbook to Newcastle*): Map of the Country around Newcastle-upon-Tyne included in a district of ten miles, 1838 (TWCMS J3274).

Commander E K Calver R N, & W Otter: Newcastle and the River Tyne, 1840 (in, Appendix to *Second Report on Tidal Harbours*, 1846).

Unknown (in John Taylor, *An Inquiry into the operation of tidal streams and running waters etc.*, 1851): Map of the Tyne from Willington Quay to the outfall etc., c.1851.

John T W Bell: Map of the Great Northern Coalfield in the Counties of Northumberland & Durham etc., 1850.

Ordnance Survey, 1ˢᵗ edition, Six Inch to One Mile: Durham (surveyed 1856, published 1862); and Northumberland (surveyed 1858, published 1864).

ELECTRONIC SOURCES

Jackson R, Journals A-F, 1749-1756, transcriptions of: www.greatayton.wikidot.com > ralph-jackson-diaries (accessed 02/03/2021).

Kleshnev V, Rowing Biomechanics, 2006: www.biorow.com (accessed 06/01/2021).

St Guthlac (image): http://www.bl.uk/manuscripts/FullDisplay.aspx?ref=Harley_Roll_Y_6 (accessed 11/02/2022).

Pictures in Print (Durham University), 2014: valentine.dur.ac.uk/pip/index.html (last accessed 03/05/2022).

Watercolour World: www.watercolourworld (accessed variously January 2019 to April 2022).

Other electronic sources consulted as per the relevant chapter endnotes.

NEWSPAPERS

Durham Chronicle

Lloyd's List

Newcastle Advertiser

Newcastle Chronicle

Newcastle Courant

Newcastle Journal

Shields Gazette

Tyne Mercury

THESES CONSULTED

Elliot N R, 'Tyneside, A Study in the Development of an Industrial Seaport' (PhD thesis, University of Durham, 1955).

Fenton R, 'Transition in the UK coastal bulk trades 1840-1914' (PhD thesis, University of West London, 2005).

Goodburn D M, 'An Archaeology of Early English Boatbuilding Practice c.900-1600 AD: based mainly on finds from SE England' (PhD thesis, University College, London, 2003).

Olaberia J-P, 'Ship design-knowledge in early modern Europe: Royal yachts and the shared knowledge of ship-designers and common shipwrights' (PhD Thesis, University of Southampton, 2018)

Osler A G, 'Responding to Change, Shipping deployments in the Baltic Trade of the Tyne, 1860-1880' (PhD thesis, University of Hull, 2005).

Rennison R W, 'The Development of the North-East Coal Ports, 1815-1914; The Contribution of Engineering' (PhD thesis, University of Newcastle, 1987).

Tanner P, 'The Reconstruction and Analysis of Archaeological Ships and Boats' (PhD thesis, University of Southampton, 2020).

Wright P D, 'Water Trades on the Lower River Tyne in the Seventeenth and Eighteenth Centuries' (PhD Thesis, Newcastle University, 2011).

IMPERIAL TO METRIC CONVERSIONS

THE WORLD OF THE KEEL and its users was one in which all measurements and calculations were made in long-established imperial units, supplemented by a few regional variants for volume and weight that originated in the coal trade. For consistency, such contemporary imperial and local measures have been used throughout this book. Those wishing to convert to metric measures for comparative purposes may find the table and listings overleaf a helpful preliminary guide.

Linear: inches to millimetres; feet to metres; and miles (statute) to kilometres

Inches	ins	1/8	1/4	3/8	1/2	5/8	3/4	7/8	8/8			
	mm	3.18	6.35	9.53	12.7	15.88	19.05	22.23	25.4			
	ins	1	2	3	4	5	6	7	8	9	10	11	12
	mm	25.4	50.8	76.2	101.6	127.0	152.4	177.8	203.2	228.6	254.0	279.4	304.8
Feet	ft	1	2	3	4	5	6	7	8	9	10		
	m	.305	.610	.914	1.22	1.52	1.83	2.13	2.44	2.74	3.05		
	ft	10	15	20	25	30	35	40	45	50			
	m	3.05	4.57	6.10	7.62	9.14	10.67	12.19	13.72	15.24			
Mls	Mls	1/2	1	2	3	4	5	6	7	8	9	10	15
	km	.805	1.61	3.22	4.83	6.44	8.05	9.66	11.26	12.88	14.48	16.10	24.14

Note: Mls, statute (land) miles.

Weight:

1 Keel (8 chaldrons) of 21.2 imperial tons equivalent to 21.54 metric tonnes

1 Newcastle Chaldron of 53 hundredweights equivalent to 2.69 metric tonnes

1 pound equivalent to 0.454 kilogrammes

Speed (nautical):

1 Knot of 1 nautical mile per hour, equivalent to 1.853 kilometres per hour (note: 1 nautical mile = 1.152 statute miles)

Area:

10 acres equivalent to approximately 4.05 hectares

INDEX

Shields Harbour, 67, 72, 75, 105, 129,
    133, 153, 156, 176, 179, 183, 185
South Shields, 34, 106, 188, 200
South Shore (Gateshead), 35, 37
Stella, 9, 14, 73-75, 92, 157-158, 160, 179,
    183
Swalwell, 58, 183, 186
Walbottle Colliery, 157-158
Walker, 106
Wallsend, 111, 127, 170, 177
Whitehill Point, 74-75, **107**, 191
Willington, 38, 108, 159, 226
Wylam Colliery, 153-154, 157

Various, England
Alnwick, 49
Beadnell, 101
Carlisle, 14, 109
Dunwich, 203, 210
Graveney, 212, 215
Ipswich, 172
King's Lynn, 203, 210
London, xix, **xxii**, 46, 97, 108, 135, 204,
    220
River Clyde, 72, 152
River Thames, 72, 90, 97, 147, 200, 212,
    220, 221, 226, 223
River Wear, 21, 59, 119
Sunderland, 45, 63, 139, 186
Whitby, 172, **173**, 186
Winchelsea, **210**

PEOPLE

Historical
Bell John, 39, 48, 52, 70, 80-81, 83, **84,**
    90, 120, 128, 138, 170, **177, 224,** 232
Bertram Robert J S, **5**, 19
Brand Rev. John, 3, 22, 54, 77-79, 83, 89,
    91, 100-101, 222, 225
Brandling John MP, 127
Bute Marquess of, 157
Caverhill Robson, 18
Chapman William, 15, 218
Charleton R J, 3, 122
Cowell George, 159
Dodd Ralph, 14-15; 109-111
Gardiner Ralph, 64, 200, 220
H.L.H, 16
Heslop Richard O, 4, 14-15, 19-21, 53,
    76, 79-80, 83, 87, 89, 98, 100-101, 104,
    106, 126-128, 140-143, 145, 148,
    171-172
Holland John, 78, **79**, 83
Mayor of Newcastle, 186-187
McKay John, 75, 112, 160, 172, 180
McKenzie Eneas, 3
Mitcalfe R Stanley, 3, 15-16, 18-20, 27,
    43, 52-54, 79, 141-142, 145-146, 193
Nicholson Joseph Innes, 1, 160
Pennant Thomas, 51, 78-79, 89-90
Rennie John, 71
Softley Robert, 4, 61, 163
Stukeley William, 76-77, 79, 90
Ure J F, 158
Viall Hugh R, 3, 9, 13, 16, 48-49, 51, 54

ABOUT THE AUTHOR

THE ENJOYMENT, MAINTENANCE, and occasional building of a succession of sailing and rowing boats has been the author's chosen recreational activity for over fifty years, and the professional, curatorial pursuit of maritime history has occupied around thirty of them.

His doctoral research and associated studies explored the Tyne's mid-nineteenth century shipping trades and two previous books comprise original findings about vernacular wooden boats in northern Britain, whilst other published works have embraced both scholarly papers and popular articles. For a decade he was a contributing editor for the international journal *Maritime Life and Traditions*, acting as consultant editor for its publisher's authoritative books on the world's sailing pilot boats. Afloat, he and his wife formerly cruised the English and Scottish east coast – from Lowestoft to Lossiemouth – under sail.

Together with the late Duncan Towns he was responsible for the preservation of the only surviving Tyne Wherry, the 50-foot *Elswick No. 2*, the last to be built.

www.ingramcontent.com/pod-product-compliance
Lightning Source LLC
Chambersburg PA
CBHW080606090426
42735CB00017B/3344